PICTURING ARCHITECTURE

PICTURING ARCHITECTURE

GRAPHIC
PRESENTATION
TECHNIQUES IN
AUSTRALIAN
ARCHITECTURAL
PRACTICE

DESLEY LUSCOMBE
ANNE PEDEN

CRAFTSMAN HOUSE

First published by Craftsman House BVI Ltd, Tortola, BVI
Distributed in Australia by Craftsman House
20 Barcoo Street
Roseville East, NSW 2069, Australia

Distributed internationally through the following offices:

USA
STBS Ltd.
PO Box 786
Cooper Station
New York
NY 10276

UK
STBS Ltd.
5th Floor, Reading Bridge House
Reading Bridge Approach
Reading RG1 8PP
England

ASIA
STBS (Singapore) Pte Ltd
Kent Ridge
PO Box 1180
Singapore 9111
Republic of Singapore

ISBN 976 8097 20 5

Designer: Annelies Siero-Jahn
Typesetter: Netan Pty Limited, Sydney
Printer: South China Printing Co (1988) Ltd, Hong Kong

CONTENTS

ACKNOWLEDGMENTS

For their help in the production of this book I would like to thank Tracy James for her work in the initial conceptual stages of the book, Professor Jon Lang, Mark Jackson and Stanislaus Fung for their comments on the text, Michael Campbell for his help with photography, the secretarial staff of the School of Architecture, University of New South Wales, Sydney, and Nevill Drury, Professor John Ballinger and Leo Campbell for their continued support and guidance.

SPONSORS

Ancher Mortlock and Woolley Pty Ltd Sydney
Campbell Luscombe Associates Pty Ltd Sydney
John Mainwaring and Associates Pty Ltd Noosa
McConnel Smith and Johnson Pty Ltd Sydney
NSW Public Works Department Sydney
Philip Cox Richardson Taylor and Partners Pty Ltd Sydney

PREFACE

An initial aim of this book is to present a range of graphic images used in the production of Australian architecture. The body of the book focuses on architectural drawing – perspective, axonometric and orthogonal images – and examines techniques and materials used in the production of final artwork. However, this book is not in the strict sense a technical drawing manual. Rather, its focus is the examination of the aesthetic values and techniques of final artwork and to question their qualities as representations of a future reality. In the recent past, the photograph and plan have been the dominant media used to document architecture. The marginalisation of other forms of representation in architecture has often led to a loss of the material appearance of wit, critical commentary, ideological force and conceptual identity. Such characteristics are difficult to infer from the photograph, the constructed building or the written text, but are more easily inscribed in drawing. This is largely because architectural drawings are involved with the processes of the architectural act – the design, documentation and construction of a building – rather than the critical processes of narration or the object decoding and fragmentation of photography. In the pre-Modern past, architectural drawings have been seen as essential to both the explanation of architecture in adding a richness to architectural commentary and to the development of the architectural craft; indeed architectural drawings were often considered an end in themselves.[1] Thus, in the context of Australia, the primary aim of this book is to redress this very marginalisation of drawing by considering graphic media not simply as a means of production (tools) in architectural practice but more significantly as representation and vehicles for the transfer of information.

A second aim of the book is to pose questions concerning the temporal status of the selected architectural drawings, that is, to question how graphic practices might be seen to characterise a visibility of cultural production in the formation of our contemporary architectural profession. Indeed, why are the graphic images included here considered important, when compared to the vast numbers of architectural drawings which have by necessity been excluded, but which have been necessarily carried out for each particular building? And further, what is the status of these images within the entire range of media used in architectural practice? To address these questions opens the possibility of two domains of analysis – firstly, the roles of the observer and artist/architect in relation to the currency of visual codes and secondly, the application to architectural production of visual codes from artistic media not normally employed in architectural representation. Furthermore, questions are raised about the very necessity of architectural drawings to make comprehensible projected built form. The impetus behind

1 An example can be seen in the drawings of Pirenesi and also the graphic work of the Beaux Arts tradition which not only represented an image of architecture but encoded this with image signifiants which provided meaningful commentary for their viewing public.

the pursuits of this book is a change in the referentiality of architectural rendering. While architectural representation in the 18th and 19th centuries allowed the client participation in the determination of architectural shapes and functional locations, the images found in this book are either abstracted or semi-representational making comprehensibility of any concrete 'future' difficult. They register a shift in representation from one in support of architectural determination to one displaying an acceptance of architectural drawing as an artifact. As artifact it can be argued that the architectural drawing has become referential beyond its source. Images selected for this book maintain a significant trace of the crafted surface and artistic intentionality. As such architectural drawing directs attention away from its orthodox role as the documentary and representational 'tool' of architectural practice. This in turn modifies the status of the long held relationship between architect and client as the drawing's meaning is not always immediately 'visible'. It is no longer simply a vehicle for transmitting instrumentally rational meanings but is multiply coded and may be read in other ways. These issues illuminate significant changes to architectural practice and focus discussion for this book's introduction.

The selection of material incorporated in this book includes three categories of graphic work. The first is finished presentation; the second, more conceptual work carried out by architects during the design process to explain the theoretical influences in their design; and the third, orthographic projections used to document complex architectural features. In each of these categories the aim has been to find well crafted architectural renderings which could stand in isolation rather than simply as adjuncts to the understanding of a building. There has also been an attempt to present renderings which architects see as being representative of their design intentions, rather than commissions carried out by a small clique of commercial renderers. To clarify the distinctive characteristics of the graphic images, each is accompanied by a statement about the design, written by the architect (often telling much more about the architect than the design) and, where available, photographs of the completed building are also included. These are offset by a statement on the specific qualities of the rendering.

Drawings in this collection cover a variety of representational types. This variety is contingent on the specific techniques used and the particular stage in the architectural process of the selected drawing. For example, those done during the design phase – explanatory drawings – are often tentative and give provision for later response to the developing characteristics of a design. Hence, overworking is often visible in the artwork, resulting in a layering or a drawn quality expressive of the processes of architectural thought itself rather than the picturing of static built forms, (eg, Cracknell Lonergan p. 50, Keith Streames p. 48, Neil Durbach p. 108). At this early stage in the architectural process drawings are often developed to appeal to particular viewers or client groups and to emphasise specific attitudes or requirements, (eg, Graham Jahn p. 44, Denton Corker Marshall p. 164, Arthur Collin and Brian Lilley p. 118, Ken Maher and Partners p. 152, Philip Cox Richardson Taylor p. 116). Other drawings in this collection exemplify those carried out at later stages of the design process, even after the building is complete. These drawings are influenced by the constraints of 'framing a picture' and publication, or have resulted from the examination of three-dimensional built form as two-dimensional art, or possibly, they result from further development and conceptual experimentation, (eg, Campbell Luscombe p. 38, Norman Day p. 168, Ivan Rijavec p. 68). Rather than attempting to limit this selection of images by specific type or stage in the design process, this book tries to explore the widest possible range of approaches. However, renderings collected for the book have been limited to the ten year period of 1981–1991. While this is a fairly arbitrary control, it does isolate a decade which markedly displays a shifting status for architectural rendering, caused in part by a specific constellation of influences and also by a changed rendering aesthetic.[2] Of great significance to the growth in production of presentation drawings in architectural practice is the development of computer aided drafting (CAD) systems. Architectural practice is not only using these as tools but also reacting and critically commenting on the dominating characteristics of computer drafting systems for the picturing of architecture. This has significantly increased the number of different techniques and representational forms used for picturing architecture. Despite the variety of drawings, there are certain issues of representation common to many: firstly, drawings generally act as the primary source of explanation and examination of architectural concepts; secondly, they control the way architectural images may be comprehended or read through their manner of detailed documentation; and thirdly, they influence the final built form to the extent that drawings are placed contractually and legally superior to the three-dimensional built form. Indeed, drawings are seen as the most influential medium in the architectural process. In this context, it is interesting to question the recent response to architectural drawings as artistic objects and as commodity able to be bought and sold as such. It is in an account of the importance of drawing to the profession and the emerging popularity of particular drawing techniques for architectural documentation that we can begin to illustrate the significance of these recent changes in strategy for architectural renderings.

DESLEY LUSCOMBE

2 These include: the number of exhibitions showing architectural rendering as an independent art form including the Museum of Modern Art exhibition of 1989 and more local exhibitions in Sydney and Melbourne; the impact of the 'deconstructive' image from American architectural publications; the growth in the use of air-brush and photographic screening techniques for architectural rendering; the use of tendering systems and limited competitions used in Australia to choose an architect (this has resulted in the architectural drawings taking on an advertising role rather than functioning simply as a client aid); the use of billboard graphics for major building construction sites; the rise in critical questioning of the theoretical and conceptual bases for buildings in Australian architectural practice (past presentations of Australian architecture have pictured it through the ethos of fit to a natural and Australian landscape and 'truth to materials' rather than questioning any more profound contextual or theoretical concerns); a growing interest and pleasure in the exploration and experimentation of the mechanics of technical drawing as an artistic medium (leading to graphics both documenting the modelled surface of building and exploring the abstract qualities of line and shape).

PICTURING ARCHITECTURE
GRAPHIC PRESENTATION TECHNIQUES IN AUSTRALIAN ARCHITECTURAL PRACTICE 1981–1991

The drawings are not architecture. They are an attempt to make physical, as much as possible, a way of thinking which anticipates something further which, if applied to architecture may become a building. In the beginning, instead of progressing toward a building, these drawings suggest a way of thinking which goes in the opposite direction. They don't want to give answers ... instead, their purpose is to sustain a certain interest in associations between architecture and our presence in space: how our presence coincides with the drawing, how the drawing coincides with the building and finally, how the building comes back to our presence.

Giuliano Fiorenzoli 'Drawings and Work' in *Architecture and Body*, Scott Marble et al., New York: Rizzoli, 1988.

This introduction examines aspects of the contemporary Australian architectural profession through the drawings it produces. As a prominent and authoritative tool of the profession, drawings encapsulate attitudes specific to an architectural visual culture which may be analysed to illustrate the current status of that profession.

The analysis of and discourse on architecture in Australia has been concerned with the idea of regionalism. From early documents such as Max Freeland's *Architecture in Australia: A History* to *Identifying Australian Architecture* by Richard Apperly, Robert Irving and Peter Reynolds, authors have been most concerned to seek unique characteristics in the imagery of buildings which may enable the recognition of an Australian architectural style.[3] This book attempts to redirect this debate and examine some practices of the Australian architectural profession. Of interest are the fundamental practices which form a vehicle for the translation of ideas into built form. By focusing on the graphic techniques used in architectural practice and using mainly Australian examples, this book directs attention to issues which have intrinsic and local significance. However, this direction is pursued without any intention of suggesting that these issues are distinctively regional or that these are the only issues of concern to the profession over recent time. Rather, it is suggesting that if we are to understand the architecture of any location, a broad spectrum of attitudes related to practice and the self-examination of the profession need to be debated.

Also significant to locating architectural practices in text is the notion of narrative voice. Any visual culture is complex. To reflect this complexity the text of this book is structured around an appearance of each artist and architect's voice. Thus the narrative of this text features a multilayered voice rather than authorial dominance. By fracturing the authorial voice an interaction between the 'usual' way of

3 Freeland, JM, *Architecture in Australia: A History*, Melbourne: Cheshire, 1970; Apperly, RE, Irving, RC and Reynolds, PL, *A Pictorial Guide to Identifying Australian Architecture: Styles and Terms from 1788 to the Present*, Sydney: Angus and Robertson, 1989.

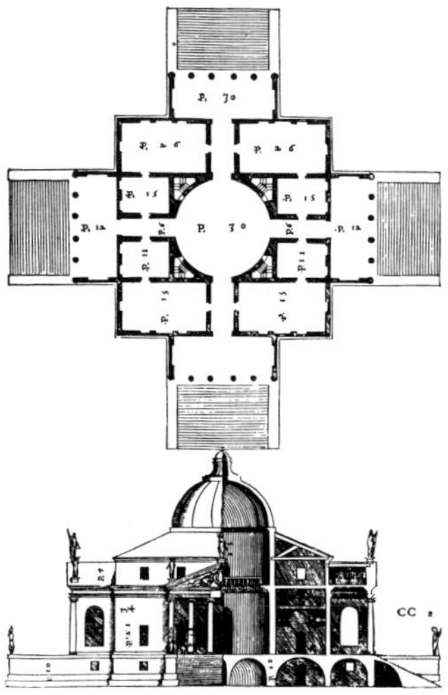

fig. 1

fig. 2

considering architectural drawing and the richness of current visual cultures in Australian architectural practice may appear.

To display this interaction this introduction highlights a schism between what has come to be seen as the more 'usual' manner from which to consider the practice of drawing and what actually appears in these selected drawings. The introductory analysis attempts to locate current practices with references to changes in professional attitudes developing over time and specific to location. Because the architectural profession has retained many of its techniques for displaying buildings from Renaissance time, it becomes important to pinpoint specific attitudinal appearances and changes.

The most significant and obvious change for the practice of architectural drawing is the status of drawings within the full practice of architecture. It is this changing status which allows an understanding of changing systems of cultural production. With growing status and authority, drawing has been imbued with an excess of meaning lifting it from being a 'tool' of the profession to a practice embodying distinctive discourses and visual concepts. This discourse can often be seen to critically question the boundaries and meanings implied by there being a recognised profession of architecture.

1. THE AUTHORITY OF DRAWING TECHNIQUES AND THEIR IMPACT ON THE ARCHITECTURAL PROFESSION

Architectural drawing has been intrinsically linked to the status of the profession from the beginnings of modernity and humanism in the Renaissance. Catherine Wilkinson suggests that it was precisely the pre-eminent role of drawing in the Renaissance which allowed architecture as a profession to emerge from its origin in building and become accepted as a conceptual art.[4] She cites Giorgio Vasari who in his *Lives of the Artists* (1568), focused on the idea of *disegno* for his analysis of status in the arts.[5] By this definition Vasari was able to separate the high arts of architecture, painting and sculpture from traditional craft. This action not only documented a separation among the arts but also instanced a separation of the design act from the labour associated with its appearance as an object.[6]

With the separation of conceptual thinking and drawing from building, discourse on design in architecture tended to be through orthographic projection and conceptual sketches. The number of treatises on architectural design grew significantly from the Renaissance till the 15th and 16th centuries, when Andre Palladio's *Four Books on Architecture* and other treatises, including those by Antonio Filarete, Giuliano da Sangallo and Sebastiano Serlio, emerged (Figure 1 and 2).[7] These treatises

4 Catherine Wilkinson, 'The New Professionalism in the Renaissance', in Spiro Kostof, *The Architect: Chapters in the History of the Profession*, New York: Oxford University Press, 1977, pp. 134–5; also mentioned in Helene Lipstadt 'Architecture and its Image: Notes Towards the Definition of Architectural Publication', Andreas Papadakis (ed), *Architectural Design: Drawing into Architecture*, New York: St Martin's Press, 1989, p. 13. Evidence of early orthographic and scaled drawing is given in Franklin Toker, 'Gothic Architecture by Remote Control: an Illustrated Building Contract of 1340'. *Art Bulletin* LXVII, pp. 65–95.

5 *Desegno* generally means design by drawing and perspective.

6 Mike Cooley gives examples of the bitter debates this action aroused during the Renaissance when the intellectual practices of architecture were seen to strip the crafts of their intellectual content. Mike Cooley, 'From Brunelleschi to CAD-CAM', in John Thackara (ed), *Design After Modernism: Beyond the Object*, London: Thames and Hudson, 1988: pp. 197–207.

7 Further commentary on these writers can be found in Rudolph Wittkower's *Architectural Principles in the Age of Humanism*, London: Academy Editions, 1977.

8 Oechslin, W, 'From Piranesi to Libeskind: Explaining by Drawing', *Daidalos*, 1 September 1981: pp. 15–19.

9 Oechslin, *op. cit.*, p. 15.

changed drawing practices in architecture from a mimetic production of the classical representation of antiquities, to a practice in which documents were made for the production of building. Professional debate became focused on the drawing of ideal but fictitious architectural images – a utopic and remote future rather than an ideal past. This heightened the professional acceptance of technical architectural drawings as the expression of architectural understanding, intention and novelty.

While texts written during the Renaissance sought separation of the conceptual arts of painting, sculpture and architecture, these boundaries have never been clearly defined with regard to drawing. Drawing for all the arts was seen as a technical tool without embodying succinct and independent values. The study of drawing as a separate and value laden art became significant with the rise in connoisseurship during the 18th and 19th centuries. Before this time drawings in all the arts utilised many similar techniques and many techniques derived from painting had an impact on architectural drawing. The proliferation of drawings increased when technically precise artistic styles focused on architectural images for their representation, as in the *scaenographia* of the 18th century (Figure 3). At this time both art and architecture became involved in the precise and geometrically correct representation of buildings. This adaption of architectural drawing techniques in art divorced the necessity for architectural drawing to be a design tool. Werner Oechslin gives the example of the numerous drawn architectural fantasies of Piranesi, stating that if Piranesi was 'deprived of actually building, it [was] because of "the adversity of the time", not for reasons of incompetence'. (Figure 4)[8] However, the appearance of Piranesi's drawings as entities in themselves triggers the attitudinal change suggested here. This blurring of the boundary between painting and architectural drawing was also evident with architectural theorists like Boullée, who assimilated various methods of representation and illusion found in painting to represent buildings.[9] Furthermore, public accessibility to architectural drawing and the drawing's status in the structure of the arts grew with the 18th- and 19th-century rise in museological collections in England, Europe and North America and display of architectural drawing in a gallery setting. This has been extended with 20th-century practices of mechanical reproduction of the architectural 'print' and further accessibility of reproduced architectural drawings through the manufacture of postcards.

In the 20th century, the boundary between architectural drawing and painting still remains unclear. Artistic movements which have accented orthographic and axonometric projection for picturing objects in space, include De Stijl, the Suprematists, Constructivists and Deconstructivists. The use of these

Ioseph Galli Bibiena Primar.us Archt. S.C.C.M. Inv. et delineavit.
I. A. Pfeffel S.C.M. Chalcogr. sculp. direx. A. V.

fig. 3

fig. 4

techniques appears to have provided artists with a conceptual and measurable clarity for the examination of architectonic shapes. Critical evaluation of these artworks responded to architectural drawings and paintings from the same evaluative framework, there being an assumed equivalence of painting to architectural drawings. Furthermore, this criticism further encouraged an acceptance by art galleries to display architectural drawings as artworks.[10]

The specific nature of any visual culture for the Australian architectural profession would involve traces of this instability of definition. However, it would also embody an acceptance of the authoritative position of architectural drawing for the practice of architecture and its characteristic as 'tool'. Many further notions having an impact on an evaluation of architectural drawing as a symptom of visual culture are intrinsic to each drawing technique used. The foundations to architectural rendering and drawing have been characteristically based on techniques of mechanical drawing. The historical development of these techniques illustrate many of the practices still evident in current architectural rendering. A brief examination of contemporary and past uses of these drawing techniques will indicate specific attitudes to representation that the recent profession is seeking to develop, for example: the close focus and meticulous rendering of architectural details through orthographic projection; the application of 'slogans' over drafted images using collage and montage techniques; conglomerate compositions developing from a layering and fracturing of drawings using multiple techniques; and abstract images which have their source in technical drawing and representation but 'play' with a reconfiguration of these images in an abstract composition.

ORTHOGRAPHIC PROJECTIONS

Conceptually, orthographics, that is, plan, elevation and section, dominate the documentary process of architectural production, providing the pictorial, mathematical and geometric bases of built form. At various times throughout this documentary process the function of the orthographic changes, for example, representation may include: the conceptual sketch, theoretical examinations of complex architectural ideas, design explanation, working drawings and so on. Specific representational codes and drafting standards are necessary in the working documents which are to be used in the building process,[11] other orthogonal representations are guided by artistic will, technique and graphic media, experimentation and professional appeal. While each of these images may be orthographic and thus share influences of parallelism and metrication, there will obviously be significant variance in

10 Example may be seen in the 1988 exhibition 'Deconstructivist Architecture' held at the Museum of Modern Art, New York, Guest Curator Philip Johnson and Associate Curator Mark Wigley. More locally the contemporary exhibition of architectural drawings of 1988, 'The New Breed' held at University of Technology, Sydney, Convenor Neville Quarry and Associate Convenor Stephen Varady or the more recent at Irving Galleries, Paddington to name but a few local examples.

11 For example *Australian Standard Technical Drawing Part 301 Architectural Drawing*, AS 1100, Part 301 – 1985, North Sydney: Standards Assocation of Australia, 1985.

mathematical accuracy and graphic technique.

The domination of the orthographic derives not only from its metrical accuracy and parallelism but also from its role in the Renaissance separation of conceptual design from building. Significance further derives from the ability of a client audience to critically evaluate a future building through the reading of plans. Robin Evans cites a particular 18th-century practice wherein:

> *... to act in the character of an architect meant the adoption of techniques which allowed a proposal to be laid forth for examination in the absence of the building itself, above all in the form of drawing. Plans, sections and elevations – the principle tools of the profession – made it possible to see a building from a distance and yet to see its multifarious internal workings at a glance; to survey it from an abstracted, privileged vantage point as if it were a dissected body and to see it before the fact of construction.*[12]

Evans also draws attention to the bifurcation of the client body through this act. The client, in Evan's case the prison magistrate, was one who had no essential tie to the workings of the prison or production of the architecture he was evaluating. Thus the production of plans for critical evaluation took the power for architectural control from those with on-site concerns and gave it to those with bureaucratic status. The comprehensibility of future built form thus dissipated architectural intention and control. It fragmented the political structuring of the architectural act.

Metrical accuracy in combination with a power of determination were significantly influential to the role of the orthographic in the mid-20th century. By this time the legal role of the orthographic had been established and the drawing provided evidence for accuracy in built form and helped establish liability in malpractice suits.

PERSPECTIVE

The dominant type of technical drawing for representing three-dimensional built form is the perspective. It can be defined as:

> *... the distortion of shape, size and distance in the aspect of the seen objects according to the viewer's eye-point. It enables the complexity of the multi-dimensional visual world to be accurately codified into two dimensions. Paradoxically, perspective preserves the identity of shapes and relationships by agreeing to warp them systematically.*[13]

12 Robin Evans, *The Fabrication of Virtue: English Prison Architecture 1750–1840*, Cambridge: Cambridge University Press, 1982, p. 45.

13 Kamholtz, J, 'Spencer and Perspective', *Journal of Aesthetics and Art Criticism*, 39, 1, p. 60.

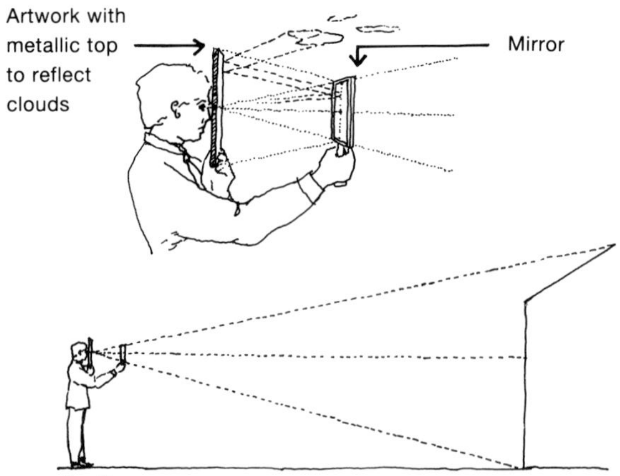

fig. 5

The technique of perspective has historically been tied to humanist symbolism from Renaissance times through texts such as Erwin Panofsky's *Perspective as Symbolic Form.*[14] It has also been historically popularised through the documentation of Brunelleschi's camera obscura 'peep show'. Mike Cooley summarises Brunelleschi's apparatus (Figure 5):

> *One of the paintings showed the octagonal Baptistry (S Giovanni) as seen from the door of the Cathedral. The optical 'truth' was verified by drilling a small hole in the baptistry panel. The spectator was intended to pick up the panel and press his eye to the hole on the unpainted side. With the other hand he was then required to hold the mirror in such a way that the painted surface was visible in reflection through the hole. By these means, Brunelleschi established precisely the perpendicular axis along which his representation should be viewed. By use of a mirror, there was a precise matching of the visual experience and the painted representation.*[15]

The two predominant characteristics of perspectival art at this time were indicative of the contributing tensions found in the relation of classical mimesis to the experimental sciences. Perspective was seen to have a capacity to imitate Nature and also to incorporate strong technical and scientific determinants. However, precision in mathematical accuracy and the geometric laws which enable perspective projections to be constructed from orthographic projections were not fully developed until the late 17th century.

As a drawing technique, perspective has ceased to carry any clear association with its original symbolic meaning which portrayed the Renaissance equivalence of humanist man with God or infinity. Yet there is a continuity of its particular codes of visuality. Specifically these include, firstly, the separation of viewer from the object: perspectives rely on geometric rules of distancing and stabilising the viewer and perspectival convergence relies on there being only a single eye. Unlike much non-perspectival art which allows an implied interaction between image and viewer, for the perspective there is no imagined interactive movement by the viewer over the spaces pictured. The viewer retains a static role. Martin Jay suggests that any movement implied in the viewer takes the form of 'saccadic jumps from one focal point to another'.[16]

Secondly, there is the application of *a priori* laws on artistic vision: perspective is geometrically and mathematically defined. Furthermore, the horizon line is equivalent to the eye-level of the onlooker and

14 Panofsky, E, *Die Perspektive als symbolische Form*, Warburg, Hamburg: Vortrage der Bibl., 1924–5.

15 Mike Cooley, 'From Brunelleschi to CAD-CAM', in John Thackara (ed), *Design After Modernism: Beyond the Object*, London: Thames and Hudson, 1988, p. 201.

16 Martin Jay, 'Scopic Regimes of Modernity' in Hal Foster (ed), *Vision and Visuality*, Seattle: Bay Press, 1988, p. 7.

17 Bahnassi, A, 'The Idea of Perspective and Cultures', *Cultures*, 4, 3, 1977: pp. 93–109. Bahnassi suggests that the horizon line in Chinese art is placed behind the viewer, allowing the illusion of interaction with the image.

dictates the vanishing points of any object in the foreground, this horizon is always at the back of the image and reflects the viewer's separation from the image – unlike Chinese, Indian or Arabic 'perspective' which is dedicated to a more interactive interplay between observer and image.[17]

Thirdly, with the incorporation of the horizon and diminution in depth, colour and texture become subordinate to depth: as the ground recedes, colour reduces in intensity but texture increases in density.[18] Fourthly, with perspective comes a notion of the frontality of objects pictured, or at least that the front view is most commonly pictured. While not being necessarily referenced by Classical symmetry and frontality, perspectives retain traces of this Classical imprint. Fifthly, while aiming to unify all that is pictured, perspective privileges particular aspects of buildings over their setting and occupancy, it gives authority to the formal and abstract characteristics of mass and line and because of the scale effect it abstracts detail to form clean line. Like the architectural photograph, the haphazardness of people and landscape are often seen to undermine the clarity of form characterised by the perspective view. Sixthly, and like the photograph, perspective rendering creates viewer expectations in that they attempt to authenticate the view as 'Nature'. However, because of the graphic medium underlying the perspective view, there is only partial and superficial documentation of this 'Nature'. As such, the perspective demands greater viewer collaboration than the photograph to mentally complete the partial image seen in the picture, to read it as something real rather than ideal.

AXONOMETRY[19]

Rather than exploring perspective's central projection, the axonometric plots three-dimensional form from a parallel projection. As a drawing type, axonometric parallel projection has been used since the Greek civilisation even though these drawings were not named as 'axonometric' until the 19th century.[20] Axonometric drawing maintains abstract qualities of line and shape within its images in a similar geographical location to that proposed for the building it represents. It can show simultaneously the plan, section and interior spaces of a building. Each retains the parallelism and measurability of the orthographic plan and elevation, thus overcoming the distortion of perspective's foreshortening. By remaining mathematically measurable, the axonometric privileges the association of line and angle and has been used in the past for such diverse applications as evidence for the capacity to build complex structures and for the display of the projectile power of precise military weapons.[21] Because of this diversity there seems to be little consistency to any underlying meaning for the axonometric.[22] The

18 James Gibson's work in psychology gives evidence for texture density as a primary depth cue in life. James J Gibson, *Perception of the Visual World*, Boston: Houghton, 1950.

19 Although isometric techniques for picturing in architecture are used, these are no longer as common as the axonometric. The technique is not as clearly based on the retention of plan and elevational accuracy within the final view and as such is not as theoretically 'clean' as the axonometric. As a drawing technique which is founded in geometric and mathematical accuracy the isometric does not open issues outside those raised through the examination of the axonometric and has thus not been examined separately.

20 Scolari suggests there is evidence that both English and French sources called parallel projections like the axonometric 'perspective' or 'perspectiva soldatesca' from the 16th century suggesting there was no clear separation between the idea of perspective and parallel projection as we know them. Scolari, M, 'Elements for a History of Axonometry', *Architectural Design Profile* 59: The School of Venice, Luciano Semerani (ed), *Architectural Design*, 55, 5/6 (1985): p. 73.

21 *Ibid.*, and Robin Middleton 'August Choisy, Historian: 1841–1909', *International Architect* 5, 1, (1981): pp. 37–42.

22 Bois, Y-A, 'Metamorphosis of Axonometry', *Daidalos*, 1 September 1981: p. 42.

fig. 6

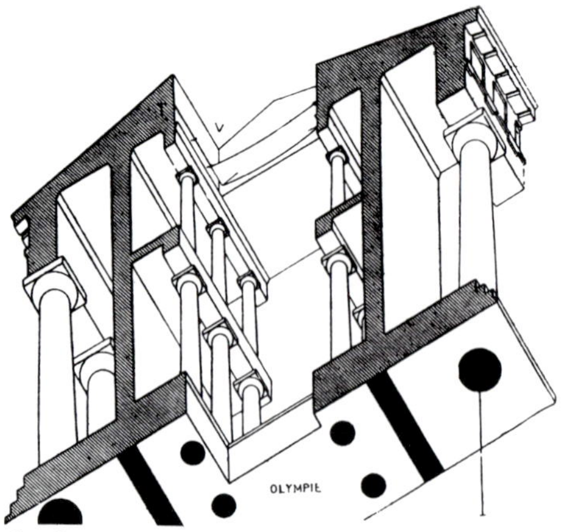

fig. 7

reinstatement of the axonometric during the early 20th century in De Stijl and Suprematist art came with the artistic examination of spatial characteristics and the celebration of spatial ambiguity (Figure 6). Lissitzky wrote:

> *Suprematism has shifted the top of the finite pyramid of perspective vision into infinity ... Suprematic space makes it possible to design forward of the surface but also in depth ... We notice that Suprematism ... has created the final illusion of irrational space with the unlimited extension of foreground and background.*[23]

There was not only the ambiguity of the illusion of spatial expansion, but also of the reversibility of image documented through the axonometric of the cube. Because of this ability, the axonometric allowed views to be created from a reverse position as seen in the detail drawings of August Choisy (Figure 7).[24] The drawings of MC Escher also created illusions of space by mixing the true and reverse nature of the axonometric thus enabling unattainable spaces to be documented by the same methods as those used to verify the 'truth' of architectural spaces.[25] These characteristics freed documentation from opaqueness of the ground and the frontality of perspective images, and allowed the fabrication of mathematically accurate but fictitious views. Within this fabrication the axonometric emphasises the abstract qualities and planar aspects of building, that is, floor, wall and roof.

The coding which underlies axonometric drawings is not strictly visual. Its most significant difference from perspective is its lack of reference to the human body of the observer. The eye of the viewer is no longer fixed by the horizon and thus, the viewer is no longer in a static relationship with the object viewed. The viewing source has instead been associated with the 'eye' of the sun as axonometry was historically used to calculate heights of objects through their shadow's angle and dimension.[26] The second important characteristic of axonometry is its requirement for geometric and mathematical accuracy, for example, the circle in plan remains a circle in axonometry rather than becoming an oval as in the perspective projection. By accepting geometric laws which are not natural to visual perception, axonometry divorces itself from being a 'natural' reflection. Thirdly, as a result of this geometric basis, the axonometric privileges colour and plane rather than depth and contour, there being no depth diminution of colour. Fourthly, the axonometric to a greater extent than perspective, accentuates or pictures building or mathematically defined object over landscape and inhabitant. Unlike the attempt at natural reflection found in Chinese and Japanese axonometric art and to an extent in urban design,

23 *Ibid.*, p. 44. See also Robin Evans 'Architectural Projection', in E Blau and E Kaufman (ed), *Architecture and its Image: Four Centuries of Architectural Representation*, Montreal: Centre Canadian d'Architecture, 1989. 34 and fig. 20.
24 Middleton *op. cit.*, and August Choisy, *Histoire de L'Architecture*, Vol. 1, Paris: Editions Vincent, Freal, 1954.
25 Escher, MC, *The Graphic Work of M C Escher*, London: Pan/Ballintine, 1974.
26 Scolari, *op. cit.*, p. 76.

20th century architectural axonometrics are seldom seen with the naturalising elements of landscape and figures. Instead there is a complete domination of geometrical measurability, clarity and the complexity of the mechanically drafted line.

■ Architectural drawing has gained specific meaning through its historical development: the metric control and power of determination with orthographic projections; the predominant ideals of imitation of nature through technical and scientific 'laws' of perspective; and the geometric measurability and reversibility of three-dimensional form with axonometry. These attitudes all relate to a scientific determinism of architectural form (that is, the ability to derive a three-dimensional image through scientific 'laws' of imaging) and a predictability of its effects before construction.

The entanglement of architectural drawing with painting has also complicated the implications of architectural drawing as simply a tool of determination for the architectural process. It is evident that architectural drawing became accepted as an art and derived criticism from within a similar critical framework as painting: an examination of the drawing's two-dimensional composition, use of technique, command of colour, light/dark contrast, values of line, and the command of artistic intent. The rise in sales of antique architectural drawings and recent publication of collections of drawings has also promoted the view of architectural drawing as artifact. As such, it is comprehensible that a self-consciousness of drawing styles and an exploration of the necessity of representation in architectural drawing should become important questions for a current architectural visual culture. The appearance of the architectural drawing as self-referential to the point of becoming its own subject of interest – a sequence similar to the appearance of abstract painting during the early 20th century – becomes material evidence for the importance of these questions for the profession. The visibility of culture evident in drawings selected for this book reflect many of the questions to attitudes of drawing and practice raised in this analysis of the underlying nature of specific drawing techniques.

While many of the images selected for this book take on the authoritative and dominant requirement of drawing – that is, the measured and geometrically accurate delineation of the materials of architectural form – others significantly explore the limits of these requirements. Some display historicist drawing styles, recognising the requirements of drawing but attempting to apply historical referencing to ways of seeing or personalities. Others use allegorical images and collage or montage techniques. These call attention to debates which are building specific, for example, drawings of the suburban house with images of suburbia – the jogger, grand car or notions of idealised garden environment – being added to the drawing, or more broadly, and of general interest to the profession, commentary on the idea of the 'high art' status of architecture with the collaging of junk mail images over architectural rendering. Still others abstract or fragment the image of the architectural composition which suggests a non-representational art form, then call attention to changes in the visual codes which have in the past determined an accepted imaging of architectural form. The focus of these abstracted images is the two-dimensional and material characteristics of drawing rather than the intention for a transparency to a referent piece of architecture. This experimentality illustrates that the practice of architecture in Australia is concerned to reinforce its position as a scientific art but also to display the artistic intentionality of its practices.

If these practices illustrate significant shift to what has appeared as normal for the practice of architectural drawing, the specific nature of this change becomes topical for analysis. As artifact, architectural drawing could arguably be evaluated in isolation from the architectural practices which the drawings inscribe. At present the critical and narrative structures from which this would proceed are those of painting and artistic drawing practices. However, these do not allow for the complex intentions and roles of architectural drawings. Of significance to architectural drawing is its referentiality to a building – whether in the ideal or real sense – and its role as a 'tool' of practice. Thus much of the status and meaning given to architectural drawing has derived from the imprint of its 'architectural' foci. This makes hollow the analysis of drawing separate from its procedural role. However, to see the architectural drawing in its representational role places the building content of its image in the dominant position for analysis. In architecture it is, after all, the built object which is the dominant focus for the profession's practices and it is the building which is most commonly analysed. Furthermore, to see architectural drawings as simply referent to a final built object is to place them in a similar relationship as drawing to painting or drawing to sculpture. However, drawing in architecture is often carried out after the object is built, thus drawing becomes a tool of representation and evaluation as well as documentation. It is proposed here that for architectural practice, drawing is multiply coded and has a surplus of meaning which exposes it as a major discursive act in the architectural profession. To focus on architectural drawing and partially dissect the procedures of architectural discourse enables the analysis of the discursive characteristics of the drawn images and exposes a visibility of cultural production for contemporary Australian architectural practices. It is through analysis of architectural drawings that some recent shifts in the discursive boundaries constructed by the architectural profession become illustrated. Of significance to this changing boundary is the increased use of geometric artistic techniques adopted from Surreal and Dadaist painting which question perceptual traditions for viewing space and professional traditions which see drawing as a documentary tool.

2. THE STATUS OF ARCHITECTURAL RENDERING AS CULTURAL ARTIFACT

When trying to understand architecture there is a predominant tendency to group the media of its representation – drawings, photographs, texts, films, models and the empirical experiences of buildings – as if they are, singularly or in combination, transparent to the reality of their referent.[27] The construction of an interrelation between these media allows a belief in the comprehensibility of a hitherto obscure (or non-existent) object. This action both separates viewer from object and places the viewer in a position of determinant judge over reality.[28]

The desire to comprehend architecture has in the past resulted in its drawings or other representations being analysed for their instrumental abstraction of empirical reality, that is, their predictive accuracy. In their capacity as representation, media are said to hold the key to meaning and thus comprehension. However, although there is a necessarily assumed relation between various media and their referential reality, representations do not simply reproduce the real object.[29] There are more complex processes than simply that of a static viewer and transparent media of communication. For example, a viewer produces a reality-effect, a context-specific subject position, contingent on the media of communication itself on the basis of his/her own visual sub-culture, while conversely each medium works within its own logic and processes while also exhibiting apparent conformity to a singular and knowable world. That is to say, the very medium of drawing itself is a determinant of a particular reality-effect where value is not absolute but relative to the reality-effect of other media, for example, photography, cinema, and text. It is this complex process of representation, determination and independence, the relativity established with a real object in relation to other media, which gives access to an analysis of representation and intentionality in architectural drawing.

With such a complex set of interdependencies the task of isolating one medium in relation to others is a difficult process. In an attempt to examine some effects of architectural drawing this book inverts the relationship of graphic image, building, photograph and written text on each page, to focus attention on

.27 See most reviews of new buildings in journals such as *Architecture in Australia*, *The Bulletin*, and historical discourse by authors such as Spiro Kostof and Nikolaus Pevsner.

28 Architectural critics respond to architecture from a position of knowledge whereby they judge the worth of objects through their status. An effect learned through the continual enfolding of interpretive practices on themselves.

29 Further discussion on the referentiality of images may be found in Jean Baudrillard, *The Evil Demon of Images*: *Power Institute Publications*, No. 3, Sydney: The Power Institute of Fine Arts, 1987.

the drawn image itself rather than return the image to its referent object for the fabrication of a reality effect.[30] By altering the direction of the gaze there is an attempt to recognise that many images in this book picture architectonic shapes without them being in any simple or referential relationship to any real or proposed object. There is also an attempt to prompt examination of these images without the assumed belief that architectural rendering should function as a transparent tool for the understanding of an external and real world.[31]

Furthermore, an examination of the differing effects and many of the internal processes of architectural media most often used with drawing for the description of architecture, that is, text and photographs, breaks its contingent location and their combined relativity to the architectural object. The individual characteristics of the drawn media can further be recognised with an examination of the impact from the common and everyday experience of built architecture, and an examination of the codes and sub-codes of visuality which determine the historicity of our society's perception of its own environment. Thus, examination can be directed to architectural drawing for its own logic of representation rather than always focus on the real object.

ARCHITECTURAL DRAWING AS DISTINCT FROM THE ARCHITECTURAL OBJECT

The techniques of drawing both construct ways by which we speak about buildings as well as document proposed built form. By so doing they both represent and document architecture. As simulacra, drawings stand for and before the built object. Unlike architecture as built, the architectural drawing has technical characteristics and qualities which stem from a two-dimensional surface, its scale and its graphic production. However, confounding this quality, the image pictured often displays the illusion of the third dimension. In contrast, architecture as built is essentially four-dimensional and spatial. Response to contact with it issues from movement through it, social and visual cultures which determine responses, temporality and the personal structuring of experiential input: ideas of space and mass; response through the movements of the eye over surfaces; the impact on the viewer of being 'ground-bound'; the perception of detail referenced by material, colour, light, shade and texture; the space's furnishings; and the confusion of each respondent's life, his/her mood, purpose and company.

These experiences are impossible to picture through the static medium of drawing. Robin Evans gives an example of the difficulty of capturing the changing qualities of space, light and atmosphere in drawing.

In his article, 'Translations from Drawing to Building', he uses the work of James Turrell, a sculptor who creates illuminated environments which react to movement and the presence of people.

> *The mainstay of Turrell's work through the late sixties and seventies was the artificially lit room ... You look into something which you know is another rectangular room with batteries of fluorescent tubes on the back of the partition through which you peer. You can see how it works. You can put your hands into it. You can even see, standing out against the haze of illumination that moves from mauve through to pink, evidence of some earlier investigator who took it into his head to climb into the illusion, leaving his footprints in the otherwise spotless, spaceless interior.*
>
> *Even then, only by deduction can you maintain either the depth of the room or the emptiness of it, for the light looks, if not solid, then incredibly dense, as if its luminosity would not so much reveal the image of anything thrust into it so much as devour it.*[32]

Evans concludes that these spaces, if drawn, would have no sympathy with the spatial meaning as experienced. Although these spaces were architectural by nature they would lose all meaning if perceived merely as a drawing. Michel De Certeau also calls attention to the experiential quality of space. He questions the discipline of objectifying space through description or representation and suggests that the production of space in any mind is a subjective act. He concludes that:

> *Beneath the discourses ideologising [spaces], there is a proliferation of tricks and fusions of power that are devoid of legible identity, that lack any perceptible access and that are without rational clarity.*[33]

Thus, De Certeau calls attention to the power of narration and representation over space as experienced. These characteristics set attributes for built architecture which are distinct from their representations. For an examination of architectural drawing the eye as an historical artifact uses visual coding to distinguish particular iconographic and technical references. These references may range from a simple recognition of the scaling effect of drawing – seeing the complete object on one drawing with its inference of power and determination to the viewer – to the use of allegorical imagery to provoke historicist allusions. These effects of drawing allow some correlation to be made between the drawing and an imagined reality but they also provide ways for reading that 'reality'. Architectural rendering may hold a referential value for built architecture which may be understood through comparison and

30 Although film is the dominant medium, this discussion is most concerned with publications of architecture. The media of film opens a broader spectrum of debate than is required for an analysis of static medium of publication.

31 This argument proceeds from the premise that architectural representations are fundamentally different to painting and drawing per se as only architectural drawings demand figurative representation as an underlying requirement of image. See discussion in Jorge Silvetti, 'Perspective and the Envious Longing for the Renaissance', *Daidalos*, 11, March 1984: pp. 10–21.

32 Robin Evans 'Translation from Drawing to Building', *AA Files*, 12, Summer 1986: p. 4.

33 Michel De Certeau, 'Practices of Space', in M Blonsky, *On Signs*, London: Basil Blackwell, 1985, p. 128.

analysis, but its logic and processes are concerned with its narrative of explanation, its aim to be a picture, the experience of its two-dimensional surface, composition, material, colour and technique.

ARCHITECTURAL DRAWING AS DISTINCT FROM THE PHOTOGRAPH

Both architectural drawing and photographic images employ ideals of picturing and the composition of subject matter. Modern accounts of photography place special emphasis on the notion that photographs hold a privileged position with the world, in that they hold reality as their referent (they look like and have been caused in part by the real object).[34] This relationship allows the observer to systematically find similarities between the picture and the actual object depicted rather than to examine the photograph purely with reference to its medium.[35] Stephen Tyler has suggested that there is a predisposition to think of thinking/knowing as seeing and as the main media for seeing, the photographic medium thus holds a privileged position for the knowledge of objects and specifically the understanding of architecture.[36]

Coding from the photographic medium is often invisible to the viewer as its referent reality is most often the object of focus. There is a belief that an understanding of that 'reality' might be gained by examining the photograph and the image of the photograph can indeed be verified through comparison with the real world. Roland Barthes suggests:

> *In order to move from the reality to its photograph it is in no way necessary to divide up this reality into units and to constitute these units as signs, substantially different from the object they communicate; there is no necessity to set up a relay, that is to say a code, between the object and its image. Certainly the image is not the reality but at least it is its perfect* analogon *and it is exactly this analogical perfection which, to common sense, defines the photograph. Thus can be seen the special status of the photographic image:* it is a message without a code.[37]

Joel Snyder attempts to clarify the strange phenomenon of the photograph by outlining many of the differences between the physiology of vision used for a perception of an external world and the photographic documentation of that world. This illustrates many areas of media technique related to the 'eye' of the camera – techniques which continue to remain immaterial to a photograph's acceptance as representation but which differentiates representation from personal and binocular perception. He states:

> *Our vision is not formed within a rectangular boundary; it is per Aristotle, unbounded ... the photograph shows everything in sharp delineation from edge to edge, while our vision, because our eyes are foveate, is sharp only at its 'centre'. The picture is monochromatic, while most of us see in 'natural' colour (and there are some critics who maintain that the picture would be less clear if it were in colour). Finally, the photograph shows objects in sharp focus in and across every plane, from nearest to farthest. We do not see ... things this way.*[38]

There are more materially significant areas of influence related to photographic modes of production. To a great extent the production of the photographic image relies on the mechanical control of the camera. However, later production processes and the use of montage, exposure tampering and fade out techniques may also be used to create specific effects. Because of the expected referentiality of the photo, these fabricated changes to the image of 'Nature' remain unexplained and are often indistinguishable in the final encoded but nevertheless 'real' image.[39] Furthermore, a photograph never appears or is never produced context free. Thus the photograph is given meaning from this context (such as the placing of the image in an art gallery, book, frame or photographic album). It is this meaning as context specific which constructs the reader's capacity to record the image content of the photograph.

The reference to reality in the photographic image and its perceived equivalence to the physiology of sight has made this the primary mode of explanation for architecture. More explicit in its separate role the architectural drawing attempts a discourse between an imagined or sometimes real three-dimensional building or world and a two-dimensional and materially visible medium. But the architectural drawing is not controlled to the same extent by the techniques of its production. The pencil or tools of production do not have the same control as the camera in relation to the photograph. It is assumed that architectural drawing is a consciously stylised rendering of a referential world, in distinction to the photograph's 'image without a code'.[40] Its subject is either a mental fabrication, an object yet to be 'real' which directs the images of architectural drawing as fabrications, or a commentary on an existing object. It is the architectural drawing's very visibility of material which limits its status as a referential medium. Thus, the characteristics and impact of the hand and the further impact of materials set apart architectural drawing from the photograph. For the photograph it

34 For discussion on the co-substantiality of the photographic image and its content object see Joel Snyder, 'Picturing Vision', *Critical Inquiry*, 6, 1979: p. 505.
35 *Ibid.*, p. 503.
36 Stephen Tyler, 'The Vision Quest in the West, or What the Mind's Eye Sees', *Journal of Anthropological Research*, 40, 1, Spring 1984: p. 23.
37 Roland Barthes, *Image–Music–Text*, Glasgow: Fontana, 1977. The first chapter of this book 'The Photographic Message' discusses the implications of the paradox of photography.
38 *Ibid.*, p. 505.
39 John Tagg, *The Burden of Representation*, London: MacMillan Education, 1988: p. 187.
40 Barthes, *op. cit.*

41 Walter Benjamin 'Rigorous Study of Art', trans. Thomas Y Levin, *October*, 47 Winter, 1988: p. 89.

is this very transparent machinery of recording which privileges its capacity as representation.

Within the architectural drawing there is also the impact of the image being a totally mythic construction having no clear pictorial boundaries. This image may be contextualised with the inclusion of 'real' surrounds but the essential focus is of a fabricated and unbounded ideal world. The ideality of this 'world' reinforces architectural drawing as a conceptual art rather than a representational art. Walter Benjamin draws attention to this other 'world' of the architectural drawing. While the focus for comparison in his text are naturalist painters of the 18th and 19th century the essential differences in the 'worlds' of the two media may be applied equally to the photograph and the architectural drawing.

> *The architectural drawing is sharply distinguished from images of this [naturalistic] sort ... Linfert takes this to be a peculiar imaginary world of architecture which is markedly different from that of the painters. There are various indications that confirm the specificity of this world, the most important one being that such architecture is not primarily 'seen', but rather is imagined as being an objective entity and is experienced by those who approach or even enter it as a surrounding space* sui generis, *that is, without the distancing effect of the frame of pictorial space ... In short, the most essential characteristic of the architectural drawing is that it does not take a pictorial detour.*[41]

Although it is hypothesised in Benjamin's text that the architectural drawing is context free – a stance which has arguably changed with the sale and exhibition of architectural drawings as art – Benjamin highlights the nature of the architectural rendering as provoking an interior or imagined hyper-reality for the comprehension of an architectural 'world'.

Resulting from this imagined world, the architectural drawing can tamper with its referent object and sight physiology, inverting or fracturing images to signify separation from the natural world while at the same time, still being referent to an architectural object which is at least potentially real. Photographs may attempt this but retain a reality effect due to the empirical nature of their referentiality to a 'natural' world and the transparency of their media references.

ARCHITECTURAL DRAWING AS DISTINCT FROM TEXT

Rather than take on the structure of language and the narrative controls of written descriptions, architectural drawing adopts graphic constraints aimed to naturalise and visualise architectural fabrications. Architectural text uses both emotive and rational *signifiants* which are employed to narrate or analyse a given built object. These obviously include the usual literary approaches taken in the writing of fiction, for example, the description of scenes or atmosphere through the use of metaphor or analogy, but as well, they include analytical and documentary approaches to description developed through historical and theoretical discourses. The reader of texts on architecture has to mentally fabricate a 'concrete' image of buildings being described, to enter an ideal but architectural 'world'.[42] This is because the rhetoric used to describe buildings is metaphorically and culturally coded and relies on canons of visuality which are historical and socially understood.[43] The language of representation (*signifiants*) triggers dream-like characteristics for the reader, as strategies for understanding. The language derives from fantasy and metaphorical sources and descriptions of existing objects, to crystallise hard artifactual shape to word pictures.[44] The mental production of word representations as 'real' shapes, fabricates an essential but false link between reading/knowledge and reality, that is, between the reader's mental image and a proposed building.[45] There is created a felt sameness, a reality-effect.

This reality-effect is structured by the boundaries and visual coding of subject specific analytical and descriptive language. By this constraint it is difficult to document any multiplicity of meaning or modification in the very structure of an 'architectural' perception in the work being described or analysed. Text thus returns and reconstructs any described architectonic image to its tradition of narration which for architecture derives from the Eurocentric limits of architectural criticism.[46] Within this such elements as ideas of structure, materials, function, order, identity, the structuring of continuities in space, concepts of distance, inside/outside, and colour are spoken of with the assurance that these are significant motivators for architectural form and that there is a commonality of meaning in the profession.

Conversely architectural drawing locates itself within conventional structures of drafting technique often with the aim of modifying the terrain of those conventions. Its strategies are concerned with a commentary about a future which is not always made comprehensible to the present. Many conventions in drawing stem from ordering systems which can be deconstructed, inverted, overlaid or reconstructed in such a way that the mental fabrication of any mythic world or 'real' object becomes difficult or often impossible to comprehend for the uninitiated. That is to say a strategy of hermetic coding is viable only

42 Quoted in Walter Benjamin (1988) *op. cit.*, p. 89.

43 Marx Wartofsky, 'Picturing and Representing' in Calvin Nodine and Dennis Fisher (eds), *Perception and Pictorial Representation*, New York: Praeger, 1979: p. 273.

44 Roland Barthes, 'Historical Discourse', in Michael Lane (ed), *Introduction to Structuralism*, New York: Basic Books, 1970, p. 153.

45 For further discussion of this reality effect see Jules Zanger, 'Heroic Fantasy and Social Reality: ex nihilo nihil fit', in Roger Schlobin (ed), *The Aesthetics of Fantasy Literature and Art*, Sussex: Uni. Notre Dame Press and Harvester Press, 1982, pp. 226–236 and Suzanne Gearheart, 'Introduction', *The Open Boundary of History and Fiction*, Princeton: Princeton Uni. Press, 1984, pp. 3–28.

46 Example of this return to tradition can be seen in Phillip Johnson and Mark Wigley's *Deconstructive Architecture*, New York: Museum of Modern Art, 1988, which documents a particularly 'new' characteristic of architecture which they name as 'deconstructive' but characteristically describe and locate it within the bounds of a Euro-American tradition of architecture. By so doing they work against any recognition of the shift in architectural terrain attempted in this architecture and present it simply as a style.

to the extent that a drawing can be thought of as having a surplus of meaning over its mimetic referentiality to a knowable real.

Thus, rather than reinforcing the dominant position of built architecture by examining drawing's representational force, or discussing only the congruent location of drawing with other discursive media such as text and photographic image, the focus on architectural drawing gives recognition to the specificities of both its modes of production and technologies of visibility. Comparison with text and photograph and the experiential nature of built architecture has isolated characteristics for architectural drawing beyond representation or documentation. These can be summarised:

1. The significance of architectural drawing is the visible nature of its surface, materials and structuring techniques for the production of images. This visibility dictates the graphic media as a discursive act between the content object of the graphic work and the two-dimensional nature of its representation. Thus architectural drawing has little functional compliance with the re-enactment of a transparent mimetic representation.
2. Architectural drawing has a recognisable visual coding which is displayed with the use of iconographic and technical references including notions of scale, frontality and codes of delineation, as well as allegorical, historicist or illusory images which produce ways for interpreting buildings.
3. Architectural drawing can represent a visualisation of the conceptual concerns of architecture or other abstract qualities of architecture including organisational devices in planning and qualities of surface and tessellation without any necessary emphasis on a 'natural' representation.
4. Architectural drawing displays a layer of surplus intention which directs its role away from mere representation to one which can remake or shift the terrain of what is accepted as an architectural concern by documenting changing conceptual foci for architecture with changed techniques of imaging and media.

This analysis thus locates a duality of aims for architectural drawing. There is an intention to be representational and documentary – to give a measurable and geometrically accurate depiction of a future architectural reality – but conversely there is also an intention to explore the non-representational characteristics of architecture or of the medium of architectural drawing, intentions which confound any easy interpretation or comprehension of image. This duality of conventions and the open boundary for the representational requirements of some architectural drawings illuminates the acceptance of the typological plurality of architectural drawings and also locates the obviously different artistic styles used for the picturing of architectural images.

3. ARCHITECTURAL RENDERING AS A DISCURSIVE ACT

It is left to question what the isolation of these features of architectural drawing can show in relation to a visibility of cultural production in the formation of our contemporary architectural profession. What debates are set up between built architecture and the drawn image? Further to this, what are the visual codes employed to image buildings? And, what is the role of the artist and the observer in the production of such imagery? A second vital series of questions can thus examine the response of architectural drawing to the terrain of current Australian architectural theory and the reflexivity of its practices. To discuss the issues raised by these questions a selection of drawings from those displayed in the body of this book will be examined. Those selected are not representational of the book's full collection but can be grouped loosely as having structured characteristics outside those authoritative and mechanical drawing techniques of the architectural profession's traditions. Indeed those selected would probably receive a great deal of criticism from the profession because of their non-representational nature. It is this characteristic which has become interesting in the light of discussion in this introduction. Selection was made, however, without any desire for these particular artifacts to be considered as exposing any *avant-garde* amongst architects or architectural renderers but those selected are drawings that through their imagery clearly point to a particular image production for the presentation of architectural 'futures'. The selected drawings embark on the notions of picturing from an attempt to provoke, in the observer, an interest in critically responding to architectural form rather than to accept the transparency of its representation. Those which will be discuss at greater depth are the surreal and abstracted images by Marc Raszewski picturing Norman Day's designs; those semi representational and fractured images done by Zbigniew Jaworski picturing Ivan Rijavec's designs; the technical and geometrically based images of Graham Jahn for his own design and Jaro Safer for the designs of Daryl Jackson; the highly iconographic images of Arthur Collin and Brian Lilley, those of Howard Raggatt for the Ashton Raggatt and McDougall's design and those which recall the mythologised iconographia of the Australian landscape in the images of Keith Pike and Greg Burgess.

If the precondition of the visualisation of buildings through authoritative and transparent forms of representation is a forgetfulness of the experiential practices and modes of production which inscribe

fig. 8

fig. 9

47 Jonathan Crary, *Techniques of the Observer: On Vision and Modernity in the 19th Century*, Massachusetts: MIT, 1990, p. 1
48 *Ibid.*
49 *Ibid.*

that building then the most easily characterised debate which these drawings raise is an attempt at a dialogue between the many media and conditions of architecture. They all rely in varying degrees on the notions of technical delineation and representation used in architectural practices but do not simply 'represent'. Indeed the buildings pictured by these drawings cannot be seen as 'wholes' but as fragments often without clear association with other images pictured. Thus, there is little hierarchy for understanding holistic ordering concepts or compositional structures. Ordering binaries of whole and part, inside and outside, form and function, composition and technique are no longer the *rationale* for understanding. Their architectural 'worlds' require a high level of observer interaction which relies to a great extent on text, photography and observer experience to fabricate any mental image or comprehension of the building, or elaborate any meaning for the architectural drawing. The images work at a different level which demands a process of understanding which is layered and outside any attempt to objectify an exterior and rational world.

These drawings display the significance of their approach when placed in comparison with recent developments which aim to represent 'virtual reality'. Two issues are immediately highlighted. The change in the ideals of representation parallels a changing attitude to an exterior 'real' world with the impact of computers on architectural picturing. In his book *Techniques of the Observer*, Jonathan Crary calls attention to current reconfigurations in the meaning of terms such as 'representation' with the development of computer techniques for spatial synthesis.[47] He suggests that they 'herald the ubiquitous implantation of fabricated visual 'spaces' radically different from the mimetic capacities of film, photography and television'[48] (Figure 8 and 9). With the arrival of space fabrication, Crary sees practices of representation moving away from any reference to 'the position of an observer in a "real", optically perceived world'.[49] The images selected for study here, either create this 'unreal' space through a mythologising context or alternately collapse the notion of 'space' for the drawing. By withdrawing the necessity of the inscribed I/eye of the observer in architectural drawing, current practices of imaging thus free representation from any tie to mimetic repetition. These practices recognise a difference between drawing, text, photography and building which for drawing highlights its artifactural role. As 'painterly' artifacts emphasis is on colour, shape and symbols. Symbols range from figurative and iconographic collaging to the adoption of specific styles of representation.

Secondly, while the meaning of 'representation' may be changing with the introduction of CAD to architectural practice. The appearance of a group of architectural drawings which are characterised

fig. 10

fig. 11

through their non-representational imagery and their collaging of figurative iconographia is in direct contrast to an impact of CAD documented by Mike Cooley.[50] He suggests that just as design became separated from building during the Renaissance, the more recent architectural developments in computer technology disjoint the labour process of drawing from its intellectual counterpart. The practices of architectural drawing seen in examples selected here, display a proliferation of 'hand-crafted' images of architectural representation. Certainly the use of allegorical, historicist and multi-layered images illustrates an intention for a visibility of artistic will and hand/tool/craft patina to any interpretation of architectural drawing.

50 Cooley, *op. cit.*

The range of iconographic imagery directs attention to the specific nature of the visual codes which reinforce these ideals of representation. For the selected images these include:

1 The multiple layering or collection of partial views of images such as Jaworski's of the Manifold residence (Figure 10), or Raszewski's image of Norman Day's Konindaris House. Jaworski's aim reinforces the notion of drawing as discourse:

> *Every project is a combination of layers. My work is about revealing the inner nature of the subject, its complexities – simplicities – functions – forms. I am trying to involve the viewer into the discourse. Elevations, plans, structural elements, details – they are all in very specific relations.*

Norman Day further comments on the reference of his images to mimetic representation (Figure 11).

> *The graphic is a complex design showing many facets of our building – in one. We produced a concept sketch based on the formal architectural plans and elevations of our building, and over that basic information we applied a number of bits of our design in a surreal manner. The lot floats over a base and a sky. Tile patterns and colours are represented as accurate suggestions of the design but also as punchy graphic elements.*

The recognition of the architectural content of these drawings becomes a subjective act on the part of the observer. It could be argued that through the faceting of imagery the drawings allude to and draw meaning from artistic periods such as Purism, Cubism and Suprematism and Surrealism as well as from the architectural imagery of its content. This allusion both references the drawing through the structure of its imagery, but also as a historicist yearning for Modernist pasts with their

fig. 12

fig. 13

fig. 14

American and Eurocentricities and heroic avant-gardism. Thus the drawing infers ways of representing and understanding the architecture through the overlaying of such information. But a significance of this mixing of visibilities is that these non-representational artistic styles have been used in representational acts and thus picture a dialogue which reflexively states the nature of architectural drawing as well as representing the building pictured. The images pick out architectural figures as their representational focus, but rely on a compositional structure derived from painting.

2. The critical commentary and image reflexivity depicted in drawings such as Collin and Lilley's series (Figure 12), which overlay and collage images from 'junk mail' onto the architectonic content of their drawings. Their collages included 'as found postcard, collaged with associated images (junk mail), masked and peeled, painted over, finished with pen and ink' with the aim of illustrating relevant events and situations, displaying obsessions, and mimicing the precesses of design. Ashton, Raggatt and McDougall's collaged images conversely take the role of testing the object of representation under various conditions (Figure 13). They 'test' the image of the suburban house as in an ideal and symbolic association with the garden, with an image of Adam and Eve; as a site for a political statement on 'labour and industry' with the image of a mine; as a myth of consumer futures with the collaging of an upper storey to the house which happens to be a Shingle Style house by Arthur Rich; and as a site for domestic 'indulgence and aspiration' with the collaging of a jogger in silk shorts. These again use ways of picturing displayed in Dadaist art of the early 20th century and therefore have an historicist nature but similar to Dadaist art the drawings call attention to the 'high culture' nature of architecture and question the validity of this status.
3. This group attempt to locate the image of buildings in the myths of Australian landscape and spirit. Greg Burgess's sand painting planning concept (Figure 14) and Keith Pike's Eurocentric view of the Australian outback reinforce popular ideals of Australia (Figure 15). By placing particular building forms within the context of this mythologised art and landscape, there is an attempt to overcome Eurocentricities which abound for the Australian profession. However, these images also express the difficulty of collapsing the necessarily Anglo-American building forms with a difficult to comprehend landscape and aboriginal spirit.
4. This group displays a layering of images but are unlike those discussed in the first of these analyses. These drawings direct attention to the illusory and geometric nature of architectural drawing and the

fig. 15

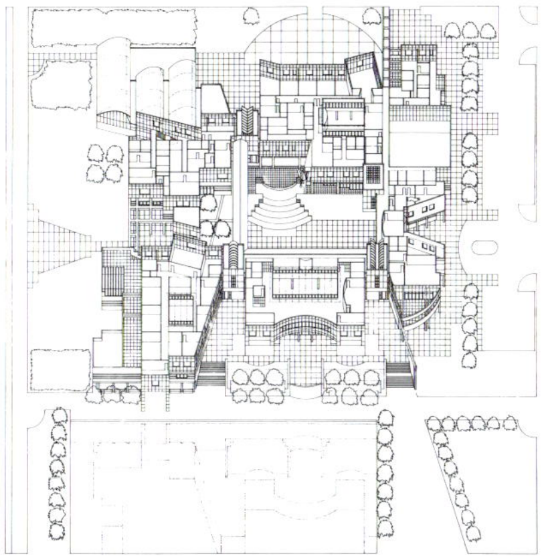

fig. 16

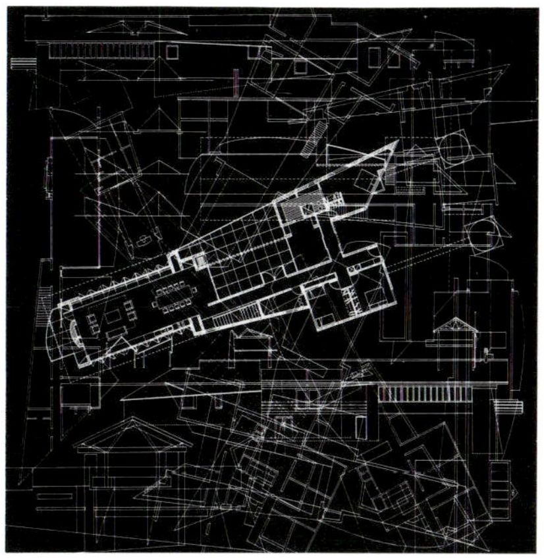

fig. 17

process of design and building experience. They take as their framing device, geometric drawings which overlay and interrupt the finite characteristics of the drawing's central focus. In Jaro Safer's drawing for Daryl Jackson this central image disappears in the abstract complexity of the whole (Figure 16). The office suggests:

> *These drawings are not easily read for they are an intended abstraction, they're for the eye to explore. The basic formula for the Safer drawing is to show the buildings in plan with their elevations projected onto one or two faces as a geometric portrayal of the inner volume. Around this centrepiece, other elevations may be drawn as a border, usually related to each side of the plan, which means that in some cases the elevation appears upside down.*

Graham Jahn suggests a more conscious display of the design process (Figure 17). He suggests:

> *We sometimes construct composite drawings which record the architectural development of an idea up to and including the final design resolution. Each step during design has language alternatives which are revealed in the plan, section and elevation. The overlaid images in this drawing are the discarded alternatives with the final design superimposed.*

These images again highlight the artifactural role of these architectural drawings and set up a dialogue between the final design and the processes which inscribe it.

Analysis of the structuring and visualising devices found in this selection of drawings illustrates a changing focus for particular practices of architectural drawing. There is an obvious break appearing between metrically accurate and legally required drawings used during the building process and those used to reinforce the public explanation of conceptual architectural concerns. This division in focus has allowed a preoccupation with a visibility of concepts difficult to comprehend through the experience of buildings. The significance of particular conceptual concerns in the Australian context is their appearance in combination with structured ways of seeing developed in modern artistic practices.

This combination makes obvious debates which underlie, but rarely surface, in the Australian architectural profession. The most obvious of these is a preoccupation with the boundaries between architectural 'space' and representation and the level of theoretical discourse acknowledged in this country's profession.

ILLUSTRATIONS

Figure 1: Sebastiano Serlio, from The English Edition of *Secondo Libro*, London, Robert Peake, 1611, reprinted New York, Dover, 1982, fol. 25.

Figure 2: Andrea Palladio, from *The Second Book of Architecture*, reprinted Dover, New York, 1965, plate 13.

Figure 3: Giuseppi Galli Bibiena, from 'Architetture e prospettive dedicate alla Maesta di Carlo Sesto, Imperador de'Romani, da Giuseppe Galli Bibiena, suo primo ingegner teatrale, ed architetto, inventore delle medisme' (1740), reprinted in *Architectural and Perspective Designs by Giuseppe Galli Bibiena*, Dover, New York, 1964.

Figure 4: Giovanni Battista Piranesi, The Arch with a Shell Ornament, Carceri, State V1., from Andrew Robinson, *Piranesi, Early Architectural Fantasies: A Catalogue Raisonné of the Etchings*, University of Chicago Press, Chicago, 1986.

Figure 5: Brunelleschi's apparatus. See also Eugenio Battisti, *Filippo Brunelleschi, The Complete Work*, New York, Rizzoli, 1981, 108, 109.

Figure 6: Theo van Doesburg and Cornelis van Eesteren, Colour Construction, 1922. Counter-construction of the *Maison particulière* 1923 Rijkadienat Beeldende Kunst, The Hague.

Figure 7: August Choisy, from August Choisy, *Historie de L'Architecture*, Editions Vincent, Freal and Co., Paris, 1964, p. 354.

Figure 8 & 9: Nathan O'Brien student work University of NSW, School of Architecture 1991.

The Australian architectural profession has often been self-critical of the level of theoretical debate engendered in its discourse. By contrast this analysis suggests that this profession does not theorise itself in text but in the visual practices of its drawing. The theoretical debates made visual in these graphic statements picture most clearly the paradox of 'colonisation' which is the most significant debate for the current profession; that self-knowledge and the constitution of the profession remains a conflict between an implanted and transliterated European model of professionalism, visuality and imaging contrasted to an Australian profession which forever seeks to gain independence. The paradox remains and will continue to be debated because each image of independence from that Eurocentric source references itself to the source in the cultural production of its visibility, with practices which give the profession its structure and which form its authority.

The second level of debate surfacing in these images is that of status for the architectural profession. Many of these drawings are difficult to interpret or 'read'. To encode a drawing with this added complexity both liberates it from any confining 'correct' interpretation but divorces it from being readily consumed by an uninformed public. Thus the drawing becomes a commodity for an elite who have been educated to read its complexity. This can be read as an intention on the part of the architect to change the accessibility of the architectural image at the level of concept. Indeed to document a separation of concept and built form and to demand recognition of different requirements for reading the differing media of architecture. While tending toward elitism this act makes concrete a theoretical agenda for architecture which is implied through its formal composition rather than the processes of synthesis to built form or the experiences and rationalities of these built forms.

The third level of debate focuses on the actual combinations which have occurred in these drawings. What is the significance of combining the structuring devices or ways for visualising found in particular painting styles of the early 20th century with the representation of architectural forms? This act certainly fractures hierarchical and traditionally coded concepts which have become the usual manner for interpreting buildings. Instead the focus works to isolate fragments of concepts and architectural images and juxtapose others in a layering which redirects architectural concepts away from traditional rationalities.

Thus in relation to the practices of architecture, drawing as a significant media provides a ground of debate for the display of significant attitudes of the current architectural profession. It also documents a visual culture which has currently taken representation from an attempted transparency to the real world to locate a media most interested in the reflexivity of its techniques.

DESLEY LUSCOMBE

DOMESTIC ARCHITECTURE

KING HOUSE - VICTORIA - NONDA KATSALIDIS ARCHITECTS

This house is a trim blade for the modern professional couple. The strategy was to clearly divide the dormitory wing and the leisure areas, thus freeing the design from the usual problems associated with grafting into existing structures.

The enclosure captures the pool on one side and the residence on the other. It weaves the circulation as a narrative promenade oscillating between the residence and the pool and winds up to the platform to view the sea and the sky.

The drawings use pencil on film and photomontage figures which are reproduced using a large format photocopier and highlighted with blue pencil. The whole polytich comprises eight panels individually mounted between glass which allows light to pass through the paper and give an illuminous effect to the drawing. The narrative structure of the drawing and the overlapping glass mounting gives a dynamic three-dimensional reading to what is normally a static two-dimensional medium.

Design Architects:
Nonda Katsalidis,
Gerard Van Beek and
Shane Williams
Drawing Artist:
Shane Williams
Size: 255 x 800 x 8 mm
Date: 1986

KING HOUSE - VICTORIA - NONDA KATSALIDIS ARCHITECTS

The bronze model was created using a technique called shell casting. This process entails producing a pattern — original model which was then encased in a ceramic shell. This is formed by dipping the pattern a number of times into a liquid clay mixture (slip).
In normal circumstances the pattern for shell casting is formed in wax, but on this occasion, in order to produce a more exacting result, the pattern was built using polystyrene foam cast with a purpose designed hot-wire cutter.
Having encased the pattern with the shell, the work was transferred to a kiln where the heat burns the pattern away. The resulting cavity is then filled with bronze. Following casting the shell is broken away and the bronze is cleaned and the patina applied.

Model: John Cherrey

HACKFORD HOUSE – TRARALGON – VICTORIA GREG BURGESS ARCHITECT

Design Architect: Greg Burgess
Drawing Artist: Peter Jensen
Size: 1189 x 841 mm
Date: 1981
Photographer: John Gollings

Situated on a 20 hectare farm beside a stream in the lower reaches of the beautiful Gippsland Valley, the Hackford family house is surrounded by undulating pastureland and fingers of bush; a wild-life lake stretches to the west.
The house poises about a north-south axis – down-valley to the sun, and up-valley to the stream source. A pool and fountain located over an underground watercourse in the walled garden, feed a waterfall and rockpools in a fern gully bridged by the house. A series of grassed terraces drop to the stream.
In the heart of the house, gravity and light are connected by stairs. A floor window to the gully below and a tower pushing through a quarterfoil roof-light opening to the sky, emphasise this relationship.
Opposing forces are in play; integrating energy is apparent.
This house is a vehicle for approaching wholeness.
As above, so below.
The rendering is lead pencil on tracing paper. Pencil is ideal for imaginatively entering and evoking the mystery of experiencing architecture – especially in the heart realm.

KONINDARIS HOUSE - BRIGHTON - VICTORIA NORMAN DAY ARCHITECT

An existing solid Brighton house has been added-to over the years in a piecemeal manner. The original Californian bungalow style of the house – with characteristic bay windows, deep roof eaves and bracket supports and roughcast render and brickwork – had been modernised and painted to become a bare memory of its original elegance. It was to be developed as a substantial family house, upgraded for contemporary living standards and especially redirected towards grand entertaining and living spaces associated with the outdoor pool and spa areas.
We chose to interpret the original architecture using contemporary and creative license so that the original building would be represented in a fresh way and additions and changes would acknowledge the original style – not by mimicry but through interpretation and discovery.
Centrepoint of the planning are the sculptured forms of a kitchen – which is at once a theatrical prop in the spacious 'theatre' of the house, and also becomes the cockpit and meeting place for the building.
New building areas are defined by flowing forms, sculptured curves and high-grade materials (granite, metal, specially constructed timber joinery). Glass has been used as a foil between the old house and new components – so the link between the two is visible and understandable. We have substantially rebuilt most of the old plasterwork, windows, doors and floors, along with a total upgrade of all services. Landscaping has been integrated into the design, so lawns, trees and paving become architectural components – they are at one with the building. We show the possibilities for uncovering historical architectural elements by interpretation rather than copying. The past becomes more understandable and the new acknowledges that past – by invention rather than quote.
The graphic is a complex design showing many facets of our building – in one. We produced a concept sketch based on the formal architectural plans and elevations of our building, and over that basic information we applied a surreal number of bits of our design. The lot floats over a base and sky. Tile patterns and colours are represented as accurate suggestions of the design but also as punchy graphic elements – they transmute into snakes at one stage. The drawing is a simple picture on the one hand but on the other it tells a complex story of our architectural intentions.

Design Architect: Norman Day
Drawing Artist:
Marc Raszewski
Size: 1682 x 1189 mm
Date: 1990
Photographer: Norman Day

HOUSE – LITTLE MANLY – NEW SOUTH WALES **CAMPBELL LUSCOMBE ASSOCIATES**

Design Architects:
Leo Campbell and
Amanda Burgess
Drawing Artists:
Desley Luscombe and
Jeffrey Mueller
Size: 1189 x 841 mm
Date: 1990
Photographer: Tim Colis-Bird

Due to the extreme narrowness of the site the concept of fragmenting the house into component parts was utilised to create 'gaps' between the parts and between the building and the boundaries. This approach gave the interiors access to natural light from unexpected and delightful sources, giving the interiors a light and spacious quality not normally found with such 'built-to-the-boundary' type houses. The components of the house break apart and reduce in mass as one progresses toward the rear of the site. These fragmented parts then form the surrounds of an internalised family courtyard space. This courtyard space is not structured as an 'internal room' or homogeneously contained by consistent enclosure, but rather in an urban sense as a designed residual space between different buildings. The last fragment separates itself both physically and stylistically from the remainder to become on the upper level an 'isolated' parent wing and on the ground level the separate informal living area.
As the client possessed little furniture, they were comfortable with the idea that the house provide the complexity of line usually given by furniture to achieve an internal visual richness. Subsequently internal walls to the living spaces become freestanding elements and the kitchen became a coloured piece of furniture within the family living space.
Axonometrics were used as the site was narrow and built-up close boundary. The exploded axonometric explores qualities of interior and exterior on the same drawing thus considering ideas of passage, spatial flow and formal composition in the one image. It was carried out with 0.25 mm Rotring pens on heavyweight film. Pantone provided colour and texture (Instantex) was covered with Pantone grey.

HOUSE – VAUCLUSE – NEW SOUTH WALES   ARCHITECTURAL PROJECTS

The house addresses a major street and harbour views at the rear. It is divided into three storeys, with the lower two levels both accessed from street level. The concern for the progression from street to reserve is primary in importance, a gradual opening of space affording views to the harbour beyond.
The planning of the house follows a regular grid of three units by three units, which emphasise the central entry axis and which unites the three levels vertically (through the entry foyer and stair) and by a higher volume. This central zone orders the internal spaces, shifting from the formal entry, deflected by the living room and re-established in the dining room, creating a cyclical motion around this implied centre which is reflected in the symmetry of the front façade versus the tension of the stepped living spaces and terraces.

The house is located on a main road amongst piecemeal and incoherent residential development. A strong image to the road was sought in a building that would enhance the geography and street form of the area. Cutting into the site reduced the visible impact of the house. Attention was paid to site coverage, and minimal interruption of natural light and privacy which resulted in the neighbours being supportive of the project. Room orientation minimised effects of traffic noise and maximised effective exploitation of views and sunlight.

All inks and drawing equipment are by Faber Castell. Ink on plastic foil (ammonia copy – negative) off which a reverse negative was taken. Overlays were applied, comprised of Letrafilm, coloured paper and air-brushing.

Design Architects:
Gary O'Reilly and
Jennifer Hill
Drawing Artist: Jennifer Hill
Size: 840 x 590 mm
Date: 1988
Photographer: Warrick Kent

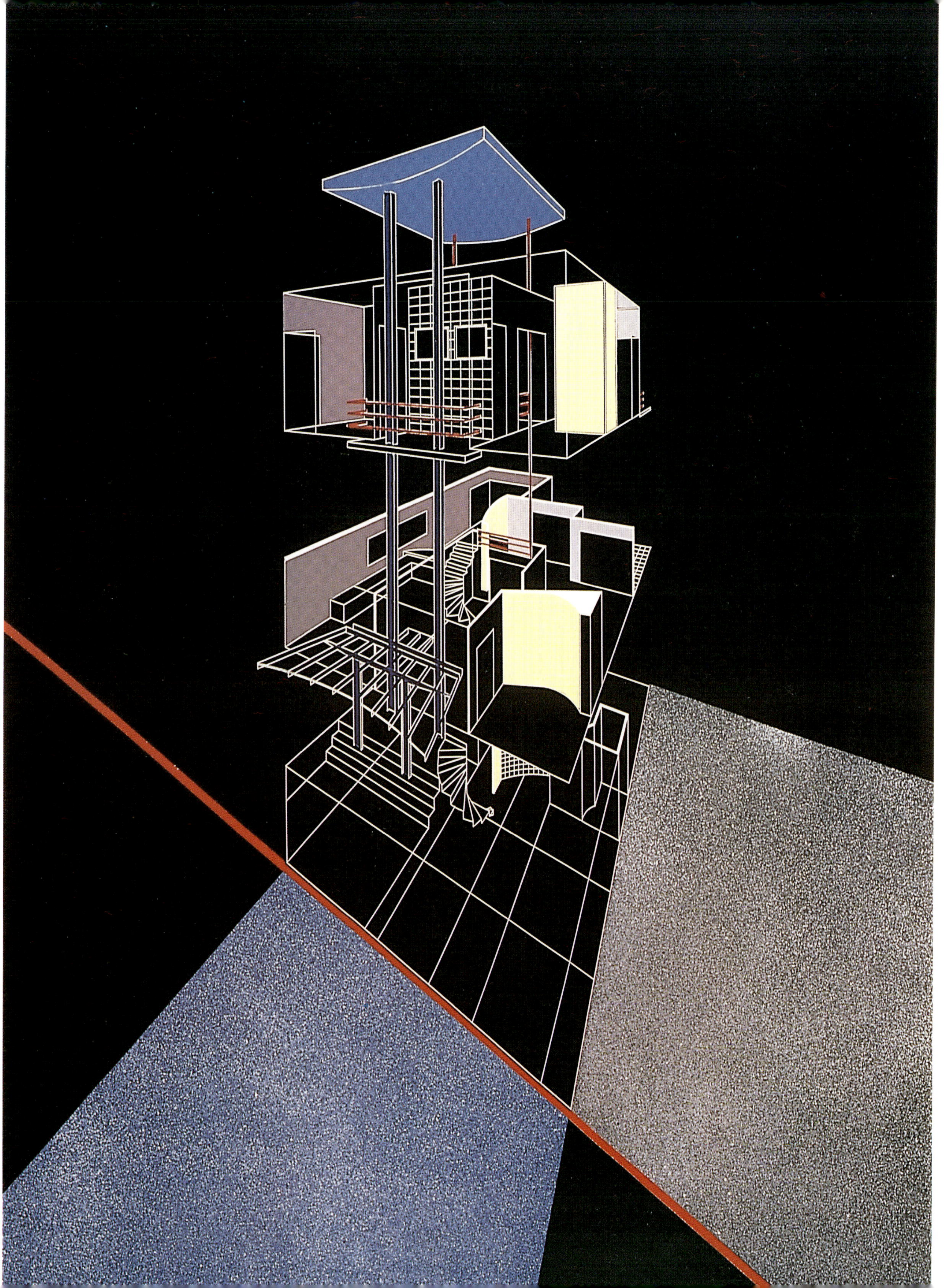

RESIDENTIAL DESIGN STUDY – WAVERTON – NEW SOUTH WALES ALLEN JACK & COTTIER

WATERFRONT PRECINCT

SQUARE

OYSTER COVE

SPORTS CENTRE/BRIDGE

KIOSK

SQUARE

In 1982 Allen Jack & Cottier was asked to study the Australian Gas Light Company site at Waverton with a view to establishing a local environment plan. The site was 9Ha in area, its south eastern boundary a steep sandstone cliff, on the North open bushland rising to the ridge on the Waverton Peninsula, to the north-east the main northern suburban rail line and to the south-west significant foreshore to Sydney Harbour.

An array of historic and existing buildings were contained on the site. The most dominant being the Bunkering Building – rising like a fortress on the South East corner of the foreshore. Three precincts were developed, waterfront, terraced ponds and central park. The design had housing developing along the south-east boundary, terracing down the cliff-face to the large central park, then benching down to individual houses and apartment buildings located about pedestrian streets. Several large terraced ponds were created by utilising an existing creek. Integrated into this area were the existing industrial buildings. The 'village' terminating in an open square on the waterfront with commercial and retail facilities a bus and ferry stop, dinghy club and marina.

A series of vignettes representational of various aspects of the development were favoured to indicate a sense of the 'village' like character. These were done as individual ink line drawings approximately 100 mm square. They were not 'set up' but done as sketches. They were then arranged and formatted on titled sheets enlarged and photocopied onto white bond paper. They were then coloured using coloured pencils.

COMMUNITY SQUARE

COMMUNITY SQUARE
(FROM ROSS ST)

TERRACED PONDS

PRE SCHOOL

BUILDING 10 ENTRY

VILLAGE STREET

Design Architects:
Peter Ireland, Peter Moncton
and Reg Smith
Drawing Artist: Peter Ireland
Size: each 100 x 100 mm
Date: 1982

HOUSE PROJECT - THREDBO - NEW SOUTH WALES JAHN ASSOCIATES ARCHITECTS

Design Architect:
Graham Jahn
Drawing Artist:
Graham Jahn
Size: 1000 x 1000 mm
Date: 1988

As part of the Lake Crackenback Village project in the Snowy Mountains, 15 individual houses were designed by 15 different architects invited by the master plan architects.

From the assessors reports: 'the house manifests a compelling architectural poetic. Its dynamic plan is unequivocally Modern, yet an air of alpine chalet is conveyed (without any resort to kitsch) by the big gabled roof end, sloping stone buttresses ... Despite its apparent complexity the house is constructed from simple, repetitive units, trusses, beams, windows and cupboard units. Most of the building can be prefabricated off-site apart from the bedroom slab and pier supports.

We sometimes construct composite drawings which record the architectural development of an idea up to and including the final design resolution. Each step during design has language alternative which are revealed in plan, section and elevation. The overlaid images in this drawing are the discarded alternatives with the final design superimposed.

The original must be created on polyester film of medium weight (003") and drawn with dense black ink. All line work must be checked on a light table for density and retouched where required.

The original is placed on matt bromide paper under glass and preferably in a vacuum press to ensure that there is even contact between the two surfaces. There is no photographic negative, as this is direct process.

The final image can be masked and air-brushed using opaque solvent inks and masking film.

Polyester film, drawing pens and ink, matt bromide paper from roll.

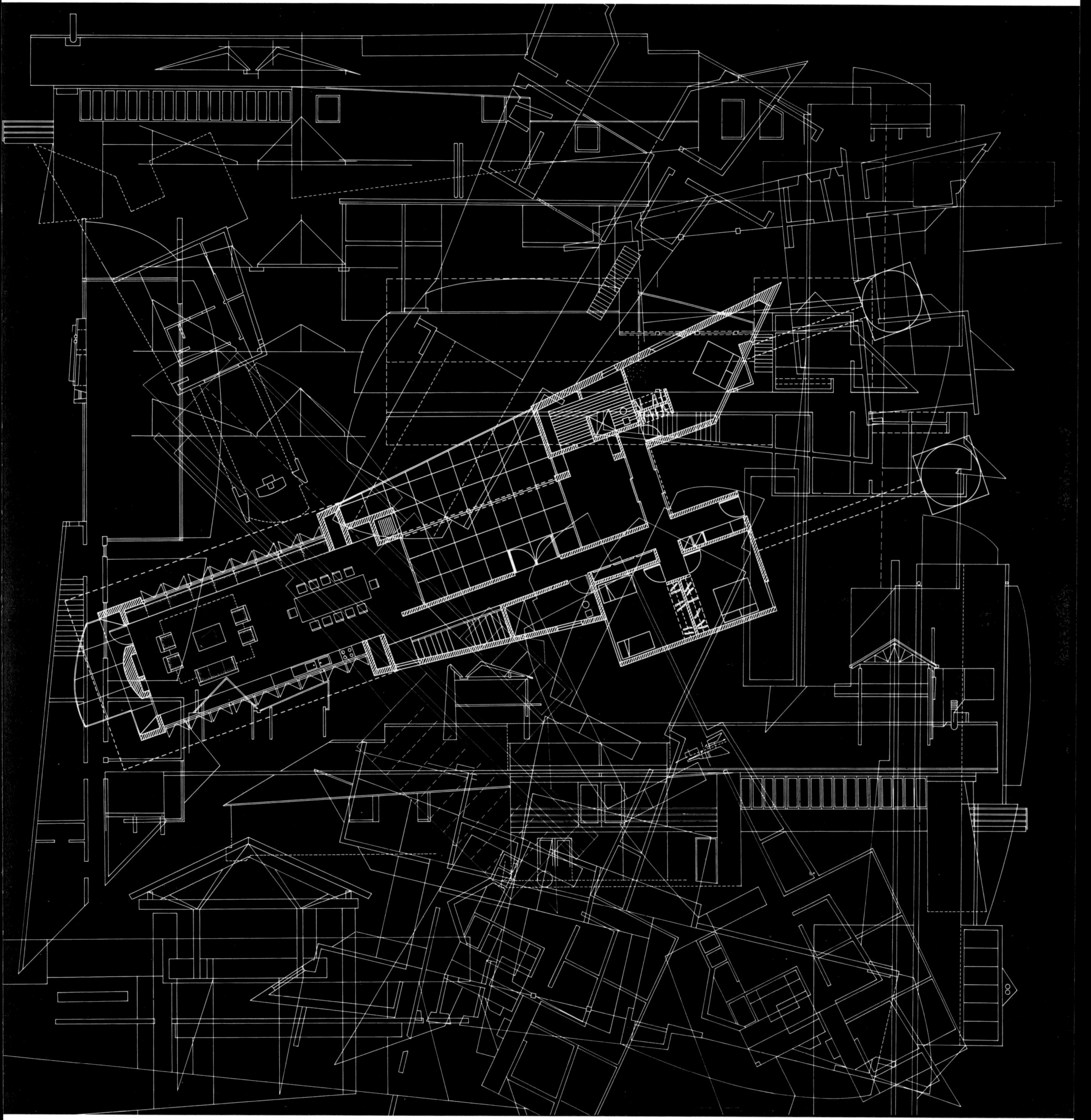

MERLI HOUSE – MERRICKS NORTH – VICTORIA **EDMOND & CORRIGAN ARCHITECTS**

This project explores the expression of elements of the House as a walled city. The surrounding European (Australian) landscape is treated as a series of vistas in the picturesque style. The courtyard is intended to be Tuscan. The client thinks he is a builder and his wife thinks she lectures in English at a nearby university. They are artists.
Pantone and ink on gloss bromide.

Design Architect:
Peter Corrigan
Drawing Artist:
Geoffrey Barton
Size: 844 x 594 mm
Date: 1983

STAFFORD HOUSE (PROJECT) MIDDLE PARK – VICTORIA STREAMES ASSOCIATES

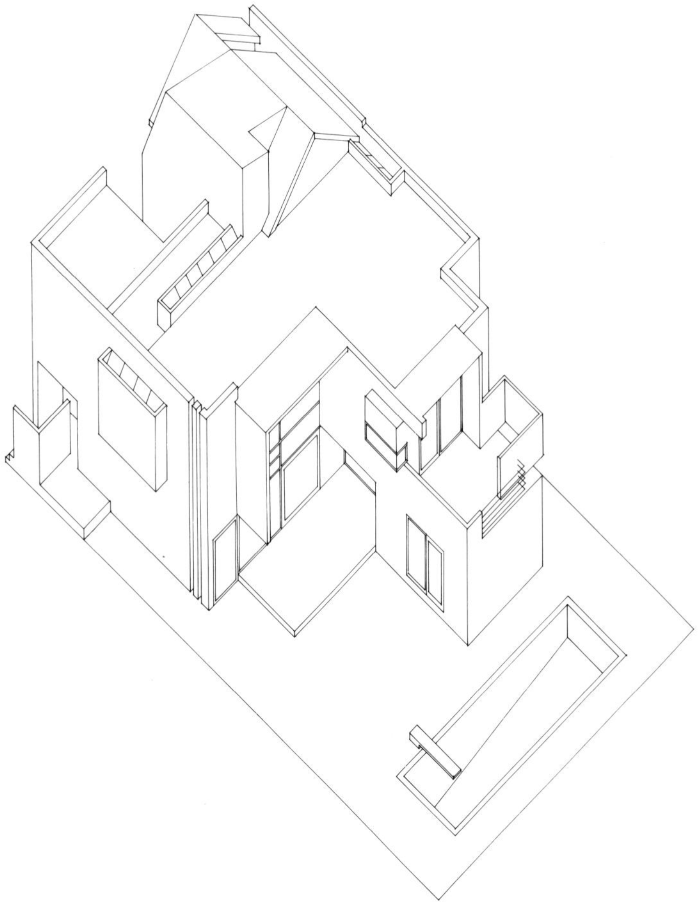

Single family house, situated at the rear of an inner suburban allotment and fronting a service right of way. The new structure is an addition to an existing two-storey garage/studio outbuilding. Town planning restrictions ensured the preservation of the existing building and required maintenance of lines of sight along the right of way. The project was an opportunity to test the formal ideas generated by my interest in the Modern movement. It is strictly Modernist, by no means contextual in the currently accepted sense of the word, gaining clues for its morphological identification from the broader environment. It makes few gestures to formalism, almost none to arbitrary quotations from expressive languages. It has few concerns beyond itself. Our interest was limited to space and its relation to material, geometry and structure.
An attempt at the articulation of a spatial order refusing mechanical juxtaposition of rooms was made by the introduction of sources of light deep within the building and by the harmony of geometric relationships made accessible by the contrast of texture and colour of the surface.
The coloured studies are a wide exploration of surface form and texture. The new centre 'block' of the building is penetrated and eroded; added to and deleted from by various forms and elements reflecting convolutions of the program. These effects on the composition are explored and analysed by the relationships of blocks of colour, and provide for alternate interpretations of form and surface. The colour palette generally used for these studies is arbitrary, though in this case colours were lifted from the early paintings of Picasso. Materials: Derwent colour pencil on detail and tracing paper.

Design Team: Keith Streames and Brendan Kennedy
Drawing Artist: Richard Brew
Size: 1189 x 841 mm
Date: 1989

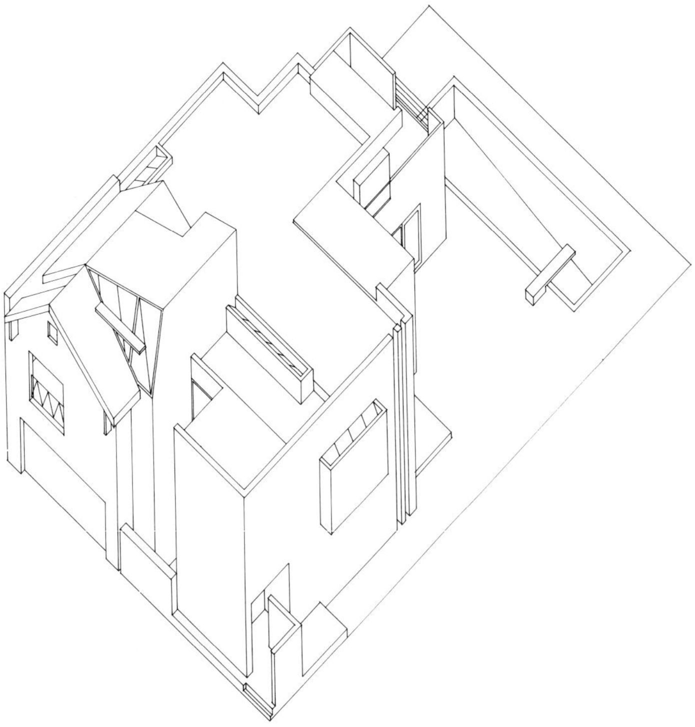

R BREW

HOUSE – SYDNEY – NEW SOUTH WALES   CRACKNELL AND LONERGAN

The existing becomes the base, womblike and strong, from which extends a pavilion-like structure below.
The new freestanding structure, vertical in expression, marks the entry.
The connection above is the pavilion.
The connection below is around water.
The entry is the loggia to the garden, the podium to the stair, the threshold to the living.
The living spaces are alcoves in the kitchen.
The kitchen is a credenza; the stair, the joinery unit.
The bathroom is the verandah, the sill is a seat, and the basin is the sleeping-bathing connection.
The garden is an outside room and the laundry and shower, the roof terrace is an outside room, the sunny garden alcove.
The street wall is a window seat and the original entry houses meters and mail.
The façade has new superimposed on old.
The house is a cabinet.
And there are some things of sentimental value inside.
Drawing is an essential part of our design process. They accumulate as a series and finally can be seen in the final object and the built work in the drawing. The axonometric is worked over with detail design sketches. Materials are butter paper with pencil outlines, Derwent colours have been used, layered to effect depth and areas of light and dark.

Design Architects:
Peter Lonergan and
Julie Cracknell
Drawing Artist:
Peter Lonergan
Size: 841 x 594 mm
Date: 1987–91
Photographers: Simon Kenny,
Ashley Barber and
Peter Lonergan

FREDERICI RESIDENCE - SYDNEY - NEW SOUTH WALES   PHILIP MOORE ARCHITECT

The existing building houses a family run pasta business with a retail outlet to the street and a small pasta factory behind. The clients required a bedroom with bathroom facilities and both internal and external living spaces. A lightweight steel stair, its aesthetic borrowed from its factory surroundings, ascends to the upper level to be encased in a glazed box. The bedroom and external paved roof deck lead from the landing. The deck provides a private outdoor escape uncommon in this high density neighbourhood. The character of the street is maintained by the façade which gives no indication of the contemporary forms and spaces held within.
The drawing is reverse bromide from Rapidograph ink pen on 110 gm drafting film.

Design Architect: Philip Moore
Drawing Artist: Philip Moore
Size: 841 x 594 mm
Date: 1991
Photographer: Philip Moore

FEDERICI RESIDENCE

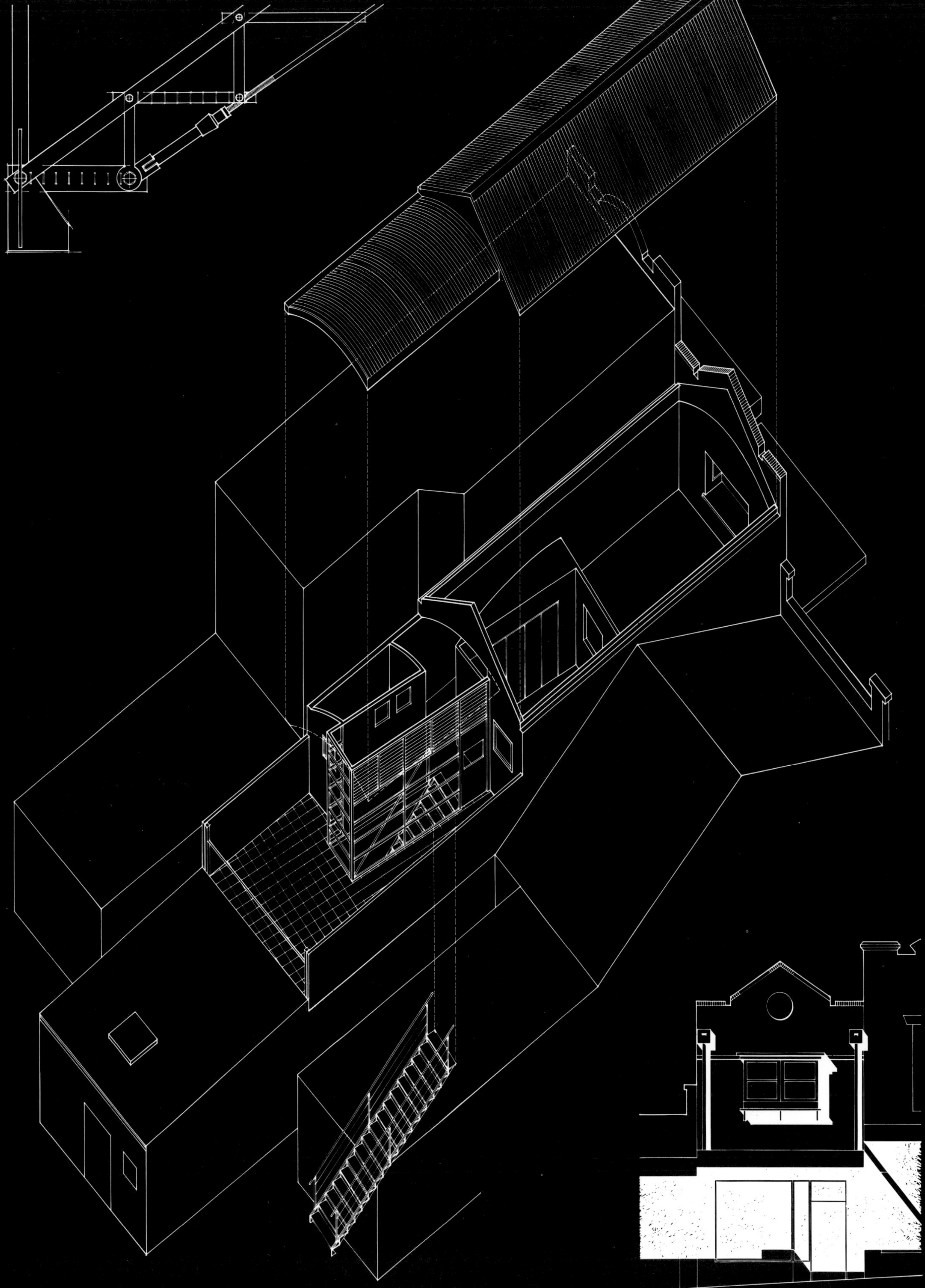

TOMSGATE WAY HOUSE - MOUNT NEBO - QUEENSLAND BRIT ANDRESEN AND PETER O'GORMAN ARCHITECTS

Design Architect:
Brit Andresen
Drawing Artist:
Michael Barnett
Size: 510 x 420 mm
Date: 1990
Photographer: Brit Andresen

The site lies within a larger property at Mount Nebo which is heavily treed with native species mainly planted in the 1950s. The clients' brief was for a single family house. In addition to the room program the most significant requirements were that the design was to incorporate images and qualities which the clients associated with traditional farmhouses of the south of France. Material preferences were masonry floor and walls and timber joinery including pine, silky oak and tallowwood which were provided from the site.
The image was achieved with the use of ink on drafting film. The axonometric projection was drawn at 1:100 scale and the external northern wall, roof and upper floors were cut away to illustrate the internal construction and spatial ordering.

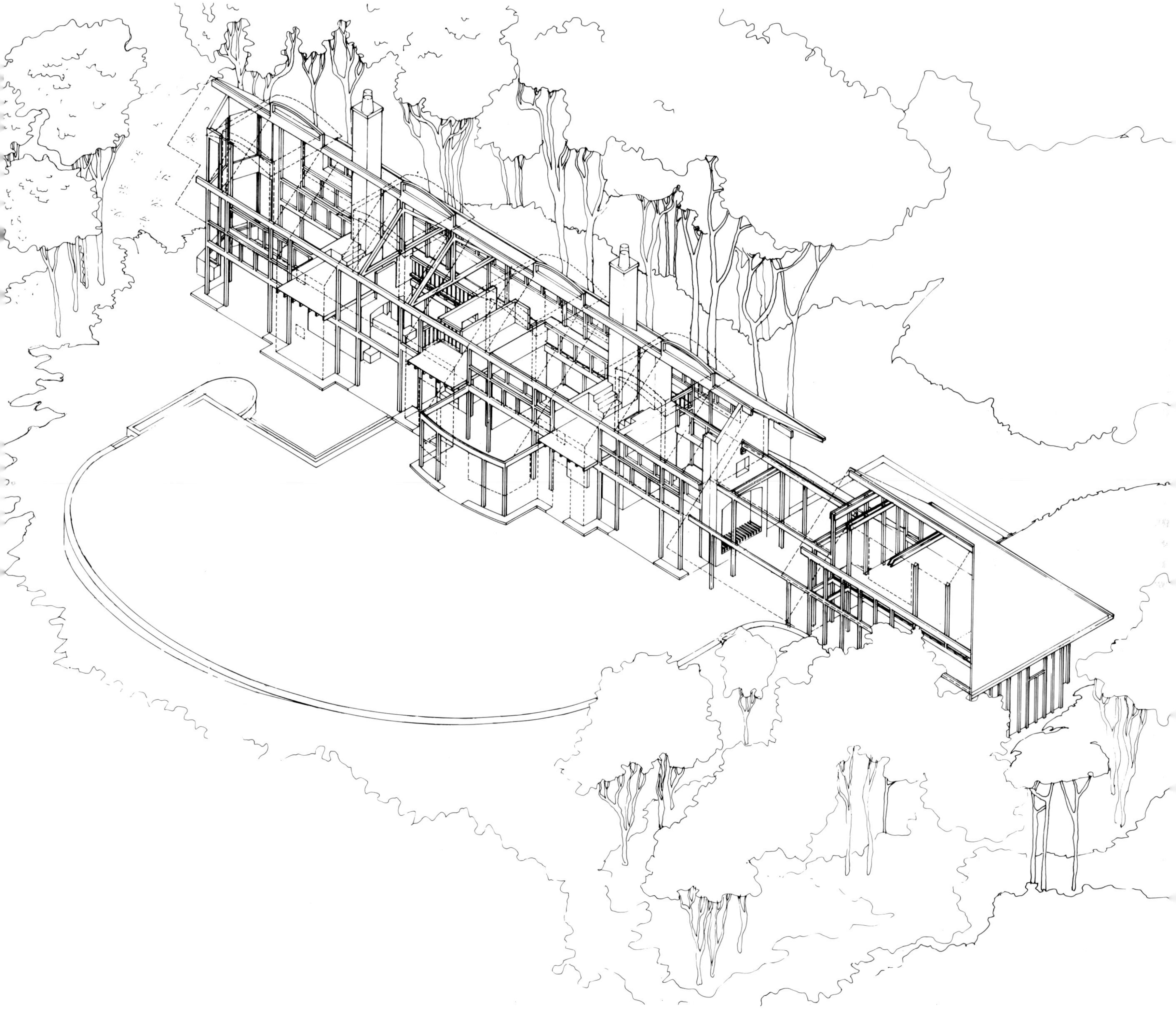

MANIFOLD RESIDENCE – VICTORIA   IVAN RIJAVEC ARCHITECTS

Design Architect: Ivan Rijavec
Drawing Artist:
Zbigniew Jaworski
Size: 1020 x 710 mm
Date: 1989
Photographer: Zbigniew Jaworski

This new residence sited on a inner suburban allotment began with the unusual requirement that car access would be provided to the centre of the house. A cubist compositional framework disguises a linear organic plan form. This framework promotes an unencumbered volumetric solution, free of the programmatic structures of conventional roof forms and thereby promotes a greater planning flexibility. The graphic image in its structure alludes to a traditional landscape format. A perspectival, three-dimensional plan provides the basic structure for the foreground on which a perspective of the house is centred, implying a horizon line above which a collage of darker perspectival views suggest the sky. A lyrical dialogue using the language of the building romanticises the Urban condition. Media: pencil, coloured pencil, ink tipped pens, applied to both sides of detail paper.

The composite graphic demonstrates a number of different drawing techniques, expressly chosen to convey the key design objectives of the project. Conventional and exploded axonometrics have been projected over plan and elevational drawings. A high density of information can simultaneously be communicated by way of these techniques. 'Guided tours' of the drawing have proved both effective and economic in comprehensively describing the project ie, without the assistance of additional plans, sections, elevations, or perspectives.

My drawings call for nothing less but a complete break with strict representation. Architectural drawing for me is a way or an opportunity to assume a position in relation to the individual architect's values and ideas embodied in his or her work. The particular concept or subject matter I seek to transform into a drawing which becomes an object in itself.

Every project is a combination of various layers. My work is about revealing the inner nature of the subject, its complexities – simplicities – functions – forms. I am trying to involve the viewer into the discourse. Elevations, plans, structural elements, details – they are all in very specific relations. I'm trying to explore them. My approach to every project is therefore different. Perspective, axonometric, isometric ... they have no strict geometric rules for me. I use them freely to serve the purpose, and the purpose is to evoke a response to the subject.

IVAN RIJAVEC ARCHITECTS

CHAUVEL RESIDENCE – PERTH – WESTERN AUSTRALIA DONALDSON + WARN ARCHITECTS

In response to the client's request for a distinctive but not ostentatious home, utilising light and space and recognising the qualities of the site in a coastal suburb, we adopted a 'contemporary attitude' to planning, form and materials. The structural system combines a concrete masonary 'service wing' with a timber-clad steel frame enveloping the remaining domestic functions. Timber floors are provided throughout, and the smooth white walls and clean lines complement the client's art collection. Integration of indoor and outdoor spaces is achieved by composing the house around a central courtyard, creating an 'outdoors room' which reinforces and complements the client's lifestyle. The importance of the courtyard and its relationship to the planning and functioning of the house is formally marked by the sculptured space over the adjacent meals area and the expressive shading canopies projecting into the courtyard. A series of louvred windows facilitate cross ventilation, utilising the cool summer breezes flowing from the nearby ocean.
The axonometric project was drawn at 1:50 scale on an A1 size sheet of tracing paper using 0.35 and 0.5 mm technical pens. Architectural elements, namely windows and staircases, were abstracted and drawn in their relative positions on the finished building. The cranked beams and canopy steelwork were included to show the spatial and formal hierarchy of the design. A photographic 'inter-neg' was prepared from the ink line drawing.
Black and white photographs were taken of some of the materials, trimmed to equal size and adhered to a sheet of tracing paper. The photographic details were arranged in approximate positions below the actual materials on the building.
A black and white photographic print of the elevation was produced by Marcello Palacios using infra-red film. The photograph of the elevation was positioned on a tracing paper overlay above the abstracted elevation of the drawing. A screened inter-neg was prepared from the photograph overlay sheet. By masking the inter-negs and double exposing, a duplicate negative was produced. A bromide was prepared from the duplicate negative with line work and photographs combined into one image. The drawing is attempting to depict modes of abstraction and to integrate mechanical reproduction techniques into the drawing process.

Design Architects:
Richard Donaldson,
Geoff Warn, Steve Parkin,
Erol Tout
Drawing Artists: John Smart
and Geoff Warn
Size: 840 x 590 mm
Date: 1989
Photographer: Garry Sarre

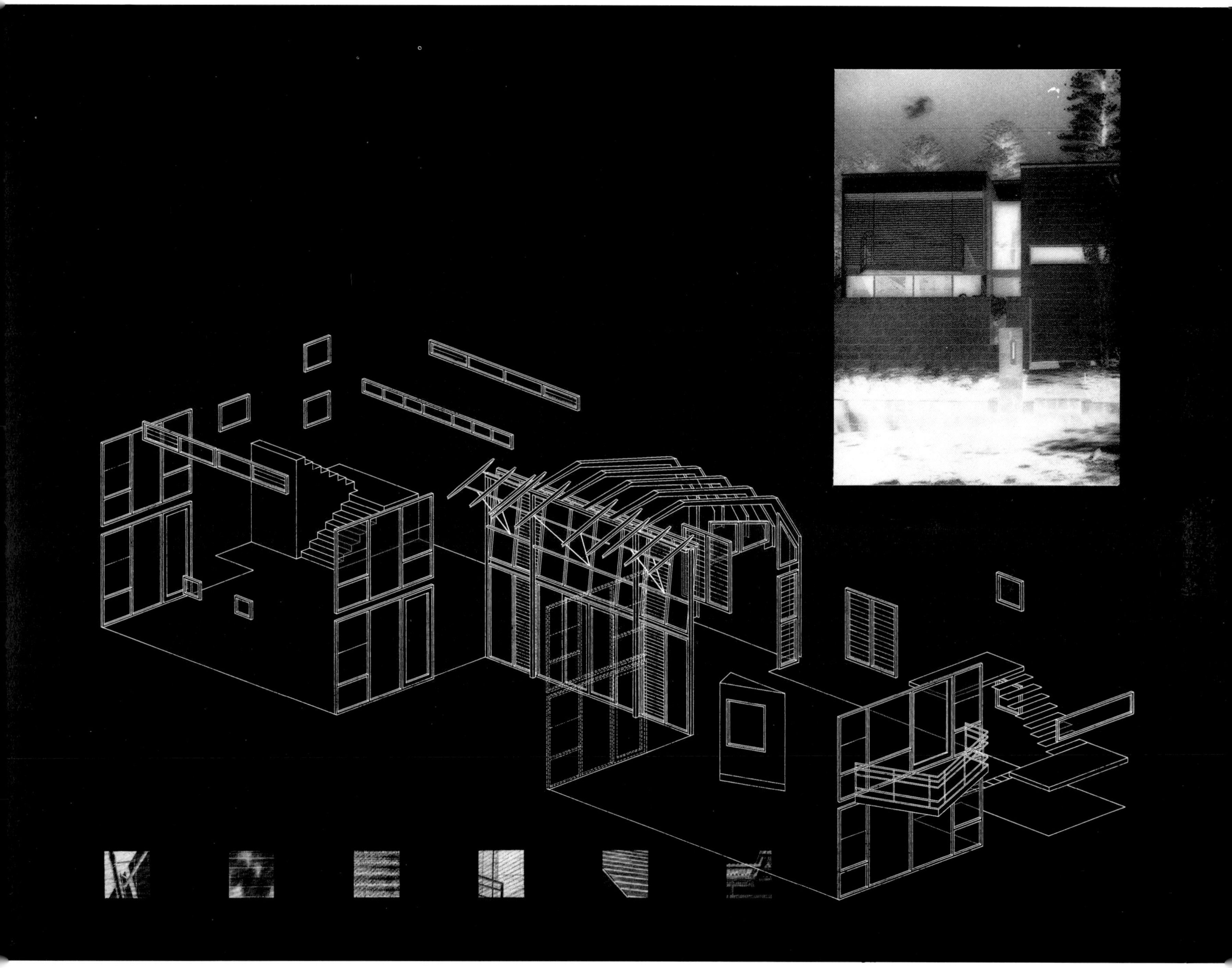

HOUSE – NEWTOWN – NEW SOUTH WALES ARCHITECTURAL PROJECTS

Design Architects:
Gary O'Reilly and
Jennifer Hill
Drawing Artist: Jennifer Hill
Size: 730 x 390 mm
Date: 1985
Photographer: Warrick Kent

In small scale terrace renovations the issues of old and new public and private and progression predominate and are overlaid to create richness and complexity. The adequacy of the existing building to adapt was considered. Rooms were maintained, modified or destroyed related to their proposed use and location. The terrace, typical of many we have renovated, is single-storey of four front rooms with an agglomeration of service rooms to the rear. It is here modified to accommodate bathroom, kitchen and laundry, centrally opening the house fully to the rear secluded courtyard. The 25 metre progression uses a series of set pieces based on colour fields and spatial manipulations that draw one through the building. Various select colours are contrasted against a colour and plain continuity of the ceiling to accentuate progression. The long progression is set against short perpendicular views across the terraces, the shifting symmetries of those rooms, and vertical views to the rooms above.

The original plan of discrete rooms along a side corridor is shifted to emphasise a central axis through the house which continues to the garden – the shift is reflected in the room colour. Colour at the rear is also used to juxtapose the shift from one wall to the opposing external wall. Equally one can see the house as a series of layers though which progression occurs.

All inks and drawing equipment used in office are by Faber Castell. Ink on cold pressed Schoellers Hammer paper. Colour and tone were added with Pantone and coloured paper.

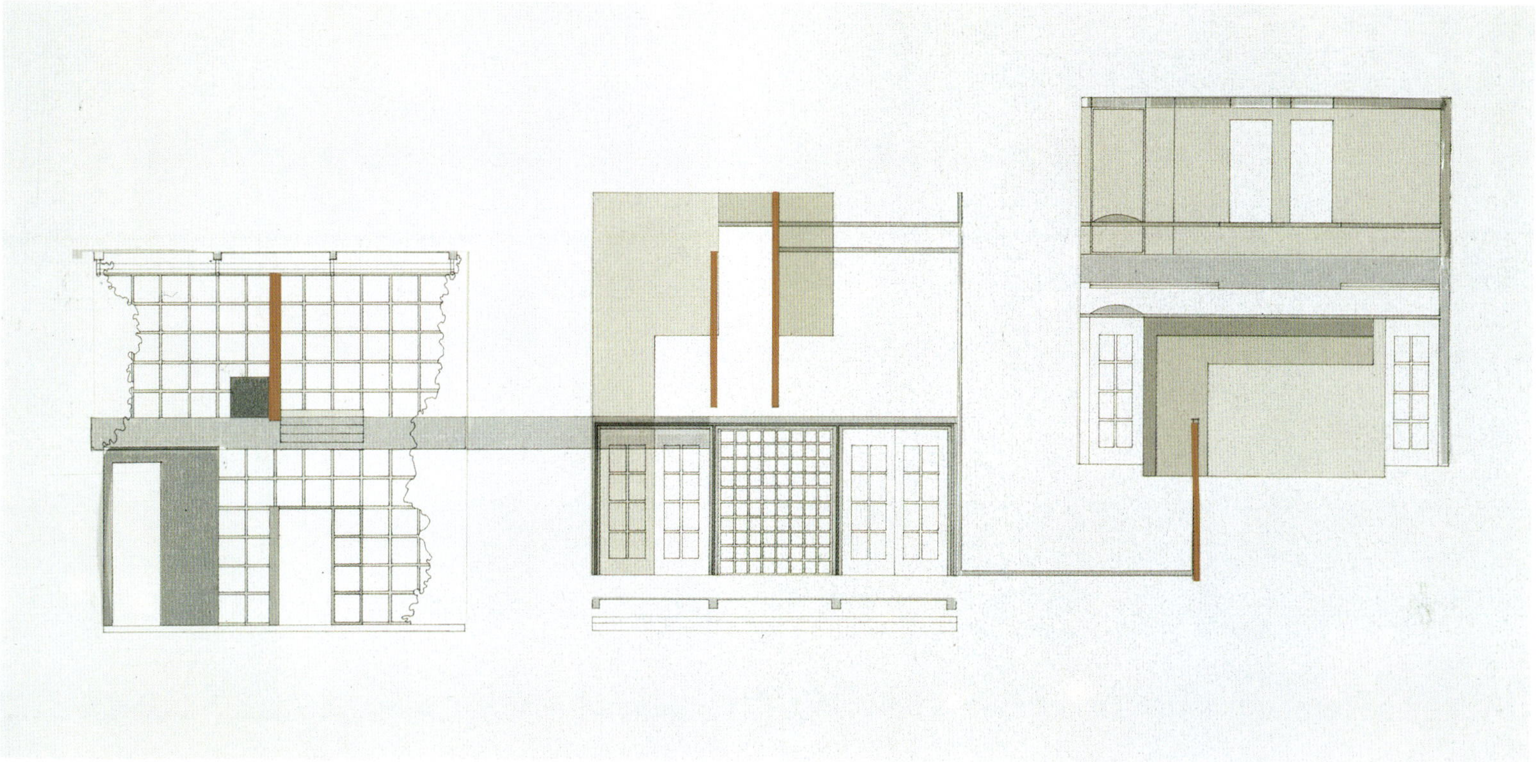

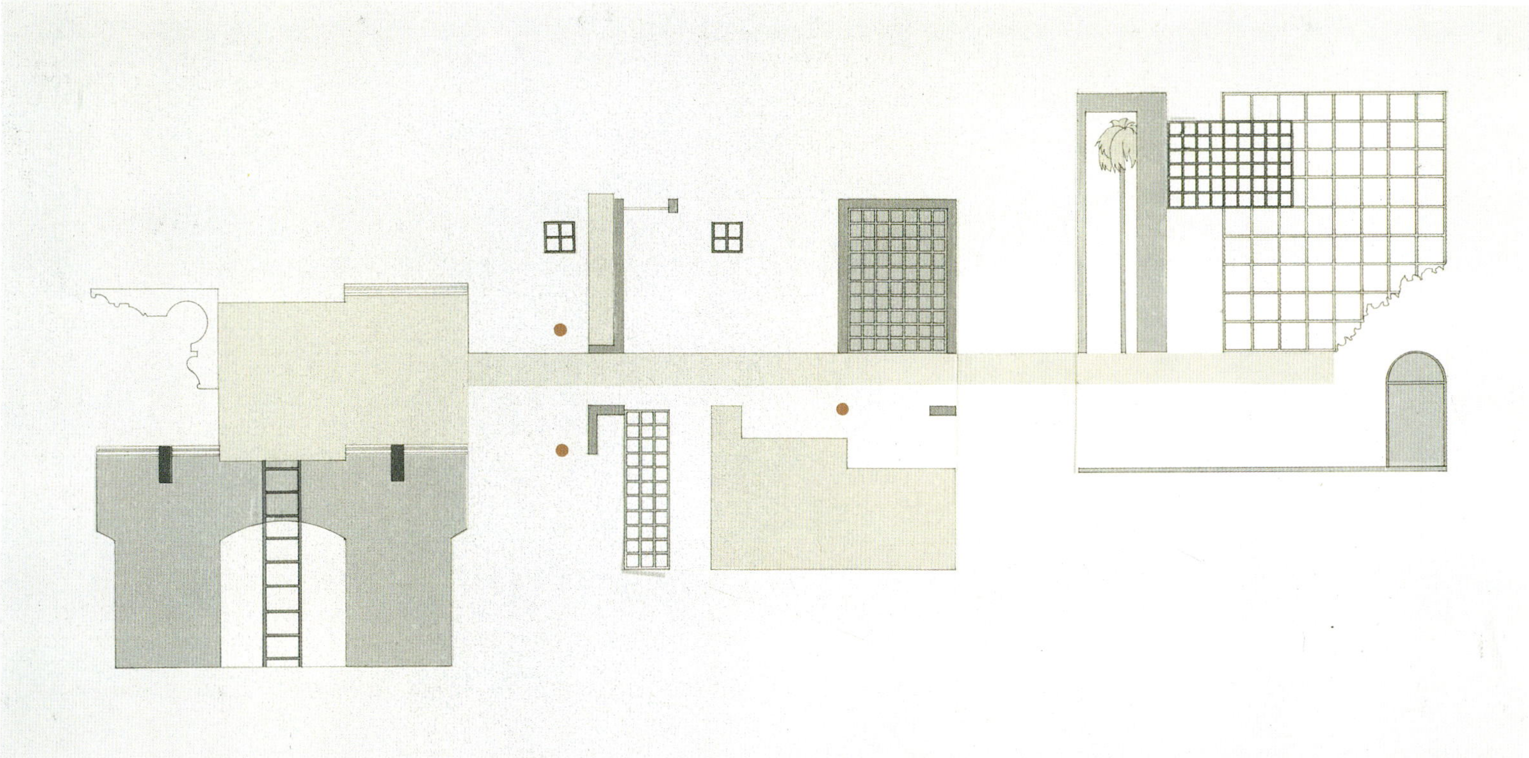

CHARMAN HOUSE – BALWYN – VICTORIA EDMOND & CORRIGAN ARCHITECTS

This 'poor theatre' extension uses elements of Twentieth Century Art, for example, Duchamp and Mondrian, to celebrate the eternal optimism of a Middle Melbourne Suburb. The client thinks he drives a truck, while his wife thinks she is a typist. They are artists. Pantone and ink on gloss bromide.

Design Architect:
Peter Corrigan
Drawing Artist:
Geoffrey Barton
Size: 510 x 440 mm
Date: 1984
Photographer: John Gollings

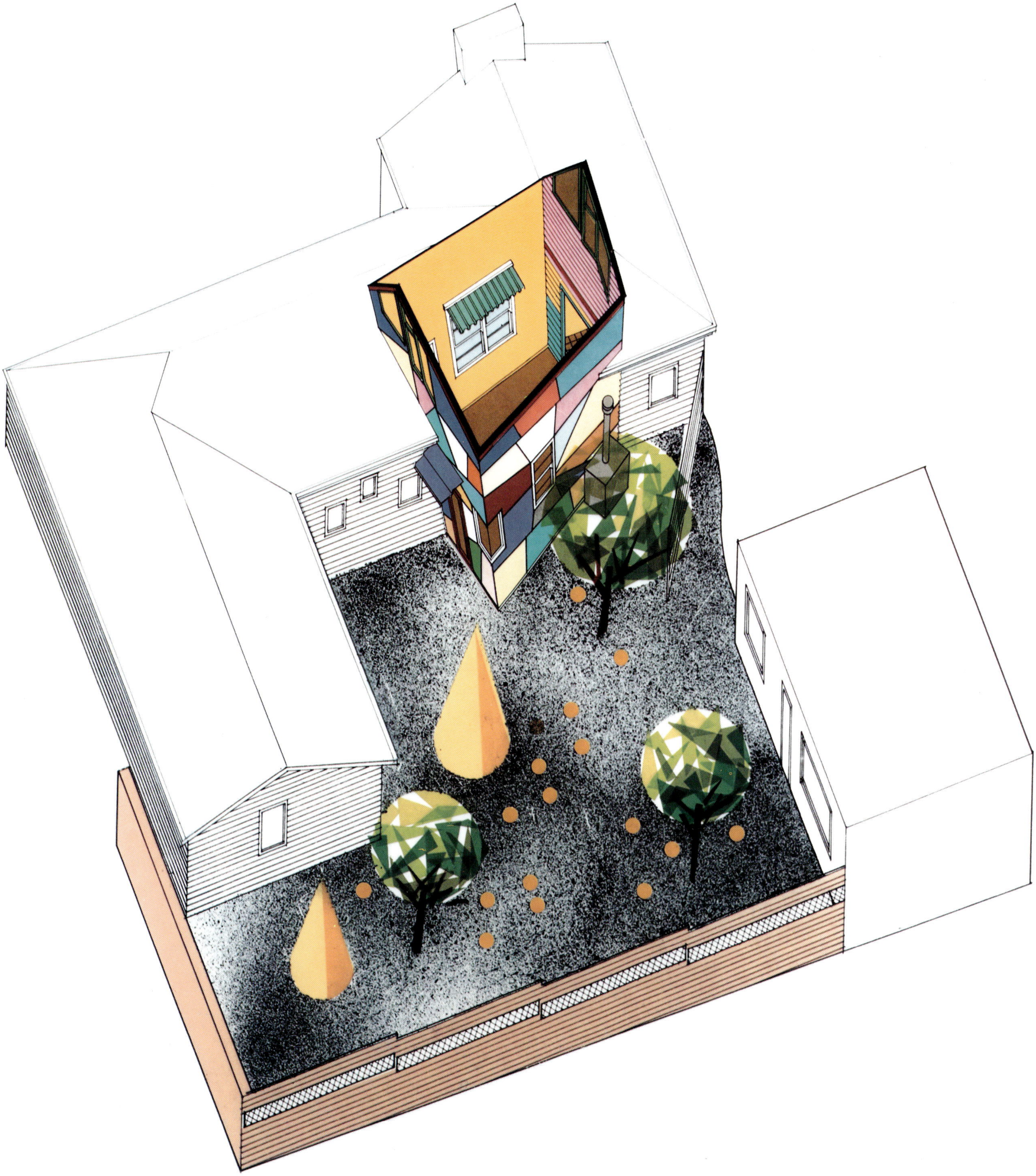

HOUSE – KENSINGTON – SOUTH AUSTRALIA **PHILLIPS AND PILKINGTON ARCHITECTS**

Design Architects:
Susan Phillips and
Michael Pilkington
Drawing Artist:
Michael Pilkington
Date: 1990
Size: 442 x 393 mm
(scale: 1:50)
Photographer: Trevor Fox

These two small attached townhouses complete a narrow 19th century mews street of single-storey, single-fronted Adelaide worker's cottages. The strong sense of enclosure engendered by the existing houses, their pattern of occupying exactly half of their frontage and their repetitive gables formed starting points for our design.

We felt committed to developing the existing spatial arrangement but modifying the form to cater to our own requirements. The demand for greater accommodation than the adjacent cottages provided, posed problems of integration with the existing streetscape.

The solid elements of our street elevation took their cue from the profile of the adjoining houses, matching height and pitch while the new roof floats above, separated by a band of continuous glazing. The diagonal northern orientation to the rear encouraged us to push the main living space out, making an L-shaped private courtyard. The setback to the dining room allows space for one car and a couple of bicycles. This 'House of Two Halves' joins at the entrance hall, which is double height and provides access to living room, dining room, kitchen, staircase and the rear courtyard.

The interior is light and airy with glimpses of other spaces across, up and down.

Our neighbour's house is a variation of our own with a smaller upper floor and larger courtyard. Its lean-to roof over the living room lowers the scale of the houses at the end of the street and terminates the composition.

Although acknowledging the street provided a strong context for instigating this design, we were keen to develop a drawing of the project which treated the buildings as discrete objects – perhaps as a reaction against some of our contextual deliberations – and to analyse if they could stand on their own.

The narrow street makes it difficult to oversee both houses and the axonometric form was used to provide an architectural view which shows scale relationships in all dimensions.

The 0/90 degrees aspect of the drawing was chosen to emphasise the building's setbacks, massing and roof treatment and to eliminate diagonal lines which tend to run into each other in standard 45/45 degree or 30/60 degree projections.

Paper: Wiggins Teape 110 gsm tracing paper.

Pen: Faber Castell TG1S, size 0.25 mm, black ink.

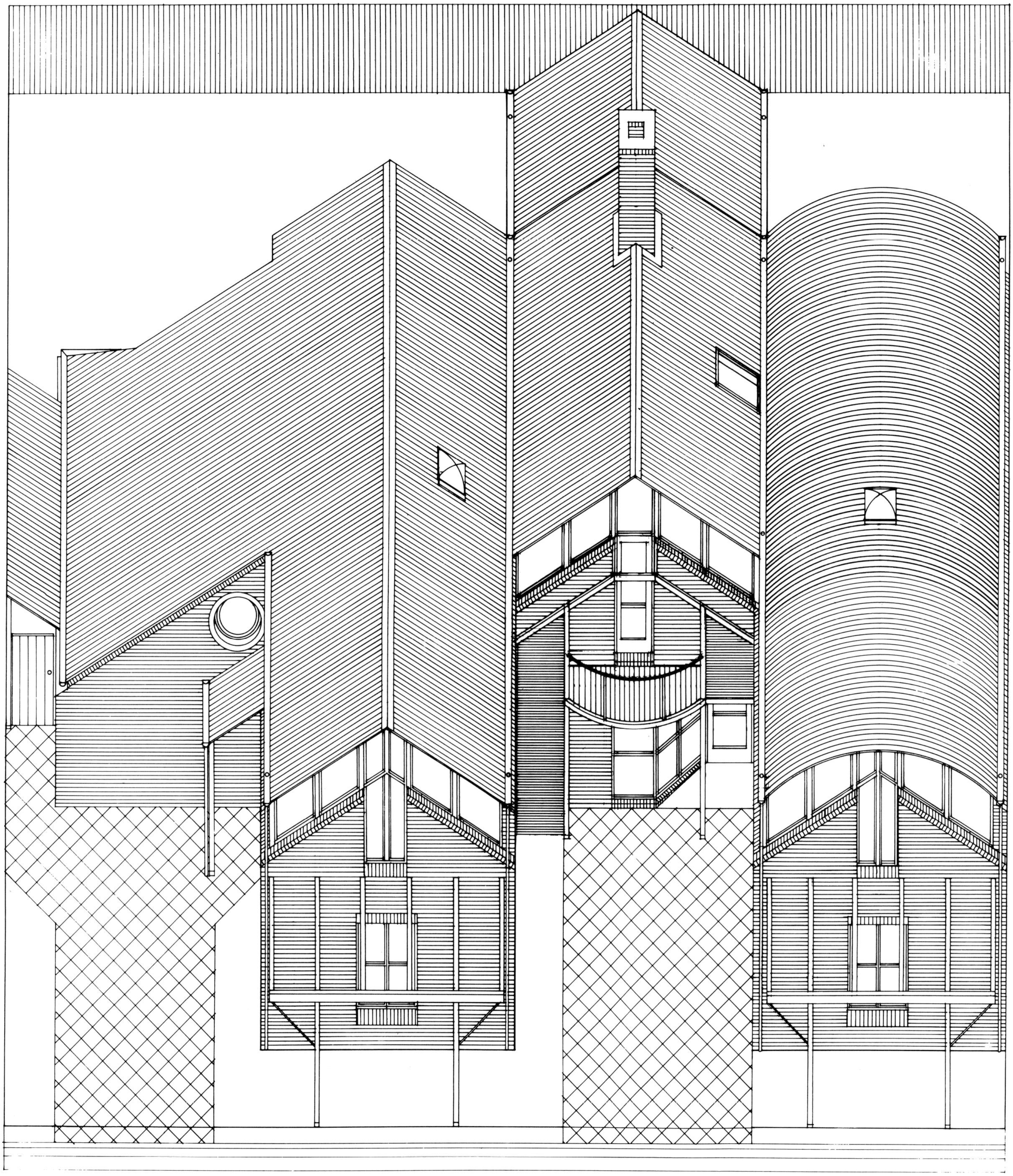

HOUSE PROJECT – SYDNEY – NEW SOUTH WALES   STANIC HARDING ARCHITECTS

We designed this house for a couple and their teenage son. They have a love of entertaining and simple living. The design attempts to create an environment being a protective shelter and a stage for confronting and enjoying life. The marriage of the rock shelf site and building has resulted in a horizontal composition. Three simple blocks are arranged around and ordered by a blade wall that secures itself into the rock ledge at the rear of the site. The house opens itself to the view, light and the activities of life.
The originals were ink drawing on drafting film that were photographed on a bromide camera and converted to a lithographic film. The film was then separated by hand and used to produce indirect screens. A screen was used for each individual colour and they were registered using a Kodak pin-bar system. It was printed using Ultrascreen inks for a satin finish on Nimbus Suedecoat 250 gsm stock.

Design Architect:
Andrew Stanic
Drawing Artist:
Andrew Stanic
(Michael Broadhead screen-printer)
Size: 1189 x 841 mm
Date: 1990
Photographer:
Andrew Harding

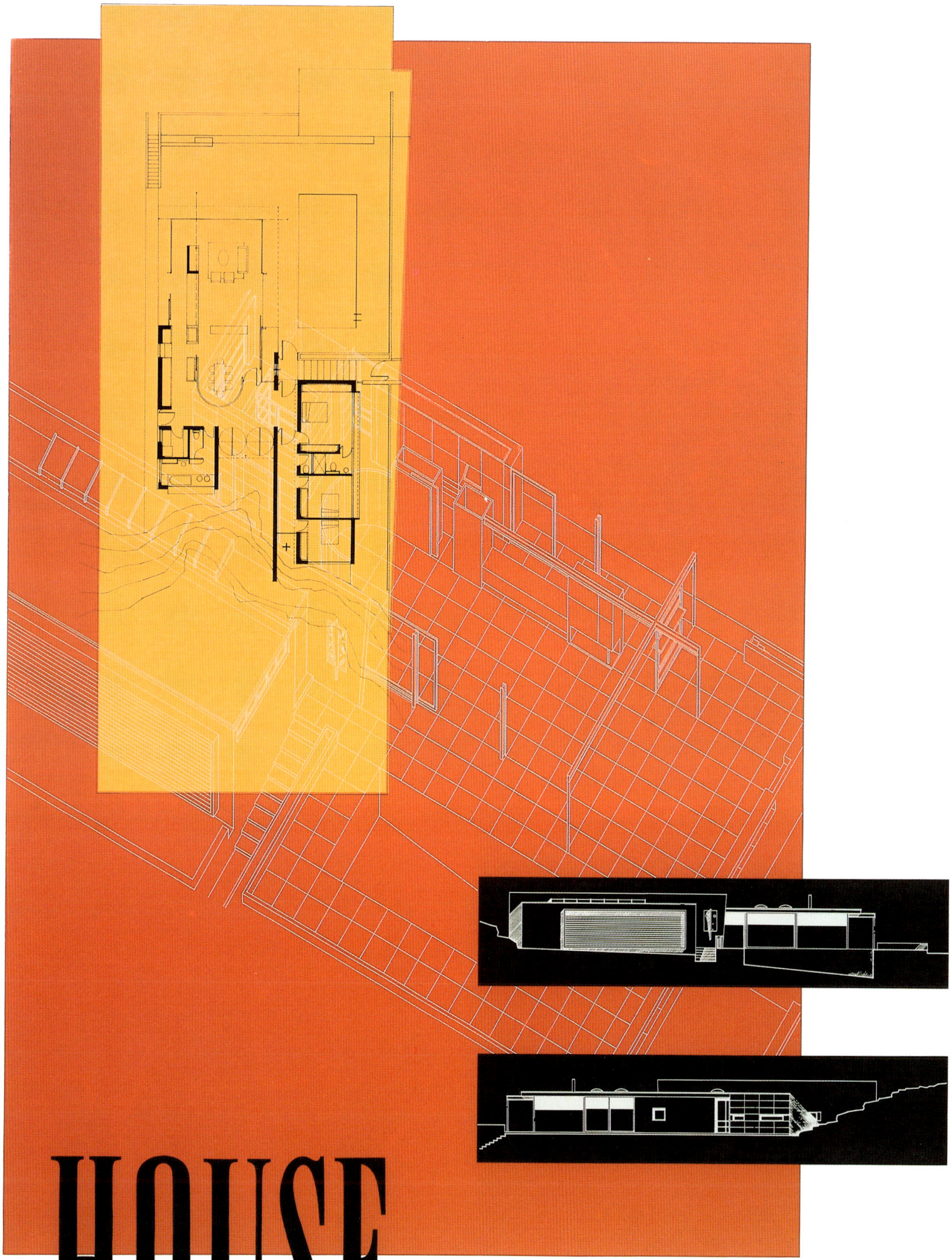

HOUSE

LARA SHOE FACTORY CONVERSION - VICTORIA **IVAN RIJAVEC ARCHITECTS**

The Lara Shoe Factory, originally constructed in the thirties, was a typical 'Modern' brick box with gridded metal windows and a fibro sheeted saw-toothed roof. The developer's brief required the building be subdivided into two apartments with the usual up-market accommodation requirements.

To maximise the illusion of space a full-height glazed screen describing a courtyard was cut into the centre of both units thereby maximising the illusion of space. The many views through the courtyards combine in memory and suggest a larger whole than exists in reality.

Internally, abstract curvilinear plastic forms are painted in strong contrasting colour which dislocates the forms from their context. Isometric drawings illustrating front and rear view of the building are projected above cut away projections which illustrate the first floors of both units. Media: pencil, coloured pencil, ink tipped pens, applied to both sides of detail paper. (The artist's general statement which elucidates some of the concerns specific to his work can be found outlined under the heading of the Manifold Residence of Ivan Rijavec Architects.)

Design Architect: Ivan Rijavec
Drawing Artist:
Zbigniew Jaworski
Size: 950 x 600 mm
Date: 1989
Photographer: Earl Carter

LARA SHOE FACTORY
IVAN RIJAVEC
ARCHITECTS

ELLERSLIE PLACE – HOBART – TASMANIA EASTMAN HEFFERNAN WALCH & BUTTON ARCHITECTS

Design Architect:
Ray Heffernan
Drawing Artists: Charles Voss and Grant Calder
Size: 1189 x 841 mm
Date: 1985
Photographers: Ray Heffernan and Richard Eastwood

The brief required the development of six large high quality residences (assigned as one double-level and five single-level units) on a site sloping down from an existing street car park platform towards the south-east. The design is perceived as two rectangular layered blocks; counterpoised along a lineal access gallery and hinged so as to slide over the edge of the other at this circulation axis.

This offsetting and lateral shift contributes to the reduction of visual impact on street and adjacent buildings, while also creating and enclosing a communal outdoor area to the north-east. It yields to site constraints of tree conservation and gradient, permitting the retention of major trees and providing partial containment of lower-level car parking.

Solid frontal planes, acting as both visual and acoustic walls, address the street frontage. Sun and views of middle and distant landscape are valued and framed, with glazing concentrated on the northern and eastern sides, where living and bedroom areas are located. Each of the units embraces the impressive outlook towards the Derwent River and by use of strategically placed windows, the tower of St George's Church (an historic landmark amid Battery Point) is framed for every dwelling; simultaneously establishing a sense of place and relationship with the building in context and reinforcing the subtle lineal axis to the east on which circulation paths are aligned. Services and circulation zones are organised along the southern edges, and windows surrender accordingly to blank walls on this elevation.

The hard-edged building expresses its Modernist language unapologetically, contrasting density plane and void upon its surfaces, and distinct in form and character from that of its surrounds. Bearing allegiance to a neighbouring building previously designed by the architect, its simple geometric forms embody an overall sense of unity, while offering privacy of entry and enclosure within its component dwellings.

Ink on tracing paper with 0.25 and 0.13 drafting pens. Original drawing at 1:100, subsequent bromide reduction to appropriate size for publication. The angle for the axonometric was taken to show the northern side of the building and its orientation to sun and view as well from above to illustrate the stacking of each block on either side of the circulation spine. One roof was left off to show internal layout and provide greater visual complexity to the composition. The dot technique was used to highlight both selected glazing areas and water surface. Depth was suggested by dotting internal features behind the glazing. Reflection on the water surface was achieved by orienting the dots horizontally distinguishing them from the 45 degree and 90 degree composition of the building. Highlighting balconies with angled paving was important to help the deep spaces recede, thus giving emphasis to the 'punctuated' walls.

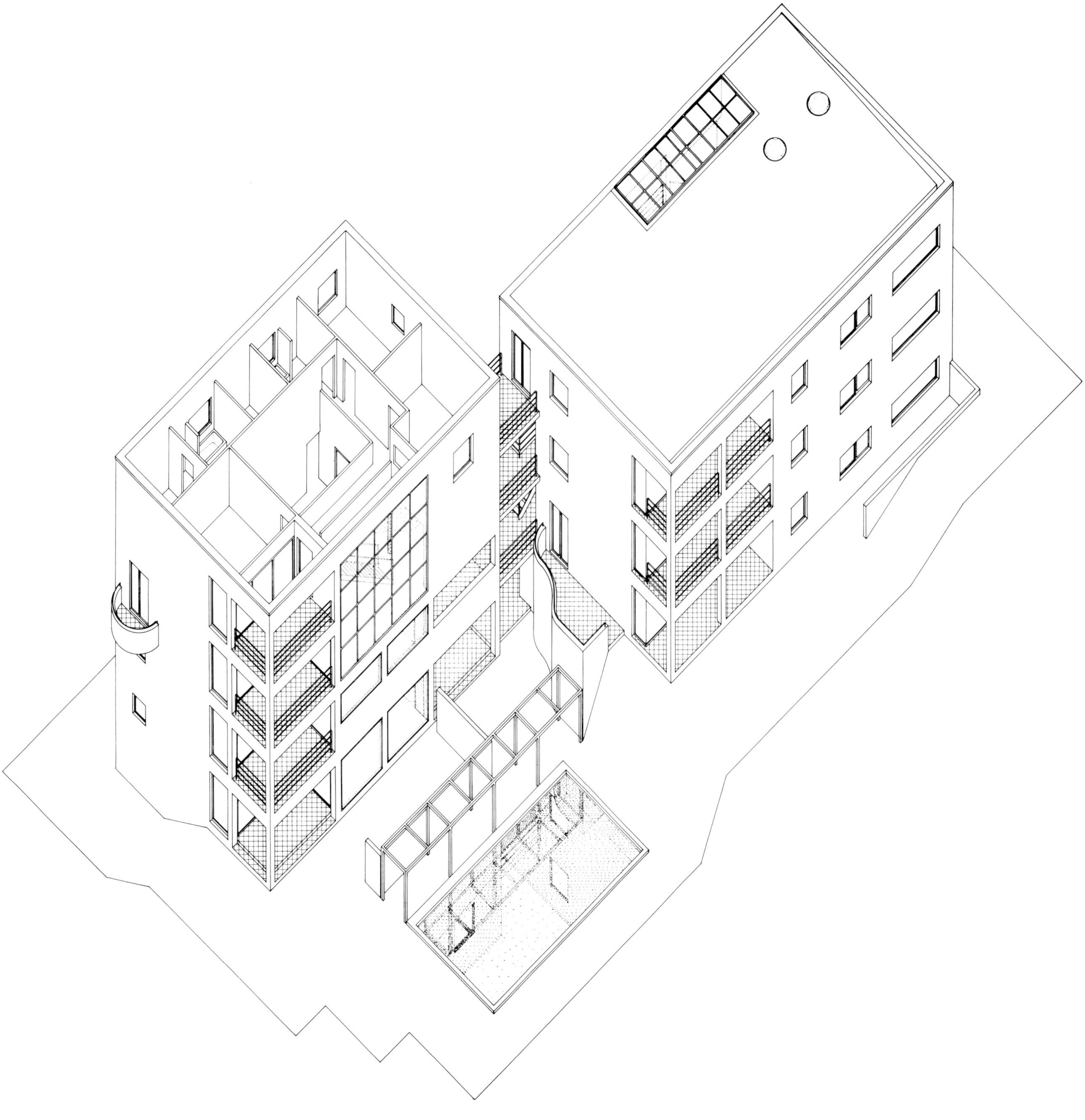

CALNIN HOUSE - KORUMBURRA - VICTORIA EDMOND & CORRIGAN ARCHITECTS

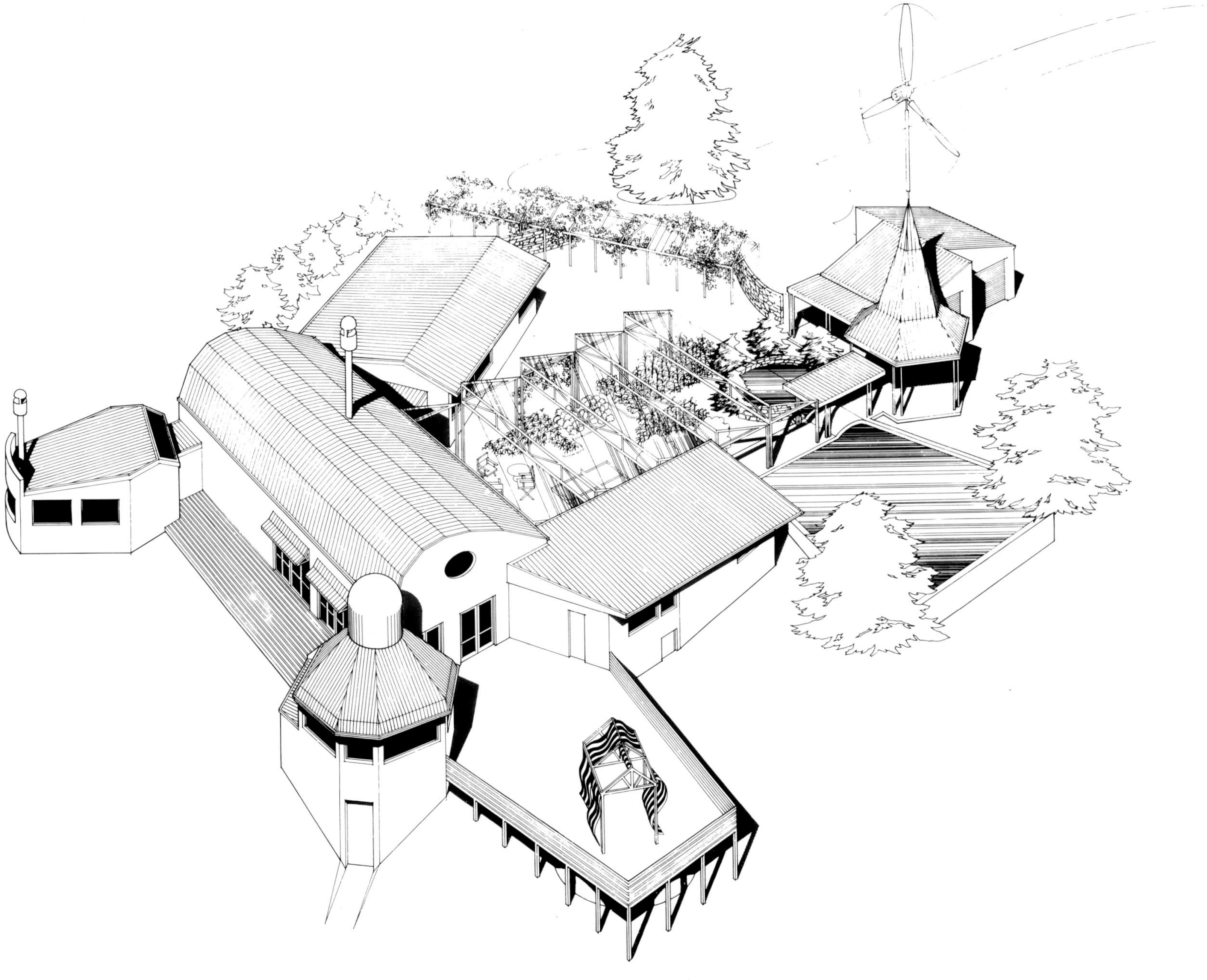

Design Architect:
Peter Corrigan
Drawing Artist:
Geoffrey Barton
Size: 900 x 725 mm
Date: 1985

This project investigates spatial hierarchy, and nestles into a hard landscape that is downright Welsh in its dourness. The wind and rain slaps in from Antarctica. In summer the blowflies are awesome. External spaces are designed to grow vegetables and party. The client and his wife have both worked in the theatre all their lives. They are artists.
Pantone and ink on gloss bromide.

McKENZIE HOUSE – MELBOURNE – VICTORIA **ASHTON RAGGATT McDOUGALL ARCHITECTS**

'The McKenzie house was built for a small family with plans to extend in the future. It is a small boldly composed house assembled with unusual shapes and materials. An enormous circle, a private sun-drenched courtyard garden for children to play in. An oversized circular window provides a spectacular vista across the Yarra River to the towers of Willsmere in Kew. Seen from the Eastern Freeway, there is the suggestion of an 'as found' piece of civil engineering, a bridge section or perhaps a gigantic piece of industrial machinery concerned with large-scale movement of people which has now been repossessed and inhabited. The McKenzie house suggests that it is part of a greater realm of things, not just a single family home but part of a greater body of buildings and structures which make up a city.' Phillip Goad – 'The Home Sweet Home Exhibition'.

The critical graphic addresses various issues of architecture beyond mere setting by means of a graphic discourse. The graphic is not just a representation of the object but a means of representing the testing of that object under various conditions. The method has been to use a standard perspective drawing as a control and then to arrange alternative settings to test themes like: Nature, Ideology, Lifestyle,

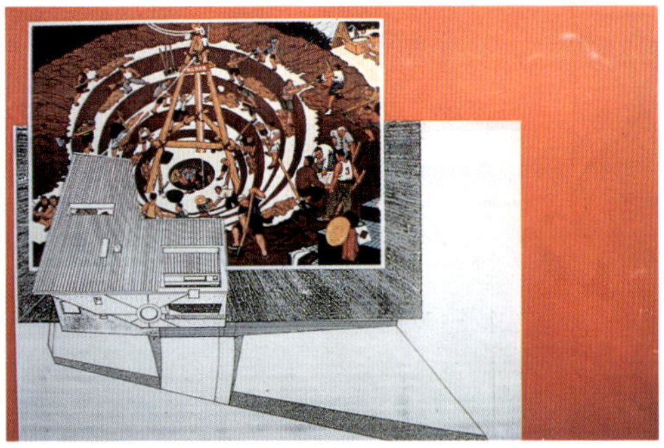

Design Architect:
Howard Raggatt
Drawing Artist:
(collage) Howard Raggatt
Size: 594 x 420 mm
Date: 1987
Photographer: Ian Davidson

Technology, Taste, or Idiosyncrasy. In the first graphic, Adam and Eve stand in the sky over the enclosed circular front garden. The background is explosive as a test of the symbolic associations of the garden. The second picture is the same aerial perspective drawing with the circular garden turned into an open mine or well upon which labour and production are centred. This graphic proposes an ideological/political test for the architecture, presenting the observer with the opportunity to examine the proposition of a politically aware or affiliated architecture. The third graphic shows a simple low angle perspective rendering of the first stage of the house with a proposed stage two renovation inspired by Arthur Rich in *Shingle Style*, 1885. The fourth graphic uses the same low angle perspective drawing of the house with a chic jogger in silk shorts dashing through the foreground and a bursting sky behind. Using every day technology the graphic tests the chic new house against potential absolutes. The sky for the graphic is a repeated and spliced sliver from a newspaper advertisement while the jogger was selected from *Sharper Image* an LA super-gloss catalogue. The purpose of the graphic is to be a kind of litmus test for the architecture by creating a new instantaneous space in which to assess indulgence and aspiration.

By using the photocopier to enlarge and shrink the images, double copying portions of the image to achieve body, and colouring the image with highlight marker and then reprocessing the graphic as photograph, the graphic becomes strongly anti-naturalistic to suggest a kind of critical narrative.

In other similar graphics we have used economical commercial colour copying technology with independent distortions of dimension, renomination of colour and massive enlargement to characterise an emphasis or create a polemical scale. Technically, the graphics are simply cut and pastes of black and white or colour photocopies mounted on A3 or A4 paper for photocopy reprocessing or photographing. Coloured paper or acetate is also used and photographed with back lighting as in the case with Adam and Eve.

HOUSE 17 – ST KILDA – VICTORIA LINDSAY HOLLAND ARCHITECTS

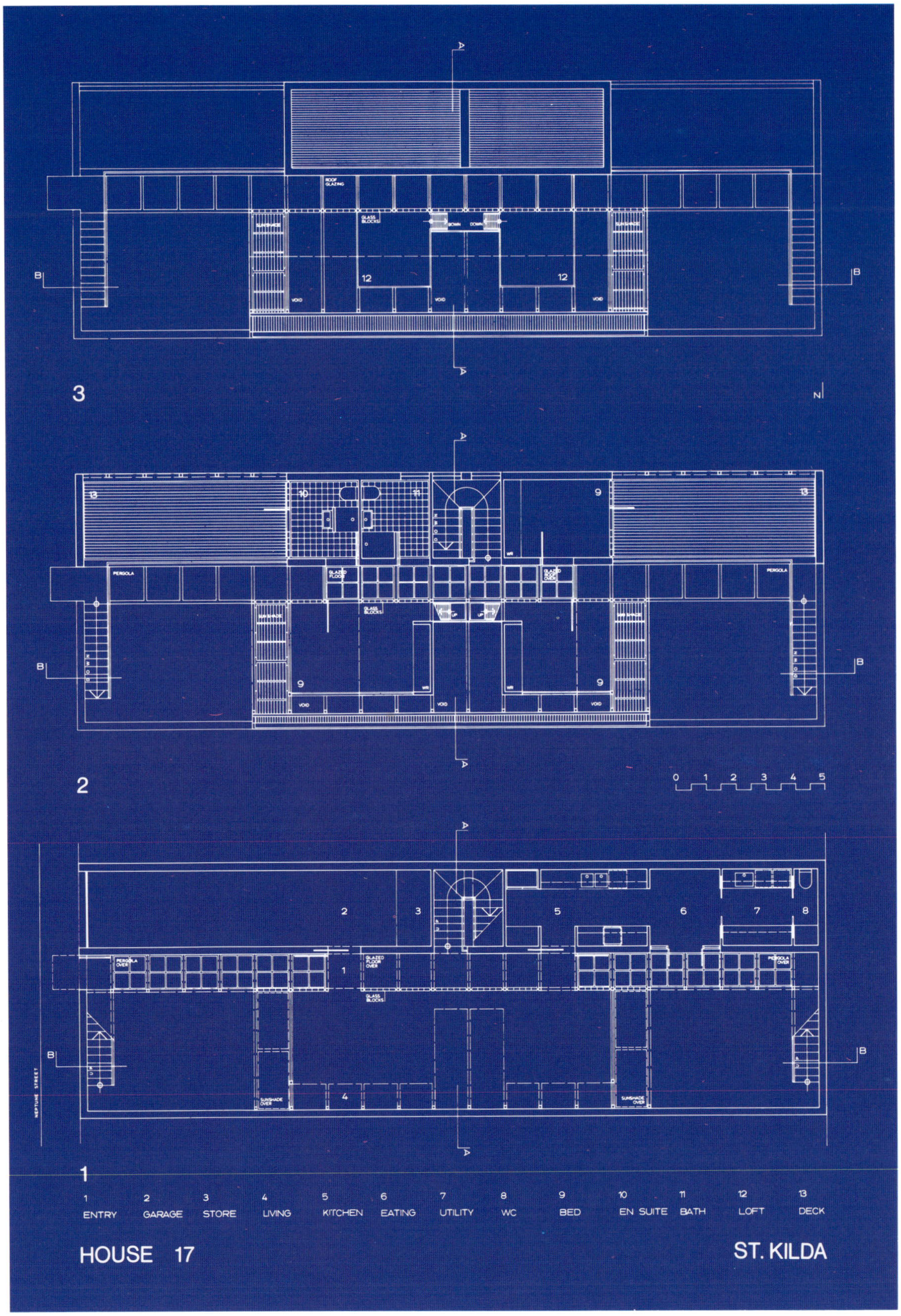

House for a restricted site in an inner Melbourne suburb, St Kilda. Site is located in an urban conservation zone. House concerns itself with issues of served/service spaces, mass/void, and transparency/interpenetration of spaces. Produce a bromide negative from an A1 size original process available from a good reprographic service. Produce a bromide negative at the required size, in this instance A4. The bromide print can be either a positive (black line on white ground) or reverse (white line on black ground) image. Resultant images can be colour modified either by colour photocopy processing or commercial colour printing. Original drawing was carried out with Rotring Rapidograph pens (0.25 mm and 0.35 mm) black ink, on A1 tracing paper (110 gsm).

Design Architect:
Lindsay Holland
Drawing Artists:
Lindsay Holland,
Geoff Crosby
and Fiona Nixon
Size: 1189 x 841 mm
Date: 1989

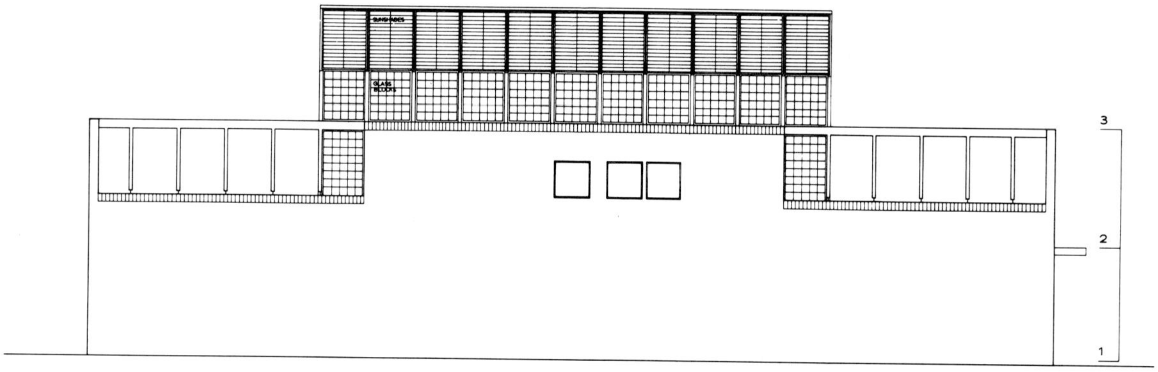

SOUTH

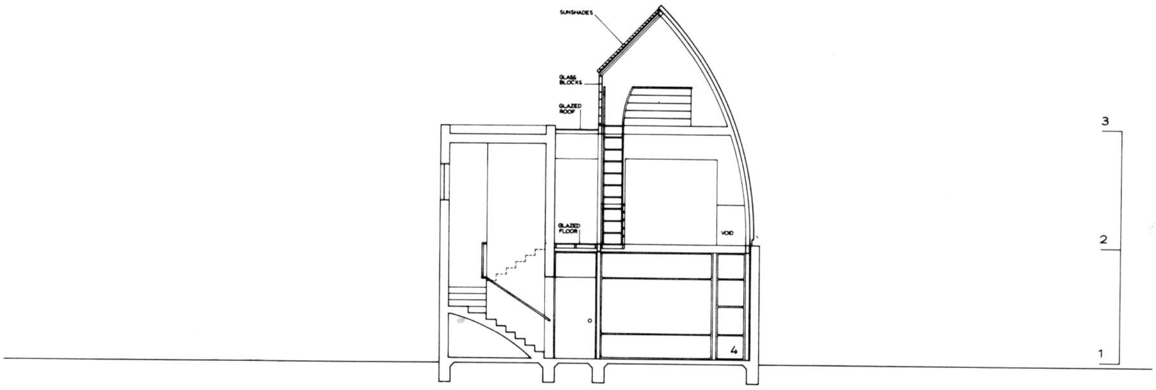

A:A

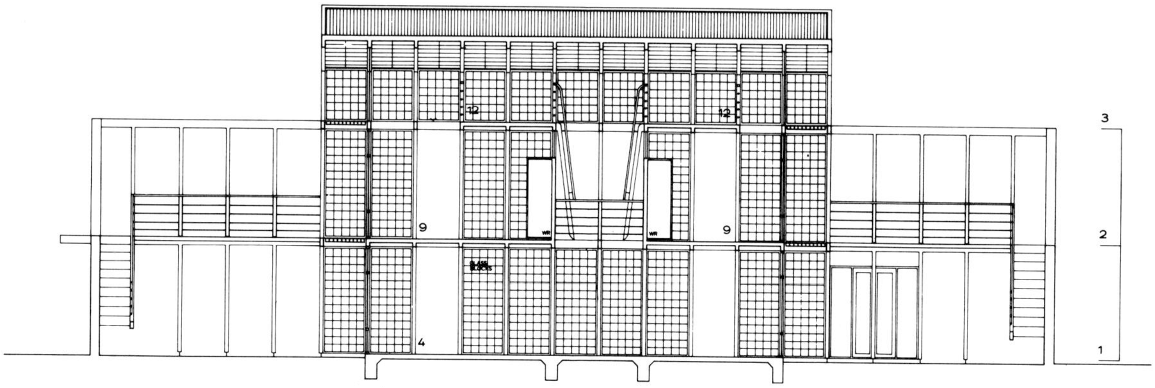

B:B

HOUSE 17

ST. KILDA

AKTION POLIPHILE HOUSE COMPETITION – WIESBADEN – GERMANY
ARCHITECTURAL PROJECTS

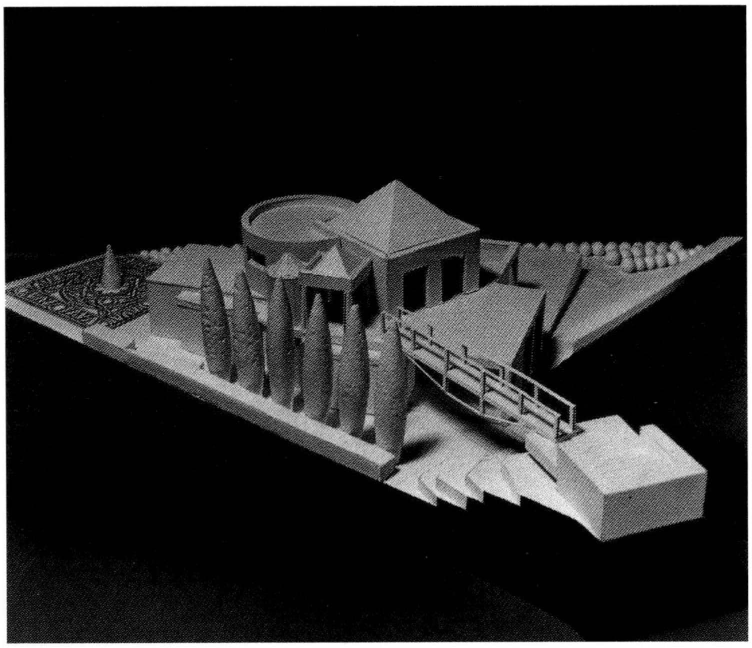

The chessboard in Francesco Colonna's *Hypnerotomachia* represents a microcosm of the integral relationship of garden and architecture throughout his book. The board as a two-dimensional ordered grid with an eight bay proportioned relationship was considered a significant inspiration for the design. The chessboard represents an ideal loci which is placed in a delicate relationship to irregular boundaries. Its notional extension beyond the site boundaries links the ideal order to the 'natural' environs beyond. Its ordered presence conceals the awkward setbacks of the site as given. It is set at an ideal datum equivalent to the height of the street and accommodates a floor below as a result of the sloping nature of the site. The chessboard acts as an ideal garden in which pavilions are located. It reduces the impact of a substantial structure on such a constrained site by concealing this bulk. It renders those rooms which occur above the ideal datum as discrete entities. The irregularities of building volumes, in order to accommodate the building setbacks, are rationalised in their relationship to the ordered grid.

The concern for the progression from street to field is primary in importance, relating to a gradual opening of fenestration within the house, affording views of the field beyond. The observer enters into the framework of the ordered grid and the circulation occurs within this parameter. A redirection occurs in the living, dining and gallery but the observers are returned to the ordered grid in the terraces and bedroom wing. The house is one of a series of investigations into the use of a cubic form with an overlayed modular grid which regulates the internal planning and allows the house to possess both a formal spatial integrity and a casual flow of space.

All inks and drawing equipment used in the office are by Faber Castell. Ink on paper, then bromides were made.

Design Architects:
Gary O'Reilly, Jennifer Hill
and Roy Lumby
Drawing Artists: Gary O'Reilly,
Jennifer Hill and Roy Lumby
Size: 325 x 325 mm
Date: 1989
Photographs: Ken Wilde

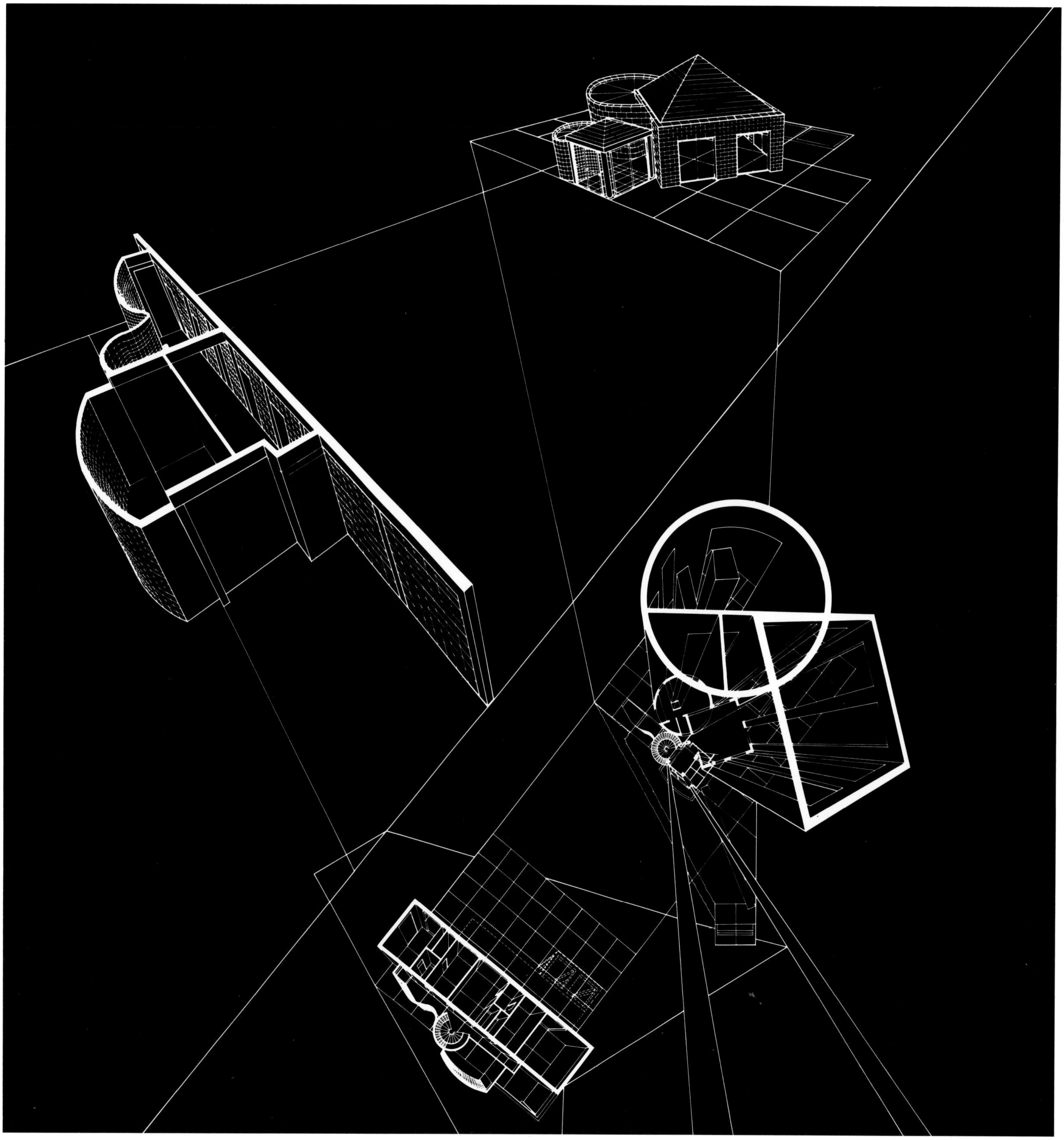

SUBER HOUSE – LUCASTON – TASMANIA JAMES JONES ARCHITECT

This house is located on a steeply wooded hillside and is approached from above so the roof design was very important. Curved laminated Tasmanian oak roof beams give the roof and ceiling some life and accentuate the view. The house is one room wide and 30 metres long so all rooms enjoy the sun, view and deck. For economy the building sits on steel columns and beams at 4.8 m centres. Walls are cladded externally with standard corrugated iron and internally with plaster panels with plywood used on the ceiling.
1:100 elevation – sepia ink on tracing paper.

Design Architect: James Jones
Drawing Artist: James Jones
Size: 265 x 240 mm
Date: 1988
Photography: Leigh Woolley

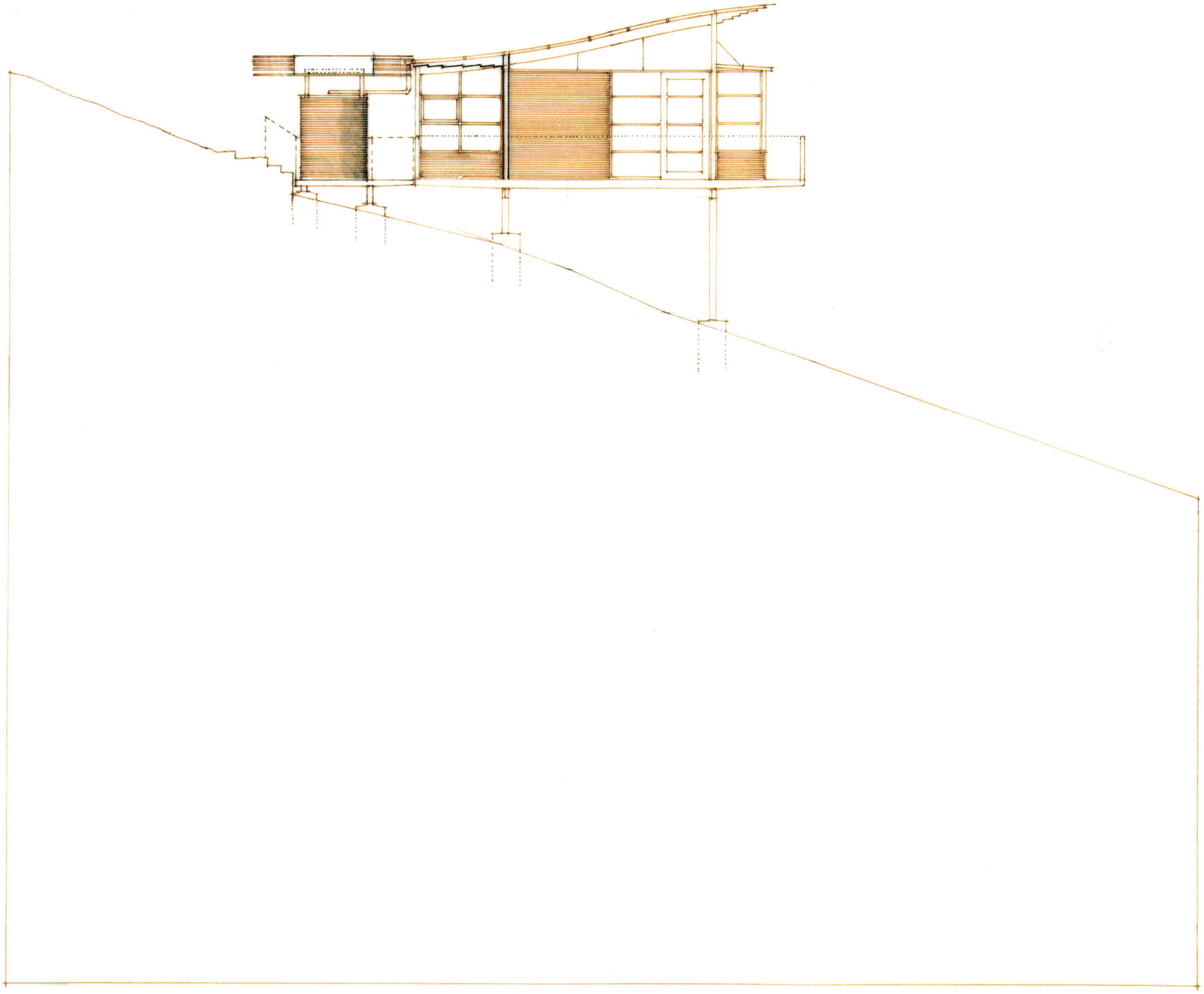

HOUSE - BRIGHTON - VICTORIA BOCHSLER AND PARTNERS

Design Architect: Nic Bochsler
Drawing Artist: Jim Tsoukatos
Size: 1189 x 841 mm
Date: 1991
Photographer: Neil Lorimer

Approaching this house in Brighton there is a feeling of expectation of seeing the sea. Just before arrival at the water the form of the house is revealed. The house absorbs all of the site, if not physically, then in its presence. Internal spaces spill out from the expanses of glass under the canopies to the boundary walls and beyond. Outlined by a strong geometry the house is a development of the Modernist, Formalist aesthetic which is made up of planes and light reinforcing changing light qualities in the day.
This drawing is the first image the client will see of the proposed building. From here the project rapidly proceeds into working drawings with only minor amendments.
Products used for presentation were: Plottex A1 double matt drafting film, Rotring 0.18 pen for all line work and 0.25 for backlining of walls, Letrafilm Pantone Catalogue Number 290-A, 365-A, 420-A, 424-A, 434-A, 475-A, 535-A, 549-A and 556-A. The trees shown on the plan have been selected from magazines and books placed under the film and traced off. Similarly the trees from the elevation have been photocopied from magazines onto clear adhesive film then applied to the image.

PATIO
B'FAST
KITCHEN
LAUNDRY
DINING
CELLAR
POOL
LIVING
TERRACE
SITTING
COURTYARD
ENTRY
PATHWAY
W/SHOP
STORE
PLANT
PWDR
E/S.
M. BEDROOM
STAIR
GARAGE
DRIVEWAY

HOUSE – TOORAK – VICTORIA   WILLIAMS & BOAG

Design Architect:
Peter Williams
Drawing Artist: Peter Williams and Jonathan Sarfaty
Size: 841 x 594 mm
Date: 1981–83
Photographer: John Gollings

The client's brief was to provide a dining space, family room and laundry/sewing area on the rear of an existing house and incorporate a swimming pool into the garden. In doing so, to be mindful of the unique 'park-like' feel of the garden behind the house, maximise the presence of a large plane tree and maintain light into the back of the building which faces due south. Attention to detail of existing Neo-Georgian building of utmost importance, compatibility with existing building a top priority. The house is two-storey and very shallow with the special quality of being set very close to the site frontage. The frontage is due north, the back is due south.
It became apparent that the key to the problem was to ignore the notion of orientation, ie, getting direct sun into the family and dining space at the rear of the building was impossible. Proximity of the new spaces to the existing spaces in the house was important from a convenience and overlapping function point of view.
The above points were incorporated into a proposal which provides three rooms placed centrally on the rear of the house about an axis of symmetry. The axis was extended along the length of the site, with the pool also set in relation to the axis. The admission of light and the view of the tree canopy was handled by use of transparent roof material.
The predominant feeling of the extension is one of lightness and delicacy with a strong relationship to the garden. Maximum realisation of the tree's presence for the client whilst still being obviously contained within the formality of the house has been very successful. This manipulation of space and form has added to our clients experience of the house in a fresh and engaging manner.
Axonometric view – ink line on tracing paper reduced to bromide negative 300 x 300 for black line on solid white background. Pantone film applied to reduced Bromide print.

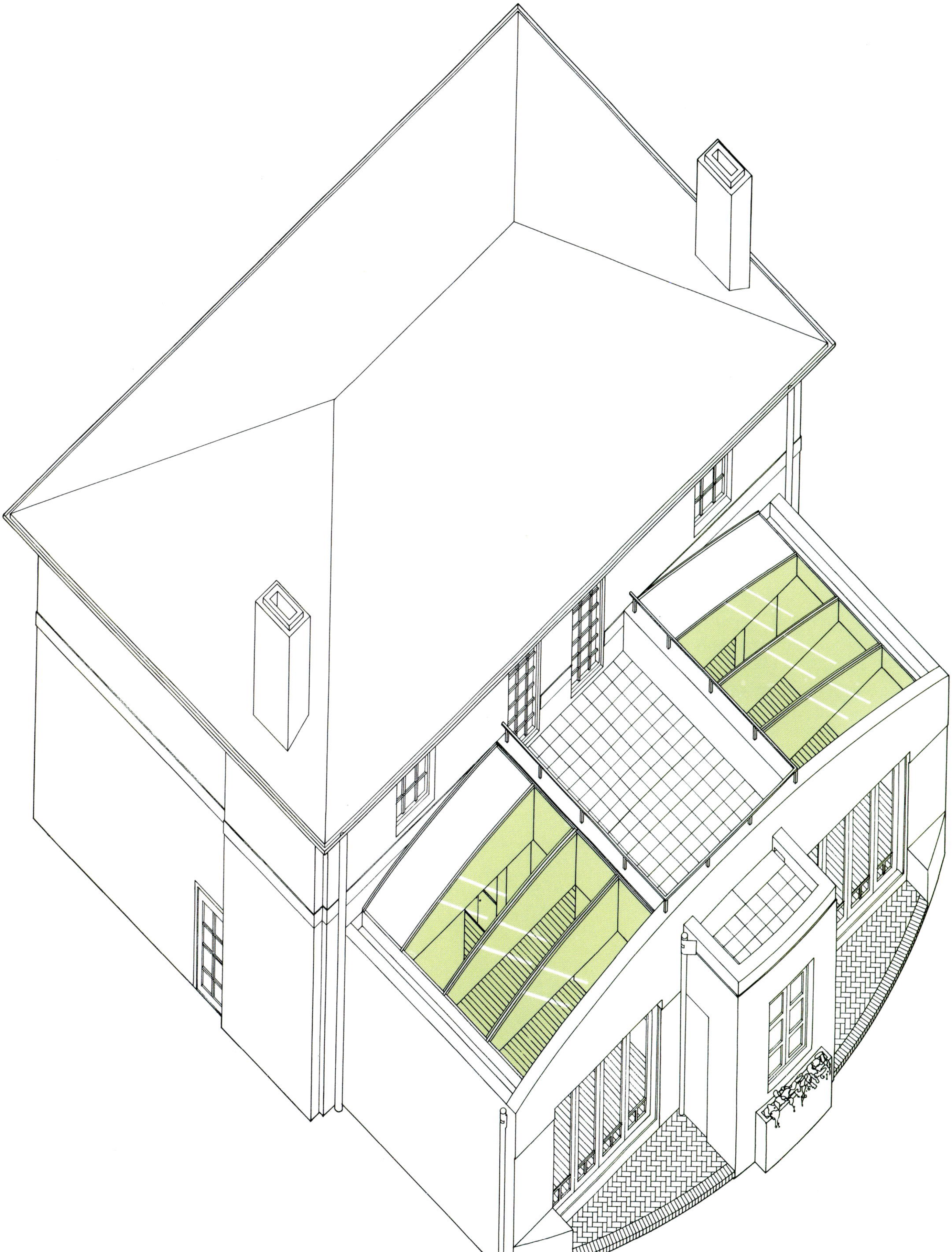

PACIFIC VILLAS – SUNSHINE BEACH – QUEENSLAND   JOHN MAINWARING AND ASSOCIATES

'Doctor Seaweed a fellow
explorer, had retired to the
peace and quiet of Calypso Bay
to build a city of sandcastles.'
Tony Edwards,
Ralph the Rhino

The site, a sand-dune overlooking Noosa National Park's southern headlands, once formed a part of the client's family estate. The inherent qualities of the site inspired the solution acknowledging the sand-dune ridge topography, the existing diversity of vegetation and the existing residential streetscape. The sand-dune form was maintained by stepping the townhouses down the ridge and carefully contouring the driveway. The five passively ventilated buildings each contained two three-bedroom thirty-metre square townhouses. All command a favourable northerly aspect both south and north.

In a small office with the technological necessities of photocopy and fax, a traditionally drafted ink drawing can provide the structure to communicate information to relevant parties. Photocopies of the 'master' can be graphically enhanced for the communication of specific information. The black and white presentation of ink drawings and relief printing are useful tools in the composition and transfer of descriptive drawings.

Virtually any textured surface can be exploited to make a print. In these drawings tree stamps fashioned from polystyrene rubber and cork have been used where appropriate to capture the nature of our coastal schlerophyll forests. Grids cut into an eraser can become paving or lattice the possibilities are numerous. Prints or stamps can be made cheaply and easily, we all remember the old potato print.

In most cases the drawings remain as monochromatic aids in the design and communication of ideas. These drawings can be taken a step further with the addition of colours. Colour pencil, water based felt pens and brushes even crayons have been used in these examples. Frottage, rubbing over a textured surface to create an image is often exploited. Relief printing has rich history and its economy, accessibility and diversity invites exploration. The drawing is ink on tracing with some additional pencil rendering after photocopy reduction to 297 x 210 mm.

Design Associate:
Richard Foster
Drawing Artist:
Richard Foster
Size: 1189 x 841 mm
Date: 1989/90
Photographer:
John Mainwaring and
M Mahady

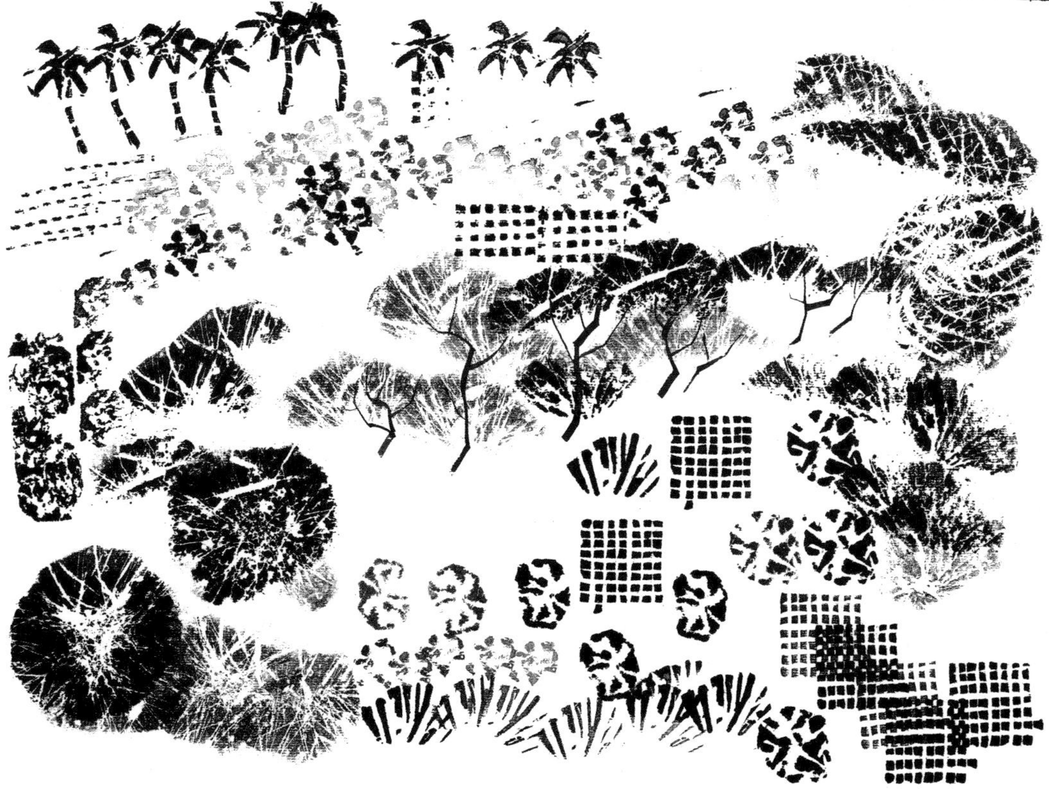

COMMERCIAL ARCHITECTURE

CORN EXCHANGE COMPETITION – SYDNEY – NEW SOUTH WALES KRINGAS AND JAHN ARCHITECTS

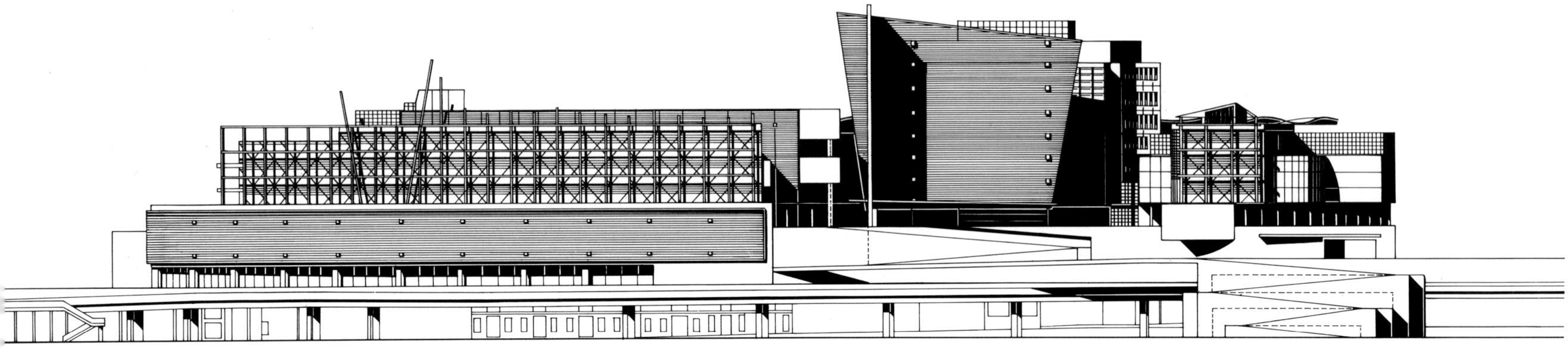

Design Architect: Graham Jahn
Drawing Artist: Graham Jahn
Painting Artist: Catherine Fisk
Size: 240 x 150 mm
Date: 1988

In March 1988, the New South Wales Government and the Darling Harbour Authority called an invited competition to use the airspace over the Western Distributor opposite the Festival Market at Darling Harbour. A concrete box deck containing the car parking was placed on columns over the roadway forming the base for buildings to be erected. A collection of five office buildings varying in size and shape were placed around a public foyer. Their glass façades were shielded from the direct western sun by timber and metal sunscreens, which protected the Festival Market and Maritime Museum building from reflected glare.
Paintings are Liquitex acrylic on plain white cardboard.

No 1 COLLINS STREET – MELBOURNE – VICTORIA **DENTON CORKER MARSHALL**

In association with
Robert Peck YFHK
Design Architect:
Denton Corker Marshall
Drawing Artist:
Barrie Marshall,
Denton Corker Marshall
Size: 841 x 594 mm
Date: 1985
Photographer: John Gollings

A 17-level commercial office building in the Parliamentary Precinct of the central city, set behind a number of historic buildings.
The building aims to sit comfortably with the surrounding generally historic built form fabric, whilst having a contemporary character of its own.
It is stepped in plan and elevational profile to reinforce a corner tower imagery, and window planes are set flush or recessed to add variation of light and shade. The precast concrete façade is natural light grey, and gridded into 600 mm squares to give a tiled rather than large panelled character.
The drawing shows the building from MacArthur Place which focuses diagonally on the site. The existing historical buildings form the street level edge, with the tower rising behind. A new six-level 'podium' building provides a separate entry from Spring Street, with main entry from Collins through the undercroft of the historic terraces.
This drawing was produced 'after the event' and based on a photograph taken by John Gollings. Its purpose was to link with other illustrations of unbuilt projects within a limited edition publication; there was no requirement for a realistic rendering in order to 'sell' the building to a client, but rather to sketch the essentials of the concept.
Technique: Ink line on tracing paper. Materials: Rotring isograph, 0.13, 0.18. Tracing paper – Hoesch Diamant Extra Special Natural tracing paper 110–115 gsm.
The drawing was sketched direct onto tracing paper laid over the coloured photograph. After the major elements of the building were overlaid, a sheet of white paper was placed between the photograph and tracing paper, and detail (trees, people, shading) added. Some line work was scratched back by razor blade to lighten the impact.

COMMERCIAL OFFICE BUILDING – DANDENONG – VICTORIA   IVAN RIJAVEC ARCHITECTS

A limited design competition was commissioned to develop a commercial office building on a mainstreet frontage in Dandenong. Our winning entry proposed a curvilinear structure composed of three principal elements; ie, a south-facing full-height curtain wall resting on an articulated base, keyed into a north-facing masonry anchor.
By way of an exploded axonometric technique the major elements of the building have been independently represented in a manner which indicates their relationship to the whole. Media: pencil, coloured pencil, ink tipped pens, applied to both sides of detail paper. (The artist's general statement which elucidates some of the concerns specific to his work can be found outlined under the heading of the Manifold Residence by Ivan Rijavec Architects.)

Design Architect: Ivan Rijavec
Drawing Artist:
Zbigniew Jaworski
Size: 1190 x 700 mm
Date: 1989
Photographer:
Zbigniew Jaworski

SOUTH DANDENONG
CENTRE
MAN-RUAVEC ARCHITECTS

CARRINGTON HOUSE OFFICE BUILDING - SYDNEY - NEW SOUTH WALES PEDDLE THORP

Design Architect:
Corinne Girard Young
Drawing Artist:
David Wardman
Size: 1189 x 941 mm
Date: 1990

Carrington House is a 13-storey office building presently under construction on Wynyard Park. It follows the tradition of a tripartite façade: firstly, a richly articulated base with its deeply recessed arcade; second, a body and third, a top.

The effect of a load bearing stone façade is achieved with a curtain wall system allowing for windows to be deeply recessed with granite cladding. Several different colours of Australian granites are further used to break down the scale of the façade. However, the chromatic interest is only subtle since the granites are used in their exfoliated form. Highly polished granite is inserted to mark the entrance portal.

A central projecting feature breaks the horizontality of the façade providing verticality to an otherwise boxy envelope. Stone spandrels are replaced in this instance by stainless steel. A common matrix ties the granite façade with the stainless steel feature by having all openings share the same treatment. This incorporates the use of black mullions with stainless steel inlay strips within the mullion. Green tinted glass is used throughout.

The basis of our work is a line drawing with all information and detail that is available from the architect. This line drawing is an important part of our process and comes from the attitude that our drawings form part of the presentation process and should be compatible with elevations and plans being prepared by the architect for the same presentation. Also it allows checking for accuracy before colour rendering. The line drawing is in fact Stage Two in a three-stage process.

Stage One: We prepared preliminary drawing in pencil or a computer outline. This drawing has all the information of the final drawing and is to establish the view and to provide a drawing for assessment and checking.

Stage Two: The line drawing is prepared by tracing the preliminary pencil drawing onto tracing paper using a 0.25 Rapidograph or Isograph pen with black drawing ink.

Stage Three: The line drawing is printed onto bond photocopy paper and mounted on 3 mm board. The print is now colour rendered using Rotring Artist Colour (watercolour pre-mixed with water) through an air-brush. We use a Thayer and Chandler or a Paasche air-brush driven by a Jun-Air compressor. Each colour application is applied individually by masking the area to be coloured with frisket paper. Final minor touches are applied by brush and pentel pen.

MAIN ESCALATOR PROJECT SKYGARDEN PITT STREET – SYDNEY – NEW SOUTH WALES
D4 DESIGN

This project came to D4 in 1988. D4 in conjunction with Susan Freeman developed the design illustrated in these presentation graphics. The brief was to come up with concepts for possible incorporation into the design of an escalator space to be the main entry to the dining halls at the Skygarden Shopping Arcade off Pitt Street Mall, Sydney. The space was very narrow and very high, similar to a canyon in which the sun only enters at noon. One escalator was placed in the space and this, of course, could go only in one direction at a time. During the day the escalator would go from the ground up four floors. At night it would be placed in reverse taking patrons from the restaurant to the street. These two modes of operation we considered set two distinct viewing sequences for the journey. D4 was to create an experience for pedestrians coming off the Pitt Street Mall; settling them down and making them receptive to information to be received in Skygarden. They were to be put in a 'retail frame of mind'.

Design Architect:
D4 Design in conjunction with Susan Freeman
Drawing Artist:
D4 Design Pty Ltd
Size: 590 x 590 mm
Date: 1988

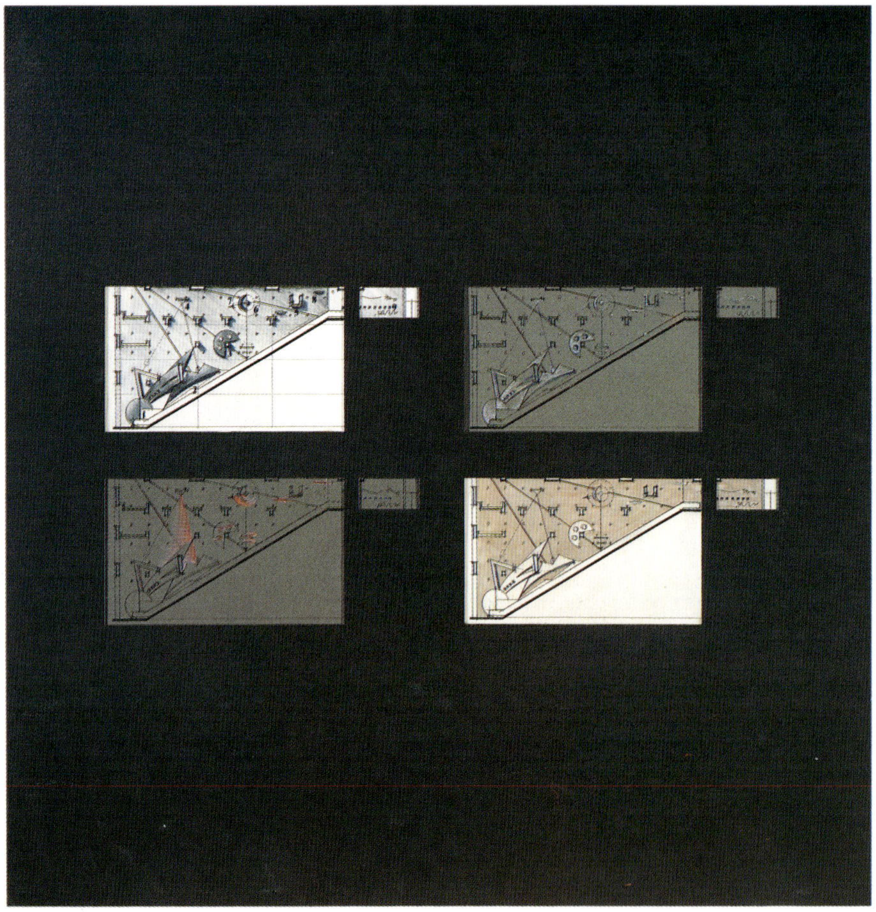

The illusions of 'Skydining' which the client desired in the dining areas would be seen as a reiteration of this initial experience. The design incorporated basic children's textbook physics experiment into the scheme so that the experience would reward close scrutiny over repeated visits. Foucault's pendulum, flywheels and a pendulum driven clock were included. These became parts of a story that took one from the ground, through trees up through more celestial bodies ... a thematic construction we felt appropriate to the notion of 'Skygarden'. Small videos located in the wall at the top levels would play looped videotapes of clouds and Michelangelo's representations of God bringing Adam to life from the Sistine Chapel.

Freehand sketches used Uchida drawing pens of 0.8 and 0.5 on Kent cartridge paper. Small areas of gold leaf were added were used to highlight. The coloured image used grey Canson paper and detail paper with drafted ink line of 0.25 and 0.35 with applied Derwent coloured pencils highlights and large areas of coloured pencil on back of paper.

CHIFLEY TOWER – SYDNEY – NEW SOUTH WALES KOHN PEDERSEN FOX ASSOCIATES TRAVIS PARTNERS ARCHITECTS IN ASSOCIATION

Design Architect: Kohn Pedersen Fox and Travis Partners
Drawing Artist: Harry Roberts
Size: 1000 x 700 mm
Date: 1990
Photographer: Patrick Binghamhall

Chifley Tower is a 44-storey commercial and retail development located in Sydney's financial district overlooking the Royal Botanic Gardens and Sydney Harbour. The building is designed to respond to its neighbours at street level and to the overall city grid at upper levels. This is articulated by stepping the building back throughout its height, culminating in a stainless steel spire. It is the largest steel-framed structure in Sydney and is clad in a façade made from Stoney Creek granite from Connecticut, USA framed up with metallic silver painted aluminium; the glazing is 20% reflective 'sky on clear'.

A delineation commission begins by chasing the appropriate medium for the expression of the architects' design. Through discussion with the architects it was agreed that traditional watercolour wash would best suit this particular design. Watercolour wash in the beaux-arts style has a venerable tradition in the rendering of architectural designs.

The technique fell into disuse in the 1950s. Perhaps it was unsuitable for international style architecture. Gouache, casein etc, let illustrators express dramatic effects more quickly than with watercolour. Watercolour wash technique, however, relies on the application of dozens of transparent washes over a light pencil outline on heavy weight art paper. The method used for this picture (one of a series of views of the building) is as follows.

Firstly a photograph from the agreed viewpoint is employed as a guide for preparing a set up drawing, using strict classical perspective method. No artistic license is used except for removal of some unnecessary foreground.

The proportions and details of the architects design are carefully reproduced. All stonework joints, copings, window mullions etc, are plotted. This work is done on heavy weight drafting film with black ballpoint pens.

This is time consuming but the result is a sharp, clean drafting. After adding some indication of tonal values with black ink in an airbrush, the set-up is ready for client and architect approval. Meanwhile a large sheet (1000 x 700) of heavy weight handmade paper is soaked in a tub, laid out on a board, secured with drum-tight flat paper surface which will not buckle when wetted by watercolour. Once approved the film drawing is reversed and the whole set-up is back-lined with sharp 4H pencils. This is also a time consuming stage, but graphite scribble on the reverse face will not transfer to the stretched artpaper.

The set-up drawing can now be transferred to the stretched paper by burning the front face. Once complete the colouring begins. The best quality watercolours come in two kinds: sedimentary and staining or dye colour. Avoid the latter as they make corrections impossible. Sedimentary colours, on the other hand, when laid down with a sable brush drop a fine sediment of pigment onto the paper, this imparts a wonderful grainy texture to the work. Care is needed not to disturb the sediment while it is drying. Corrections can be made by scrubbing off the dry sediment with wet sea sponges.

The pigments used for this picture are the traditional water-colourists comprising: French ultramarine, cerulean blue, burnt umber, burnt sienna, rose madder (genuine), Davy's gray, sepia, raw umber. The washes mixed from the above are generally complex 'greys' achieved by mixing a pure colour with its complement. These are prepared in small bowls and applied to the drawing. Pure pigments must only be used in the thinnest washes. Brushes have to be genuine sable hair (synthetics don't work). My favourite is a large No 12 which is 50 years old, in superb condition, which was used for all but the finest detail in the picture.

RIVERSIDE TOWER – BRISBANE – QUEENSLAND HARRY SEIDLER AND ASSOCIATES

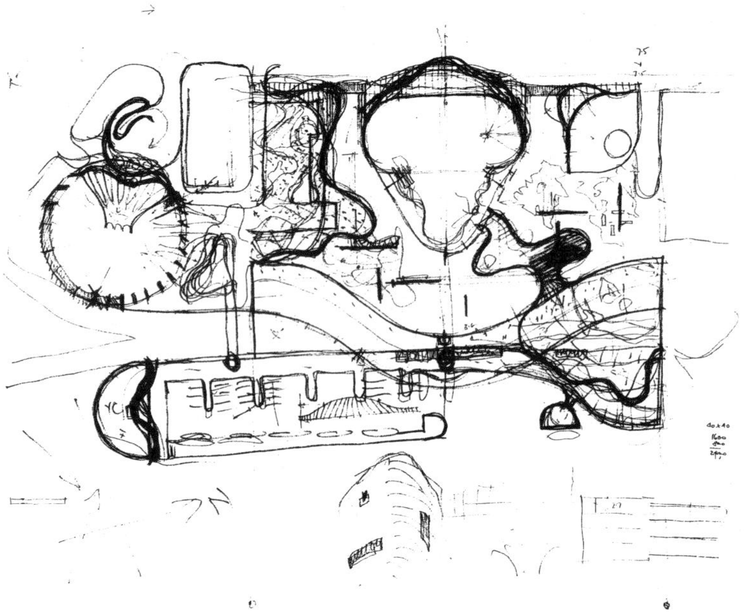

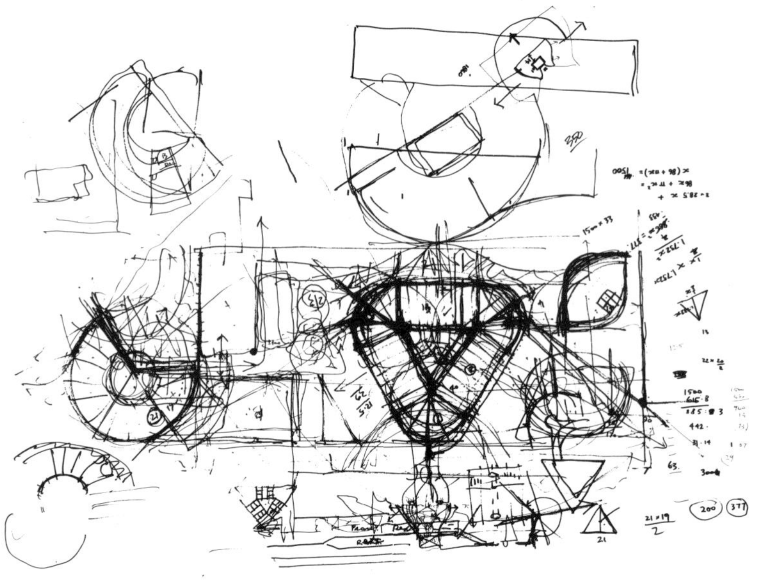

Sited along the Brisbane River, this commercial development of 50 000 m² of offices, a 350 room hotel, restaurants and shops is being built in two stages. The first, the 38-storey office tower, takes on a shape which responds to the requirement of giving as many offices as possible a clear outlook over the water. The triangular configuration achieves this for two-thirds of the 1 500 m² floors, facing full height glass walls. Fixed external sunshades are fitted at varying angles responding to the orientations. Planted terraces recessed in the façade relieve the monotony of sealed air-conditioned office space.

External columns in front of the 15 m high entrance lobby are gathered in groups of three into a projecting hyperboloid pier. This in turn is braced back against the core by isostatically determined radial ribs, exposed on the ceiling. A sculpture by Norman Carlberg forms a focus.

Drafting pens with black ink on high quality film. Completed drawings were then photographed by high resolution cameras and printed on high contrast photographic paper to the same size and mounted on double weight cardboard. After drawings are mounted on board, Pantone coloured film is applied to give a full colour presentation.

Design Architect: Harry Seidler
Drawing Artist: Mark Butler
Size: 1000 x 700 mm
Date: 1983–86
Photographer: John Gollings

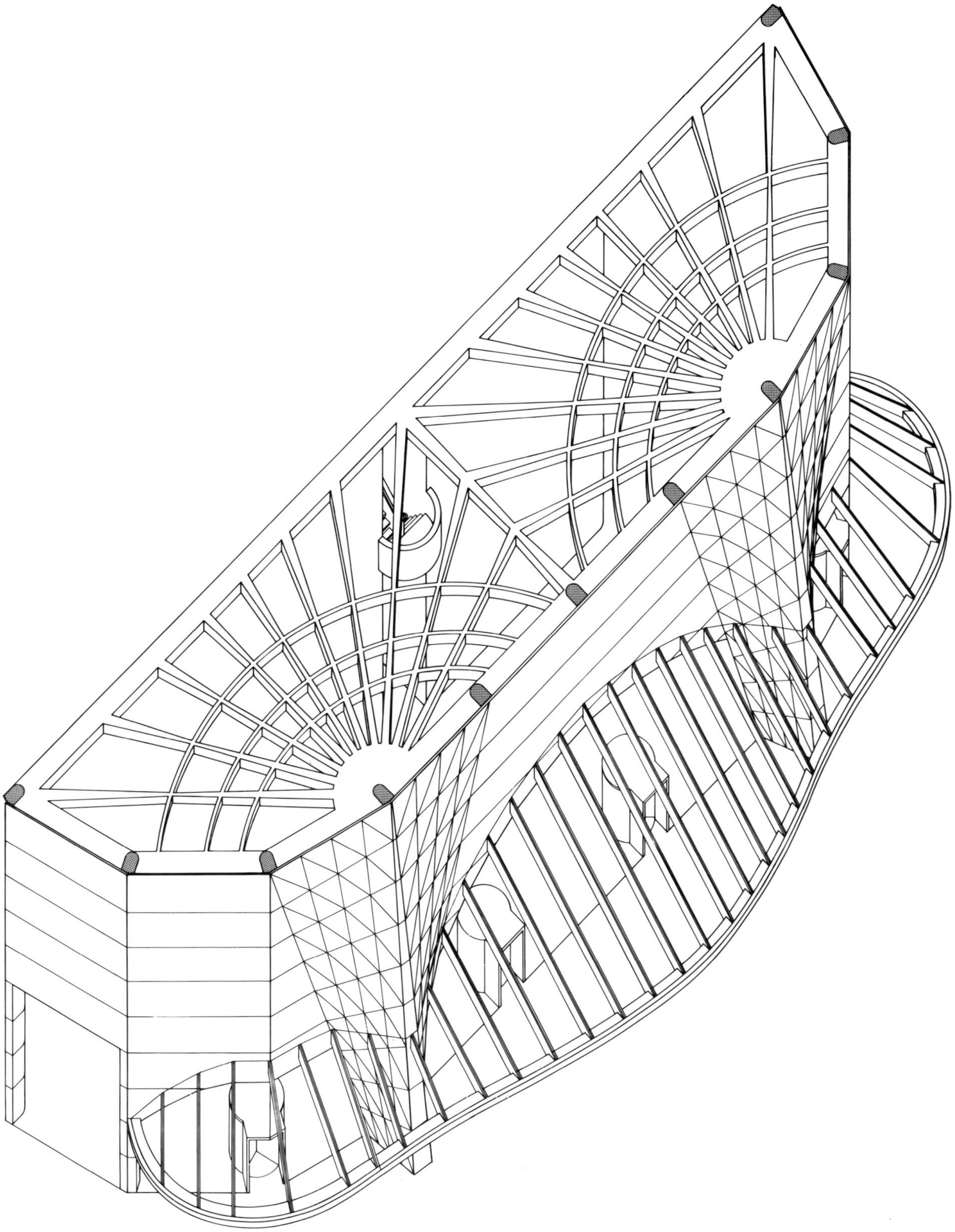

101 COLLINS STREET - MELBOURNE - VICTORIA DENTON CORKER MARSHALL

Design Architect: Denton Corker Marshall
Drawing Artist: Barrie Marshall, Denton Corker Marshall
Size: 1000 x 700 mm
Date: 1987
Photographer: John Gollings

A 56 level commercial office development. It consists of a tower building set back 30m from the street, with a five-level podium maintaining the predominant parapet line of the remaining historic buildings in the street.
The tower is a mid-grey granite clad shaft, with horizontal strip windows, symmetrically 'buttressed' on each face with metal clad frames with infill glazing. Towards the top, the glazed buttresses step back as open framed balconies.
The podium is based on a metal clad framed grid, with infills of grey granite and glazing; flush, recessed or with inset balconies. Vertical aluminium plates project at irregular locations, reinforcing the texture of the façade in response to the detail of adjoining buildings, and the light and shade of the street.
The drawing shows the tower from Collins Street west, its entry façade. The drawing was produced for presentation to the client. Its purpose was to illustrate the solidity and imposing presence of the building (a tacit client requirement). Later drawings of a more 'commercial' character would be commissioned for marketing purposes.
Technique: photocopy of ink line drawing onto detail paper, then coloured with colour pencil.
Materials: detail paper 53 gsm – Fenton C300.
Colour pencil: Derwent (Cumberland) Venus (Spectracolor) Berol (Eaglecolor)
The set-up was based on earlier perspectives of alternate proposals. Tracing paper was overlaid and the major building volume, floor levels and surrounding buildings traced through in pencil. Detail was then added relevant to the new design. The drawing was then inked with 0.18 mm Rapidograph, a photocopy onto detail paper taken, and this sheet coloured lightly with coloured pencil. The colours were not 'realistic', but presented the drawing as a 'tinted', essentially black and white rendering.

CROWN STREET PROJECT - SYDNEY - NEW SOUTH WALES TRAVIS PARTNERS

Design Architect:
Frank Stanisic
Drawing Artist: Frank Stanisic
Size: 750 x 1000 mm
Date: 1990

The Crown Street Project comprises 236 residential apartments, 3500m² retail and commercial space and a basement car park for 283 cars. This predominantly residential project covers two inner city blocks in Surry Hills, Sydney. The design concept is a restatement of the typology of the inner city residential block: buildings along the perimeter streets creating large, sheltered landscaped courtyards in the centres of the blocks; larger and more prominent corner buildings; lower rows of infill housing; the use of mainly face brick and painted concrete to reflect the character of the surrounding environment; the proportioning of windows and other façade elements to refer to older buildings in the area and the balancing of large scale monumental shapes with small elements.
The drawing presents the proportioning, materials and colouration of the Crown Street façade of the mixed use/apartment corner building and was prepared with other street studies. It illustrates the fragmentation of form of the new building and the incorporation of an existing heritage building into the new street façade. The elevation was traced over a rough pencil set-up. The part plan was included to clarify the entrance to the apartment building from the corner. Materials include Derwent (Cumberland) Colour pencil and fine felt-tip pen on Charette Yellow trace 904.
The drawing was prepared as both a design study and presentation drawing and has been used for discussion, publication, presentation to the client, council and residents. The technique is deliberately rough and sketchy with emphasis on speed and controlled spontaneity rather than precision and correctness.

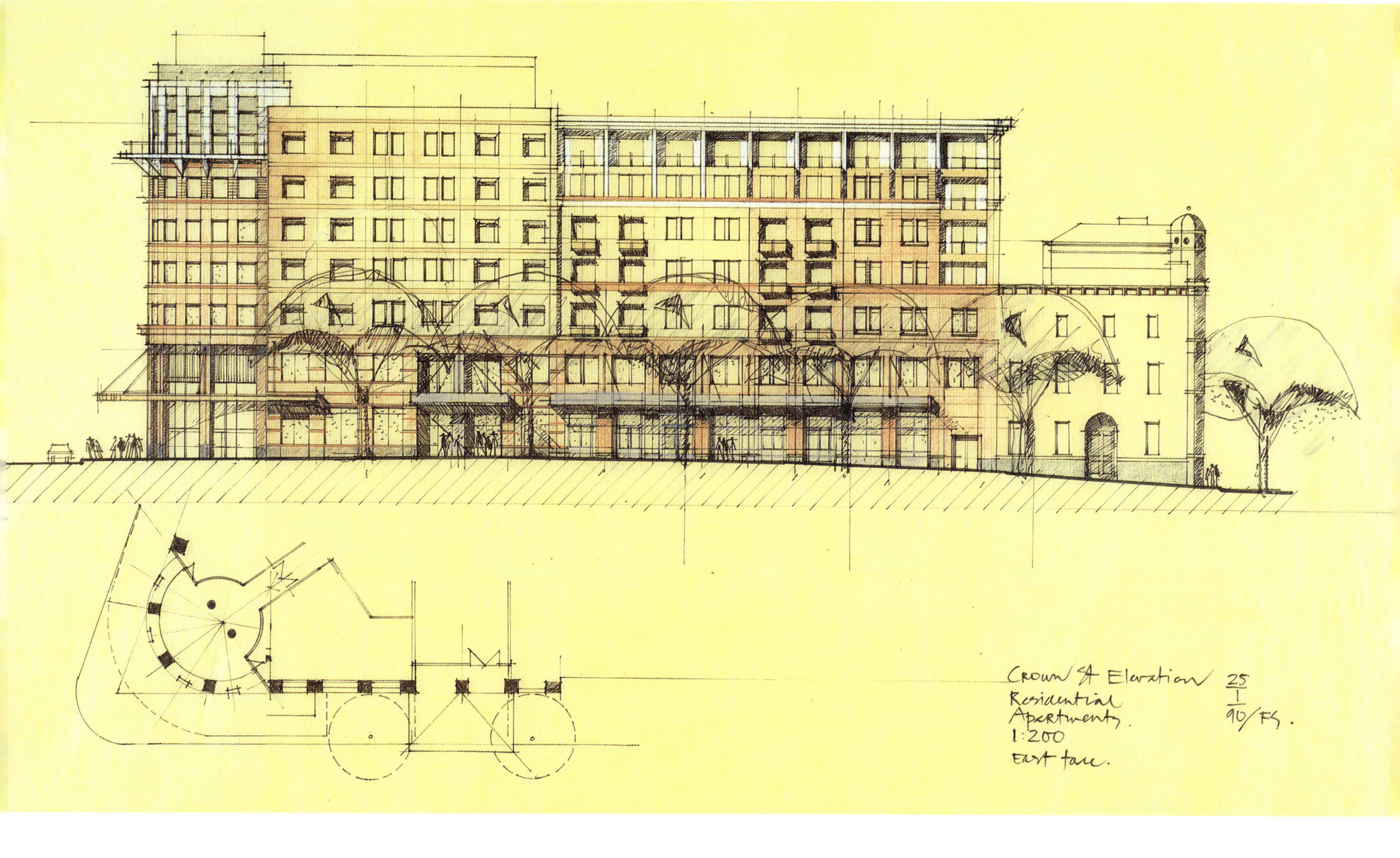
Crown St Elevation
Residential Apartments.
1:200
East face.
25/1/90/FS.

FIRST GOVERNMENT HOUSE COMPETITION – SYDNEY – NEW SOUTH WALES
NEIL DURBACH ARCHITECT

At an urban scale, the proximity of the site to Farrer Place, Macquarie Place and the larger outdoor facilities of Circular Quay and the Botanic Gardens provide ample open space for the site and its vicinity. Provision of further open space would undermine the distinctive spatial nature of the locality. Our proposal reinforces the perimeter of the site. Adherence to the geometry of the original street pattern allows the old and the new to stand side by side, held in an existing order. The liberating aspect of the grid is thus expressed; it accommodates many ages and epochs simultaneously.
The ways through the site clearly belong in the public realm. They connect Young and Phillip Streets and are part of a legacy of streets and lanes which underpin the rich urban ambiance of the locality. The introduction of interior plazas or atria makes for vacant and ambiguous spaces whose unsure urban quality would be mocked by the genuine dignity of Farrer Place.

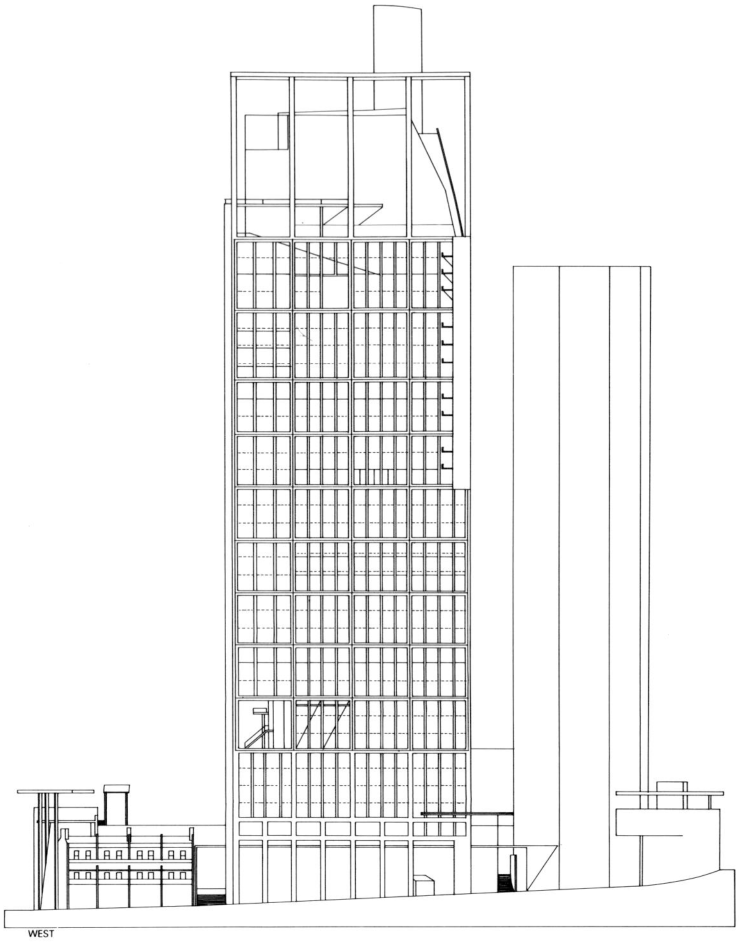

WEST

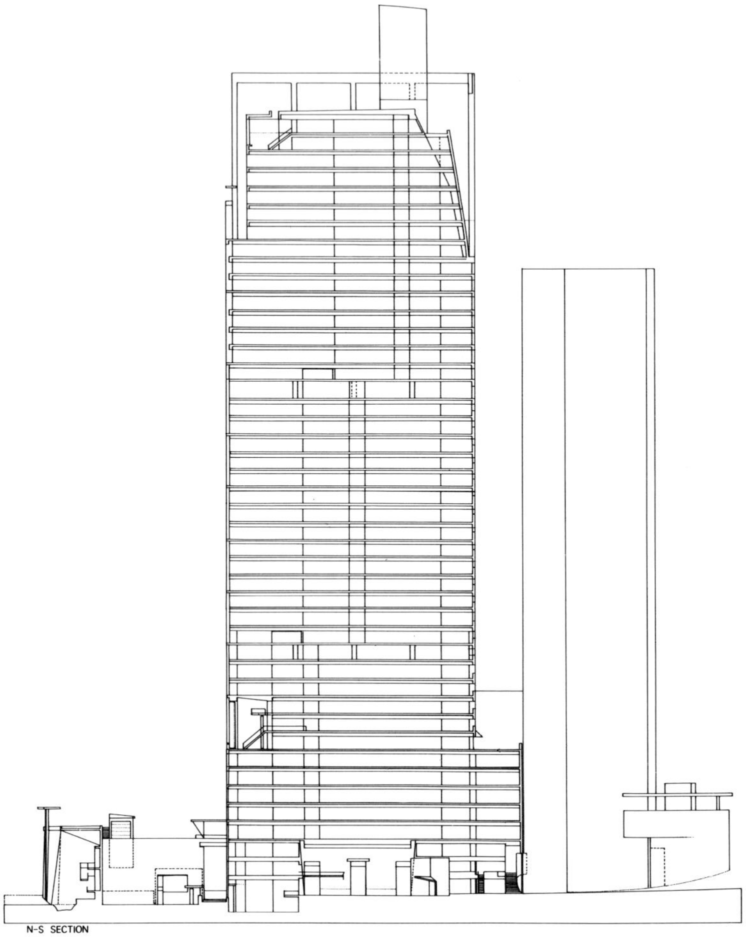

N-S SECTION

The building is essentially a concrete structure clad, in part, in sandstone. The museum for the First Government House ruins is composed of a box and a large roof sheltering the ruins. Together they constitute a façade to Bridge Street which reflects the scale and depth of the adjoining sandstone buildings.
The Museum is organised as a circuit, entered through the box from Phillip Street. The route leaves the box, brushes close to the excavated ruins then raises to provide an overview and culminates on the roof terrace where a view of the city reasserts the contemporary nature of the site.
The new tower is conceived as a connecting element as opposed to an heroic gesture standing alone. An eight floor datum, generated by the flanking buildings on Bridge Street and reflected in the Museum, as woven through the façade of the tower. The tower itself responds to the different scales of the surrounding buildings through its articulation. The height of the Legal and General tower is picked up, a large room on the eighth level orientates towards the Harbour; indeed the whole building has a horizontal aspect set up by the planes of the long sides and terminated by the flying cornices. Thus it intimates connections and mediates between its high-rise neighbours. The new tower is framed in bronze-clad steel, with parts of the north and south façade clad in grey-green granite.
The major drawing is 0.25 Rotring pen and ink on film which was later photographed back onto film. Sketches were A4 cartridge using Eagle Prisma colour pencils.

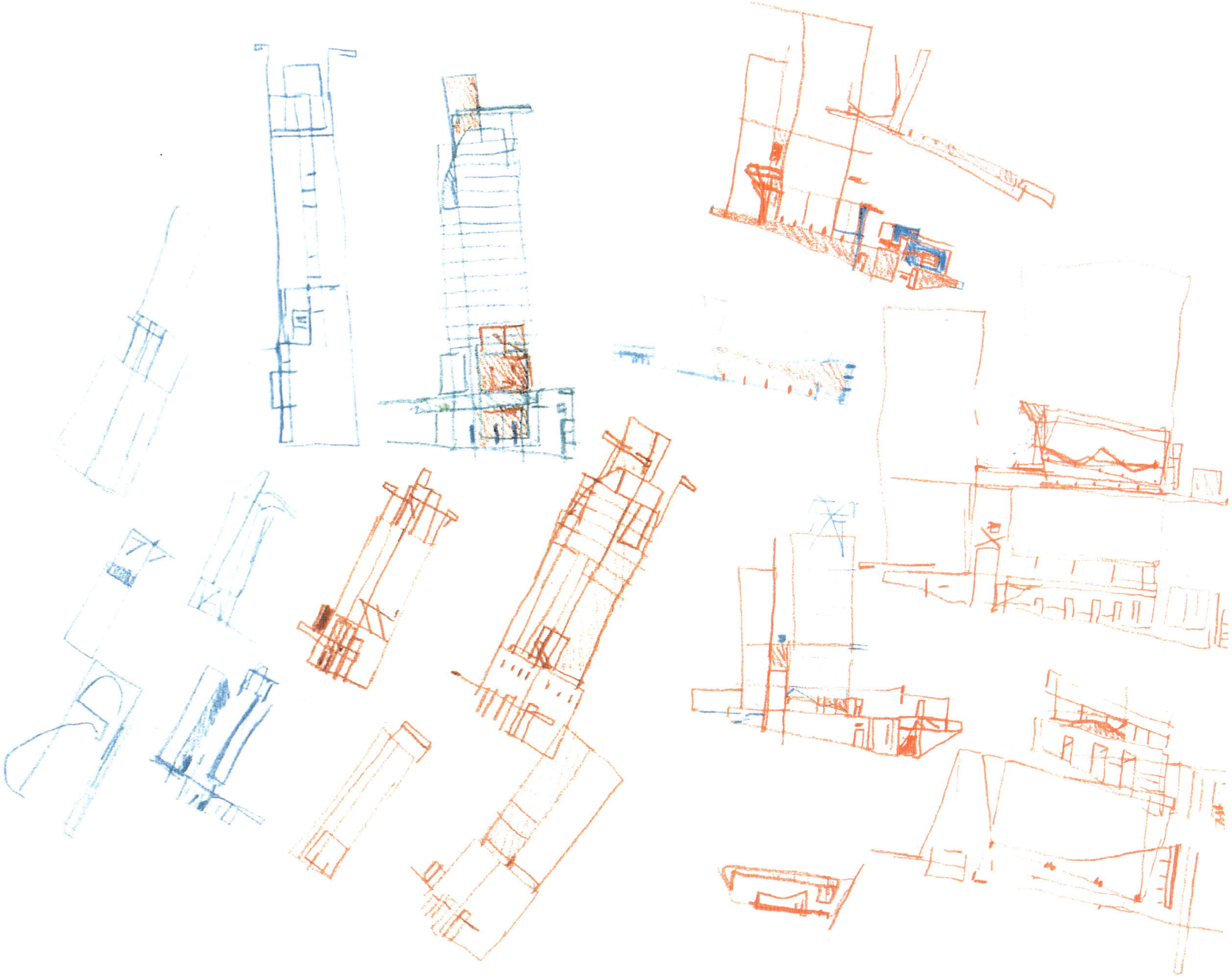

Design Architects:
Neil Durbach,
Harold Straatveit and
Harry Margalit
Drawing Artists: Neil Durbach,
Harold Straatveit,
Nic Murcutt and Andy Wilson
Size: 1682 x 1189 mm
and 240 x 170 mm
Date: 1989

GROSVENOR PLACE – SYDNEY – NEW SOUTH WALES HARRY SEIDLER AND ASSOCIATES

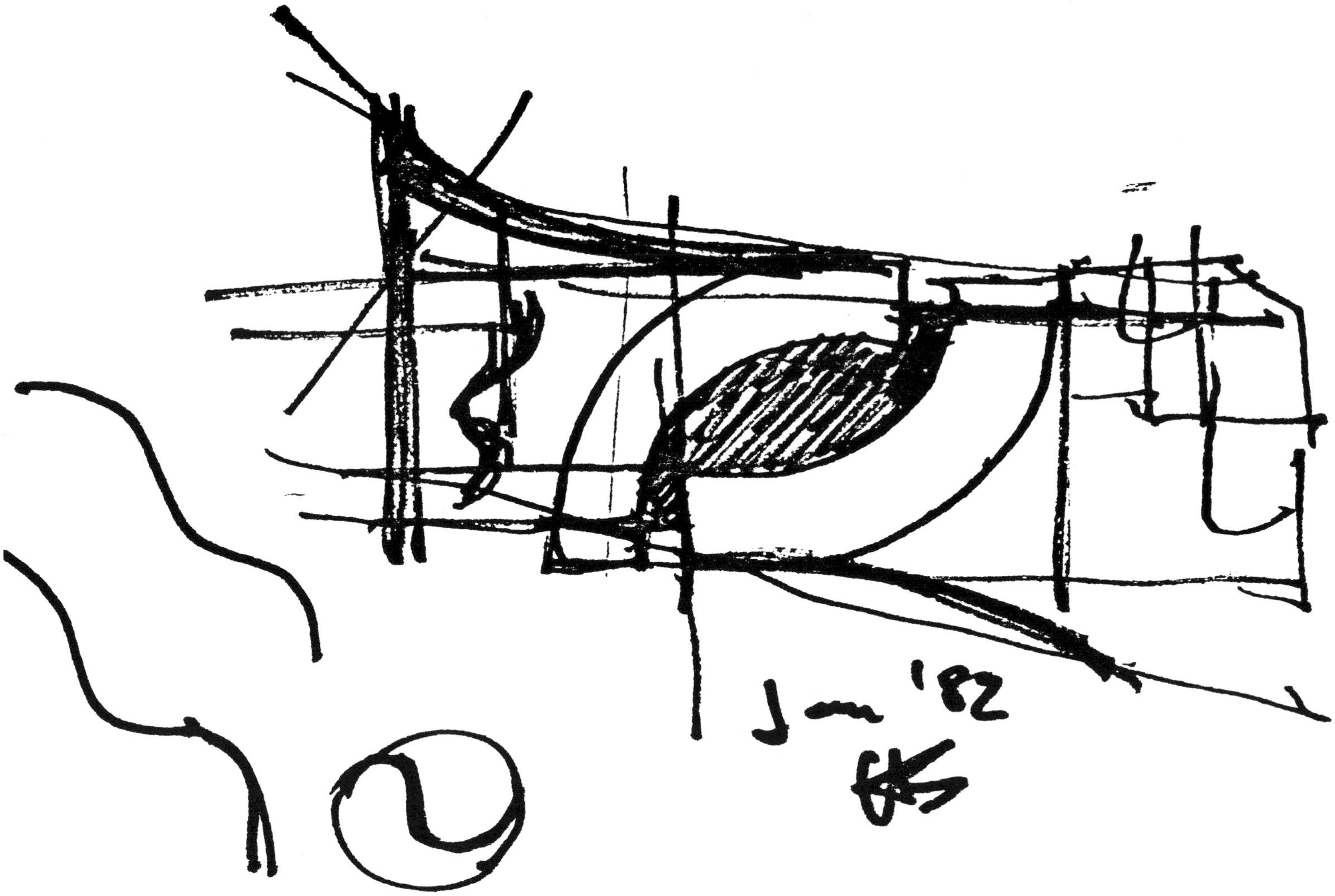

Located at the northern end of the city, the site enjoys fine panoramic outlooks toward the harbour to the north-east and the open space of Lang Park and Darling Harbour to the south-west. The 46-storey office tower's opposing quadrant shaped floors (each 2 000 m^2) maximise these sweeping views. The simple geometry allows the 14.6 m deep column-free construction to use identical steel floor beams and identical granite faced façade elements which speed and economise construction. The core is of slip-concrete.

Energy saving technology has been applied to generating power from roof-mounted solar collectors and economic night-time electricity. Energy is stored in a huge ice-bank in the basement for daytime peak demand for air-conditioning.

The tower is surrounded by public plazas, both open and glass covered. In the high entrance lobby there are three large wall-relief paintings by Frank Stella.

Drafting pens with black ink on high quality film (no pen used smaller than 0.25 for good reproduction, reduction resolution). Completed drawings were then dyeline printed onto high contrast gloss paper. The prints of the drawings were then mounted onto double weight cardboard. After the drawings were mounted on the board, Pantone coloured film was applied to give a full colour presentation.

Design Architect: Harry Seidler
Drawing Artist: Tony Caro

Size: 1000 x 700 mm
Date: 1982–88

Photographer: Max Dupain

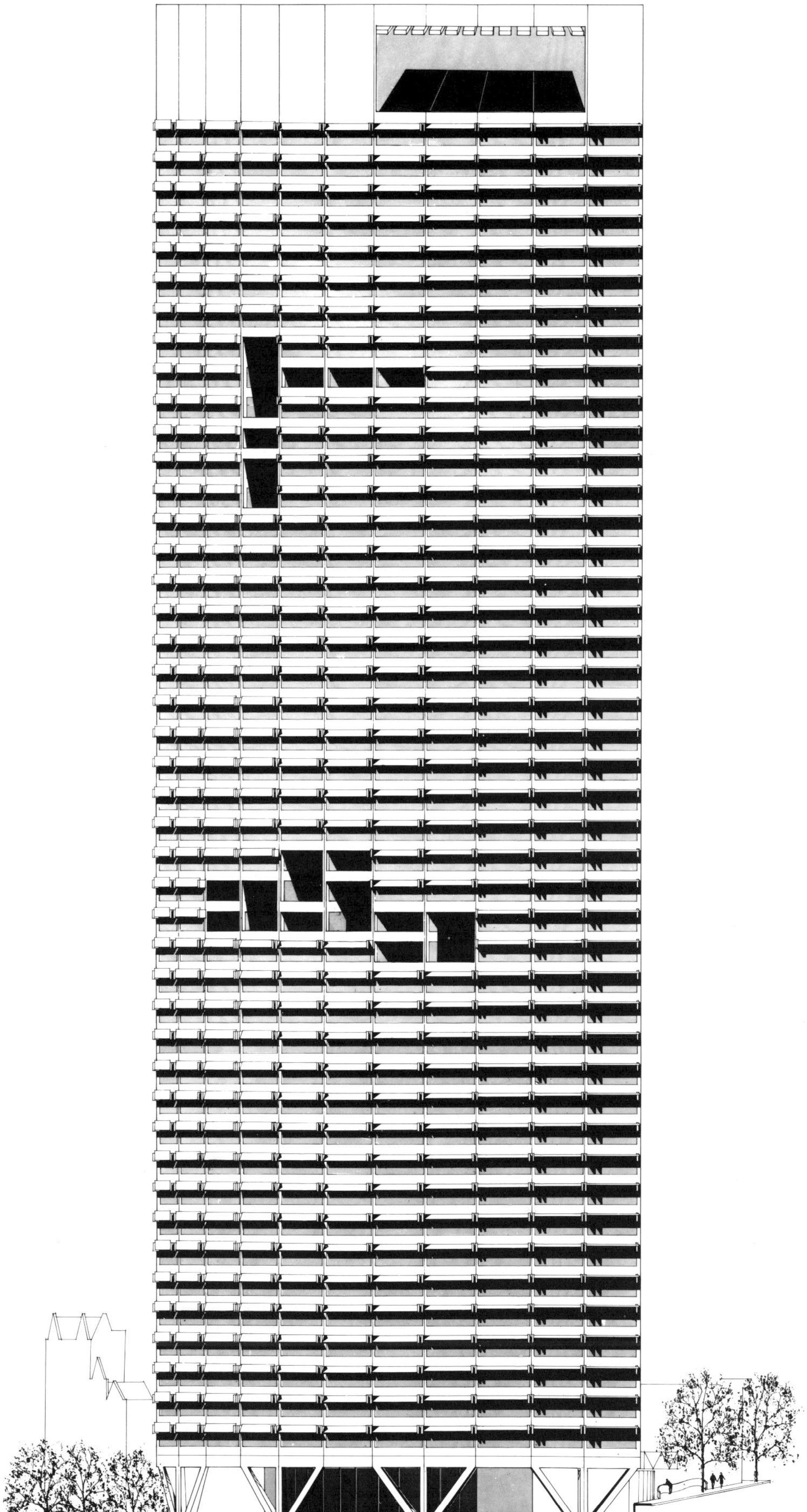

CAPITOL CENTRAL - SYDNEY - NEW SOUTH WALES LAWRENCE NIELD AND PARTNERS IN ASSOCIATION WITH TRAVIS PARTNERS

Capitol Central is a development proposal featuring the refurbishment of the disused Capitol Theatre in Sydney. The theatre is a 1920's atmospheric picture palace, one of the few remaining in the world outside the USA. The proposal included a major commercial and hotel component to provide long-term economic viability for the theatre and to assist in the general rejuvenation of the southern CBD.
The brief for the perspective was for an 'opening night' at the theatre including a view of the entire development. Materials included Columbia Math Board in dark blue/grey, Windsor & Newtons Designer's Gouache, Derwent coloured pencils.
The perspective was set up on tracing paper from a full set of architect's drawings. Numerous photos were taken on location to record neighbouring buildings and street scenery. Tracing was transferred onto board with Sarel White transfer paper, and rendering was carried out with a mixture of body colour, wash and air-brush augmented by a small amount of colour pencil work.

Design Architect:
Aladin Niazmand
Urban Design: Micheal Harrison
Drawing Artist: John Richards
Size: 850 x 600 mm
Date: 1990

CAPITOL
THEATRE

GLOUCESTER STREET OFFICE BUILDING PROJECT - SYDNEY - NEW SOUTH WALES
CAMPBELL BRADLEY FIRTH ASSOCIATES

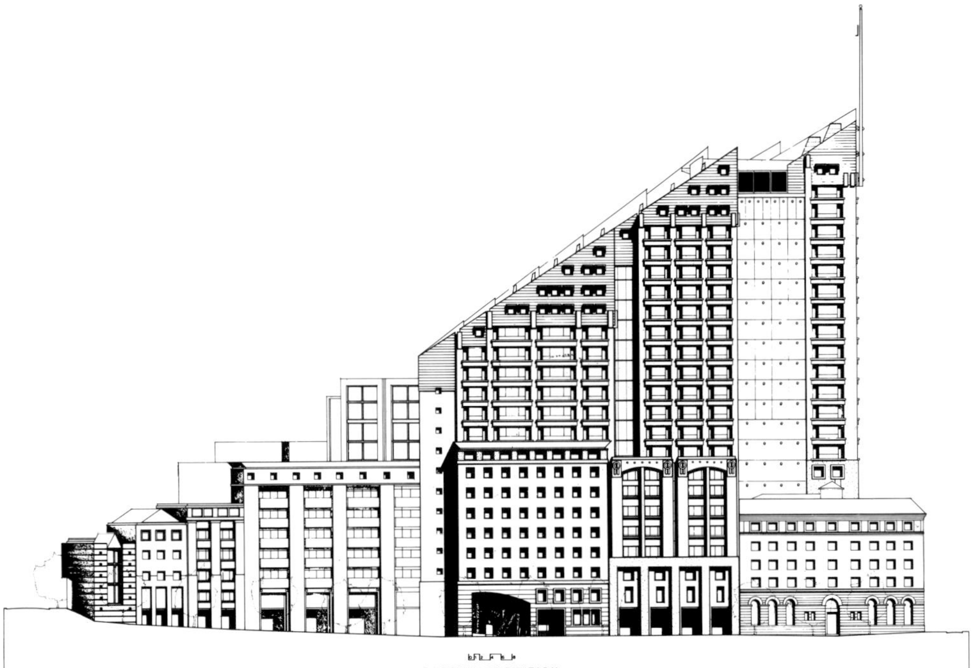

EASTERN ELEVATION

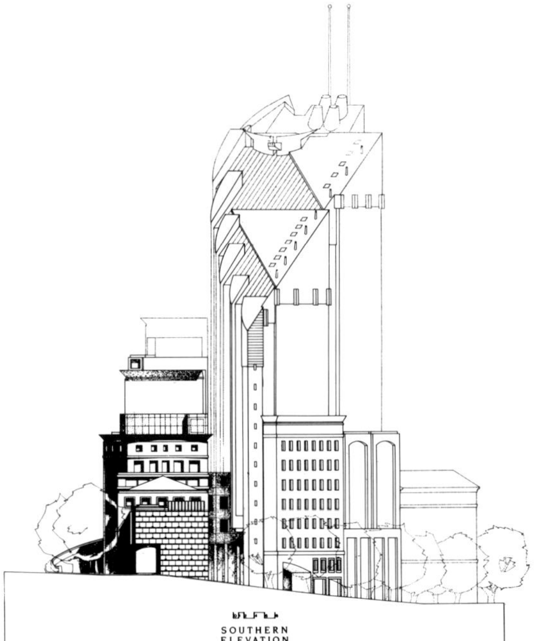

SOUTHERN ELEVATION

This scheme was carried out as a tender to the Sydney Cove Redevelopment Authority. Its brief demanded a strict adherence to an envelope which resulted from the back-projection of shadow diagrams. The resultant shape imposed a steeply sloping roof-shape to a ground plan which was narrow and angular. The brief also demanded an acknowledgment of the present building's heritage which formed part of the historical 'Rocks' area. While attempting the maximum floor/space ratio possible the scheme attempted to fragment this envelope by giving the appearance that the site included a number of discrete buildings. This was done by: creating a public pedestrian-way through the site continuing a vista existing along Gloucester Street; composing a multiplicity of building façades which each 'represented' a building and could be read as the 'corporate image' of the leasee without hindering interior planning; and attempting an interface between retained National Trust buildings and the new office tower with the use of historicist forms below the eight-storey cornice.

The graphic image was to be a Classical 'close focus' of a detail of the building. It was completely hand done and textures were built up with the use of fine Rotring pens usually 0.25 and 0.18 on heavy grade drafting film. There was an attempt to display the complexity of materials and tones with changing textures providing a rich patina of surface detail the architects wished to achieve on the final building.

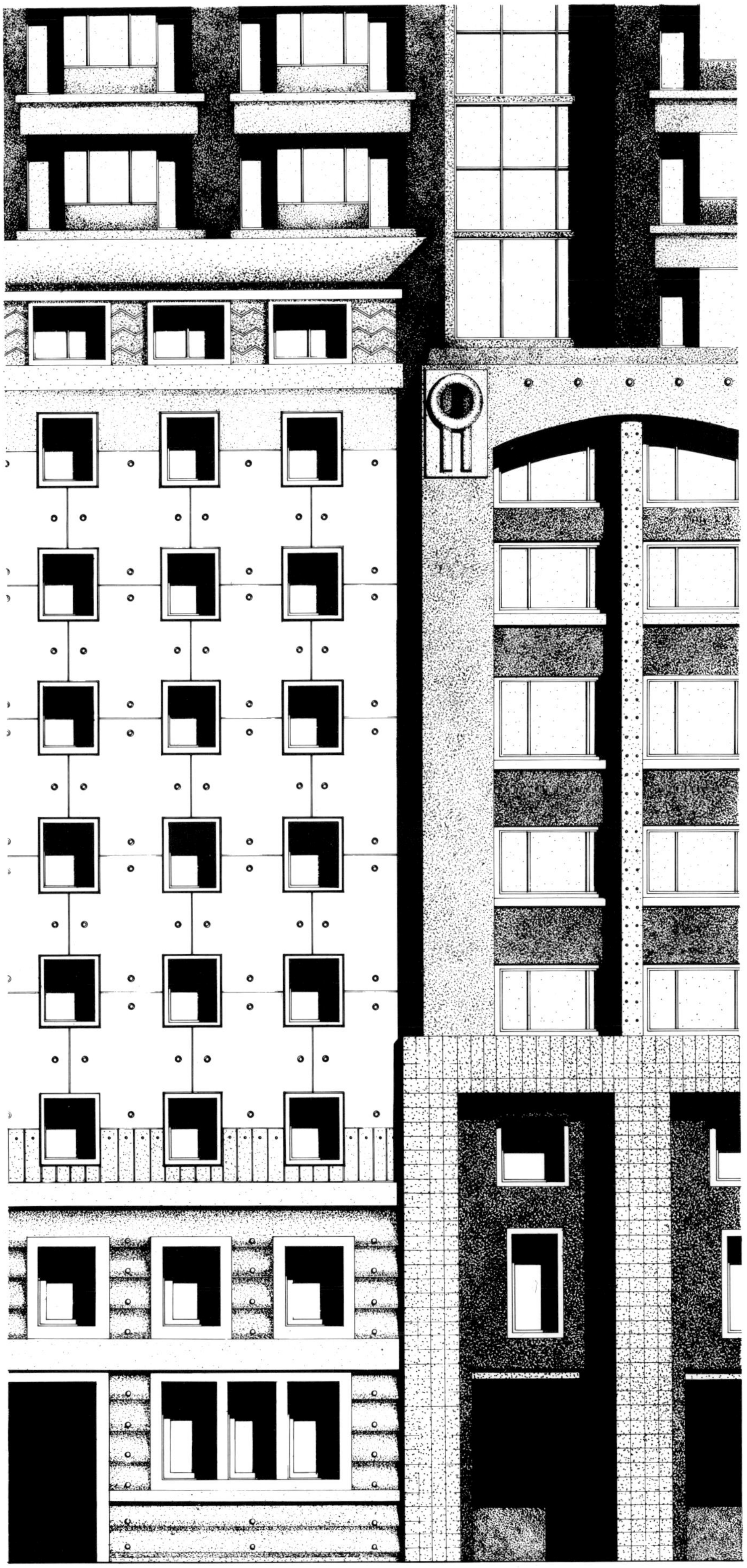

Design Architect: Leo Campbell
Drawing Artists: Tracy James
with Sally Basset,
Jeffrey Meuller,
Julie Cracknell,
Philip Birchmore,
Leo Campbell,
Peter Lonergan and
Mandy Burgess
Date: 1989
Size: 1189 x 841 mm
Photographer: Chris Pilz

URBAN PROPOSAL, PYRMONT PENINSULA – SYDNEY – NEW SOUTH WALES PHILIP COX, RICHARDSON, TAYLOR AND PARTNERS

This major planning proposal for Pyrmont Peninsula forms a part of the current rejuvenation of Sydney's urban waterfront. Presently, the majority of land is occupied by under-utilised industrial infrastructure and vacant land. The concept is for a series of precincts integrated into a comprehensive mixed use residential, commercial, recreational and local amenity development. Emphasis is placed on open space networks between precincts, definition of major axes and boulevards related to outer context, and to incorporation of the many historic buildings and structures in Pyrmont within a homogenous master plan. Provision of waterfront public access related to both park and built edges is implicit in the concept, with the purpose of creating distinct urban, rather than suburban or rural, environmental quality. Issues such as openness and closure, grandeur and intimacy of space, views and vistas, hard and soft landscape all contribute to an enriched townscape theme.

The planning of such a large and complex urban environment requires numerous graphic communication techniques adapted to suit a considerable audience ranging through the general public, the developer and various government departments each having particular interests. Generally, the techniques have to be fast, effective in communicating ideas, and seductive in impression. Much of the planning is generated by three-dimensional sketches based on visual studies examining the type of environment desired. Most initial sketch studies were done using simple black felt markers on detail paper primarily for design purposes. These were refined as planning was developed, and eventually translated in pencil onto Bainbridge board (No 80) for presentation. Soft-end sable brushes applying gouache and watercolour are used as a rapid flexible technique for producing bright, atmospheric perspectives, rather than the harder commercial quality of professional perspective artists. Definition of forms and emphases is made by working over the loose colouring with felt marker and Rapidograph. Each painting takes about 2–3 hours allowing some 3–4 illustrations in one day.

Design Architect: Philip Cox, Richardson, Taylor and Partners in association with Devine Erby Mazlin Pty Ltd
Drawing Artist: Philip Cox
Size: 1189 x 841 mm
Date: 1990

BAR
BIG CRAB

ARCHITECTURAL SCHEMES ARTHUR COLLIN AND BRIAN LILLEY

The act of drawing should mimic the process of design. The end result is a record – it should be beautiful and dynamic.
Draw at many scales simultaneously – details and the overall view must inform each other. Exploded views and sections are best but by all means STRETCH the perspective to suit your purpose.
Develop all details three-dimensionally, naturally.
Always **illustrate the relevant events and situations.** Don't cut up expensive magazines for figures, junk mail has people in natural poses.
Openly display your obsessions and prejudices on the drawing – get it out of your system. Once they're down on paper, you can work with them and throw away what isn't required.
If something is important, copy it or tear it out and **stick it on the drawing.** Don't redraw unless there's time to make improvements. Remember, **draw fast, think faster!**
Erase what you don't need by drawing or painting over it. Most things can be converted into something useful.
Introduce the passage of time to your drawings. Don't just provide before and after views but illustrate the important stages of the process as well (for example, make a film and paste on the stills).
A multi-layered stack format allows you to show so much more. Use clear or translucent materials up front (acetate, trace, perspex, or glass) with a hefty backing board behind (something that won't go wrinkly with paint). Use the board for fast intuitive expression and the front layers for more detailed work. You can draw on the rear side of clear sheets as well. Use chandler's grommets to fix the layers together or space them out on bolts for **glorious 3-D.**
Repetitive elements or non-spatial ideas can be **represented quickly and simply with symbols.** Many organisations have popular symbols which can be **appropriated** or **customised.** Textures, patterns, shapes, and colours carry their own associations, but you can add **your own** to **code the drawing.** Code systems should overlap and develop a life of their own. Have a key or legend handy for easy reference.
Introduce a chance element. Have someone else choose the colours, draw a layer without reference to the others or mask off parts of the drawing till the very end. Total control is as boring as a minimalist lucky-dip.
Computer images on their own tend to be a little flat. A little wax crayon line work on the hard copy may be all that's needed.
Sometimes things are best expressed with words. Type onto trace, Xerox back-to-front onto transtext and fix to the back of a transparent layer.

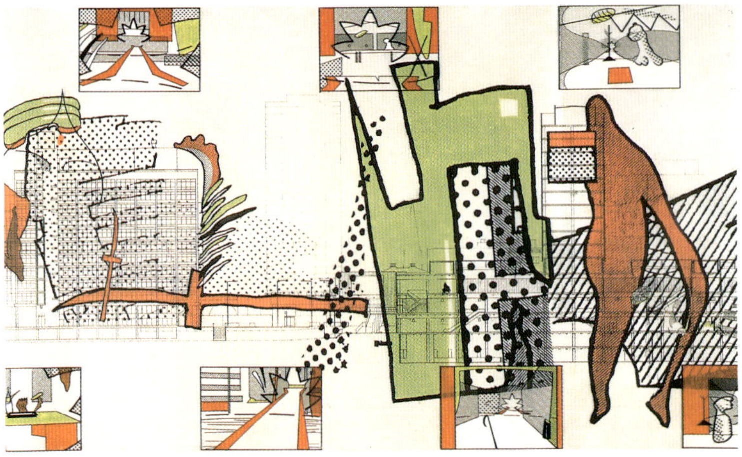

1. As found, postcard, collage with associated images (junk mail), masked and peeled, painted over, Dulux 'sample' colours, finished with pen and ink.
2. Simulated computer drawing: drafted ink drawing on trace (transtext), textural photocopy enlargements overlaid. Wax crayon on back. Acetate cover sheet with permanent master and wax crayon, grommeted together.
3. Dulux sample colours and hammertone over found images (masked) and peeled on backing board. Acetate cover sheet with drafted ink drawing on front, wax crayon and text (transtexted) onto the back and grommeted together.
4. Drafted ink drawing on Mylar, charcoal and graphite shading applied back and front (transtexted) symbols and menu onto back.

FAMILY
Tote-em!
SPRINGCLEAN SPECIAL
Travel simulator
Pet deck
CUSHIONED COMFORT
Crawling car
Price the part
Buffet circle
Room service trolley dispatch
Tube packing
Massage furniture
Dash
FASTLANE
TIGER TINT STRIP
(microprocessor interface)
INFORMATION
ADVERTISING
PURCHASES AND
VALET BAY BOOKINGS
WELCOME
The unique selling point of FAMILY Tote-em PLC is the attitude towards servicing - a concern not only with the automobile but with the family that inhabits it.
The service units are easily disposed of, as new product lines appear based on customer response. The recyclable plastic can be traded in or ground down and used to make customized furniture
Given the right site and package to fit, FAMILY Tote-em swings into action immediately - the lightweight thermoplastic shells allow easy transport of complete units with a minimum of in-situ work.

ARTHUR COLLIN AND BRIAN LILLEY
ARCHITECTURAL SCHEMES

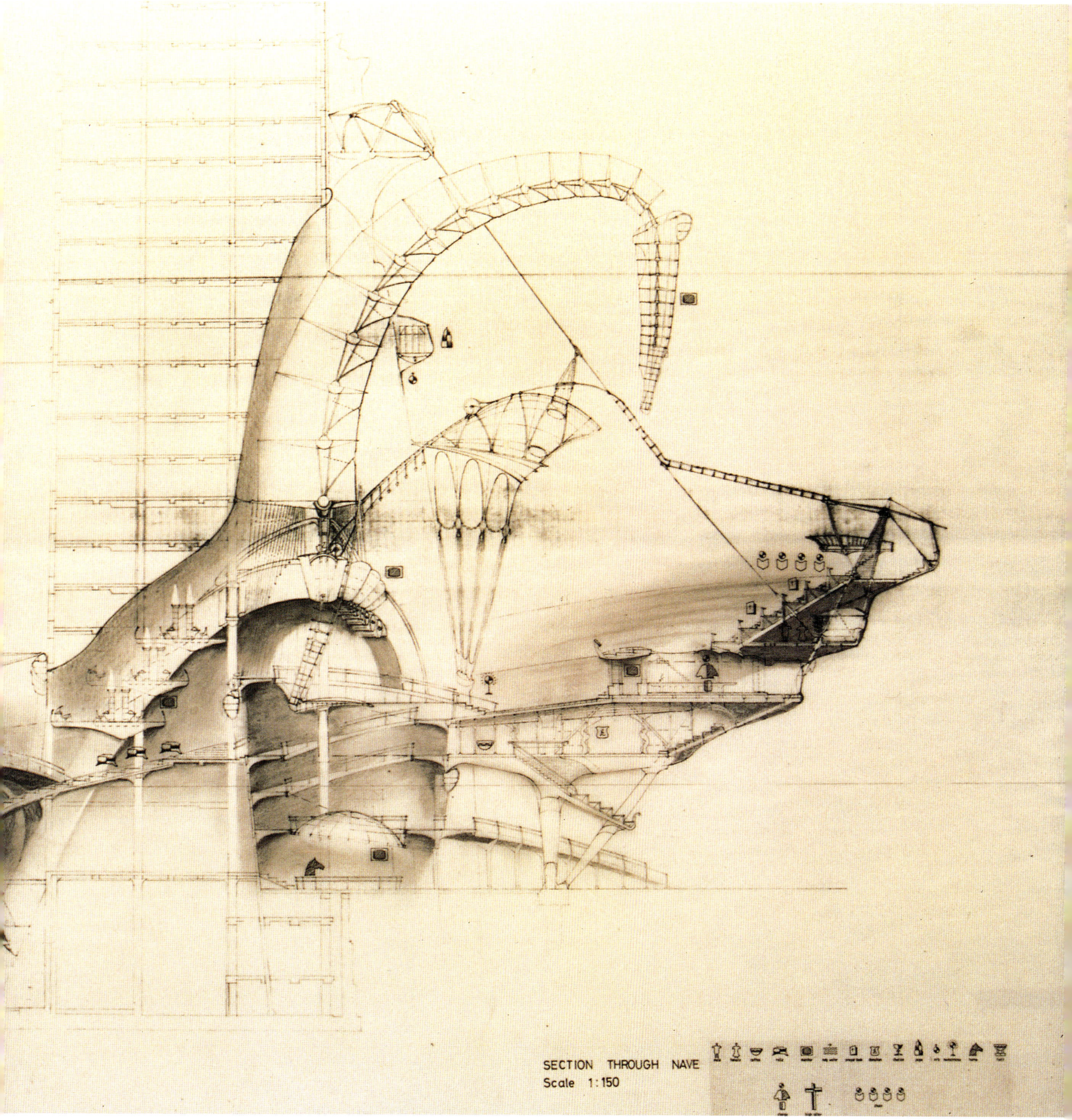
SECTION THROUGH NAVE
Scale 1:150

MLC BUILDING – 44 MARTIN PLACE, SYDNEY – NEW SOUTH WALES CLIVE LUCAS, STAPLETON AND PARTNERS

The old MLC building was constructed in 1938 to a competition winning design by the Melbourne firm Bates, Smart and McCutcheon. It was purpose-built and when the building was to be refurbished for general office use the creation of new ground floor tenancies and a new foyer, incorporating the original insurance hall, was appropriate.
The foyer design is inspired by the Art Deco Egyptian-esque character of the original design. A combination of familiar 1930s period Art Deco motifs from various sources have been used in an arrangement primarily to frame an architecture created by a forest of precast plaster up-lights.
The predominant materials are coloured terrazzo, polished red granite and painted plaster used in combination with brass, chrome, stainless steel, copper and aluminium trim. The stylism is overblown, based on, but not copying decorative design of the 1930s.
Ink line on heavyweight film.

Design Architect: Ian Stapleton
Drawing Artist: Pamela Jeffery
Size: 1189 x 841 mm
Date: 1988
Photographer: Ian Stapleton

IRIRIKI RESORT PROJECT – VANUATU DEVINE ERBY MAZLIN

The site was one of the Vanuatu islands situated in the tropical South Pacific Ocean. The landscape character of the proposed resort was emphasised and the island's natural attributes including lush rainforest vegetation, land to water interfaces, beaches and cultural elements such as buildings were important to the function of the resort.

Landscan, Landscape Architects and Devine Erby Mazlin (Qld) Architects regularly use colour rendering drawings as a basic tool in community design concepts and proposed projects. Finished colour rendering drawings are typically developed for public display, fund raising and other similar presentations. The Iririki colour rendered drawing was intended to communicate an image of a 'village' resort.

B1 medium grade tracing paper was used for the initial image which was drawn with fine medium and heavy grade felt pens. An ammonia print on B1 heavy grade ammonia paper was used as the basis for the rendering. The fundamental approach to the colour rendering of the drawing was to create a semi-realistic image with a sense of depth. This was achieved by applying washes of light coloured markers to the ground plane and building up intensities of colours to simulate the finishes of various elements in the design. It was coloured with Faber Castell Pastels, Yoken Markers, air-brush and Derwent colour pencils.

Important man-made elements such as buildings were rendered with darker muted colours to highlight their importance and convey an image of tropical landscape character. This rendering approach also helped to integrate buildings into the overall graphic image. Coral and yellow coloured markers were used for such landscape elements as the creek and swimming pools. This helped to relieve the 'flatness' of the green areas and portray an interesting and vibrant image. Texture in the rendering was also an important aspect of the technique. It was used to achieve a sense of depth and a semi-realistic image. Areas of vegetation and water were rendered in layers of marker colours to achieve a mottled tone of darks and lights. Groups of buildings were treated in similar fashion but not to the same intensity. The relative height levels of buildings were graphically simulated to differentiate the architecture from landscape.

Ocean areas were of particular concern because they occupied significant space on the drawing and were seen as critical elements in the experience of an island resort. A light coat of yellow pastel was applied around the edge of the island to express beaches and areas of shallower water. After the pastel 'wash' was applied these areas were masked off and deeper ocean areas were air-brushed in graduated intensities from the light tones of beach/water interface areas to darker, richer colours in deeper water.

Design Architect: Devine Erby Mazlin, Qld
Drawing Artists: Les Wood, Chris Newton, David Toohey
Size: 1000 x 700 mm
Date: 1990
Photographer: Peter Edwards

RECEPTION AND ADMINISTRATION
CASINO
NIGHTCLUB AND DISCOTHEQUE
CHAPEL/ MUSEUM
HANGING TREE
BEACH
EXISTING RESORT
INCLINATOR
EXISTING GUEST ROOMS
EMERGENCY WATER RESERVOIR
LUXURY HILLTOP CONDOMINIUMS
LUXURY WATERFRONT CONDOMINIUMS
RAINFOREST
TERRACED GUEST ROOMS
JOGGING TRACK
150 ROOM HOTEL AND
CONVENTION CENTRE
BOARDWALK
BOATEL AND MARINA
SERVICE JETTY
SNORKELERS COVE
SUNSET BAR
TERRACED GUEST ROOMS
PEACEFUL GARDEN AND WATER FEATURE
FARES
WATERFALL
RECREATION FACILITY
LAGOON BEACH POOL
TENNIS COURTS
LOOKOUT
HELIPAD
STAFF QUARTERS
SERVICE AND MAINTENANCE YARD

HYATT RESORT - COOLUM - QUEENSLAND BLIGH VOLLER ARCHITECTS

Design Architect:
Graham Bligh
Drawing Artist: Greg Rogers
Size: 1189 x 841 mm
Date: 1989
Photographer: Alison Taylor

The building design at Coolum is ostensibly set out to be village-like, domestic, small scale and non-domineering. The concept has endeavoured variety in subtle ways as opposed to having common design images throughout the site. To this end, apart from the Central Tower, no building is higher than two floors and the use of single storey buildings has been carefully considered to bring the scale down to the ground level. To some extent apparent depth of façade, overhangs, shadows, textures of light through lattice and pergolas, pitched roofs and the use of corrugated steel have all endeavoured to establish the resort as Australian.
It was decided to illustrate the resort site to highlight details which could not have been fully described in a photograph. The resort was visited to get first-hand and photographical references.
A4 colour photocopies were made of both detailed and general photographs. A scale grid was drawn on one copy which featured the whole resort. The grid was then scaled up and drawn on a full-size underlay resort concept. Necessary detail was plotted on this grid. This was then traced onto the Daler illustration paper on a light table. Constant reference was made to slides, colour copies and photographs as the details were lightly pencilled in with Derwent Terra Cotta coloured pencil. The edges of the illustration were masked with low tack tape before applying colour. The sky was drawn using several layers of Carb-Othello coloured charcoal, working from light colours to dark. Cloud effects were created by removing colour with an eraser. The small enclaves of buildings were drawn in coloured pencil before the surrounding landscape was started. The environment of trees and Mt Coolum was painstakingly rendered with many layers of coloured pencil.
The finished illustration was sealed with artist quality fixative.

SULLIVANS COVE IDEAS COMPETITION - HOBART - TASMANIA   LEIGH WOOLLEY ARCHITECT

Design Architect: Leigh Woolley
Drawing Artist: Leigh Woolley
Size: 1189 x 841 mm
Date: 1986

A competition run by the Tasmanian Chapter of the Royal Australian Institute of Architects in 1986 to encourage design debate on the future of Sullivans Cove, Hobart.

The proposal recommended a process for analysing development (with example applications) rather than developing a grand plan. This was an attempt to ensure that the existing character of the area was assessed with the qualities which identify it being used to test any development proposals. This would have a significant influence on the design of public space, which constitutes much of the area, and its interface with adjoining development. The qualitative aspects of design would be promoted ahead of the individual design statement.

Graphically the panel is composed of a checkerboard background of images reflecting the Cove's character, its diverse history and uses. The proposed approach identifying specific qualities desired in future design are overlaid. These are then applied with example solutions. The approach over time would be to make the area a more responsive environment. The graphic work endeavours to reflect this process.

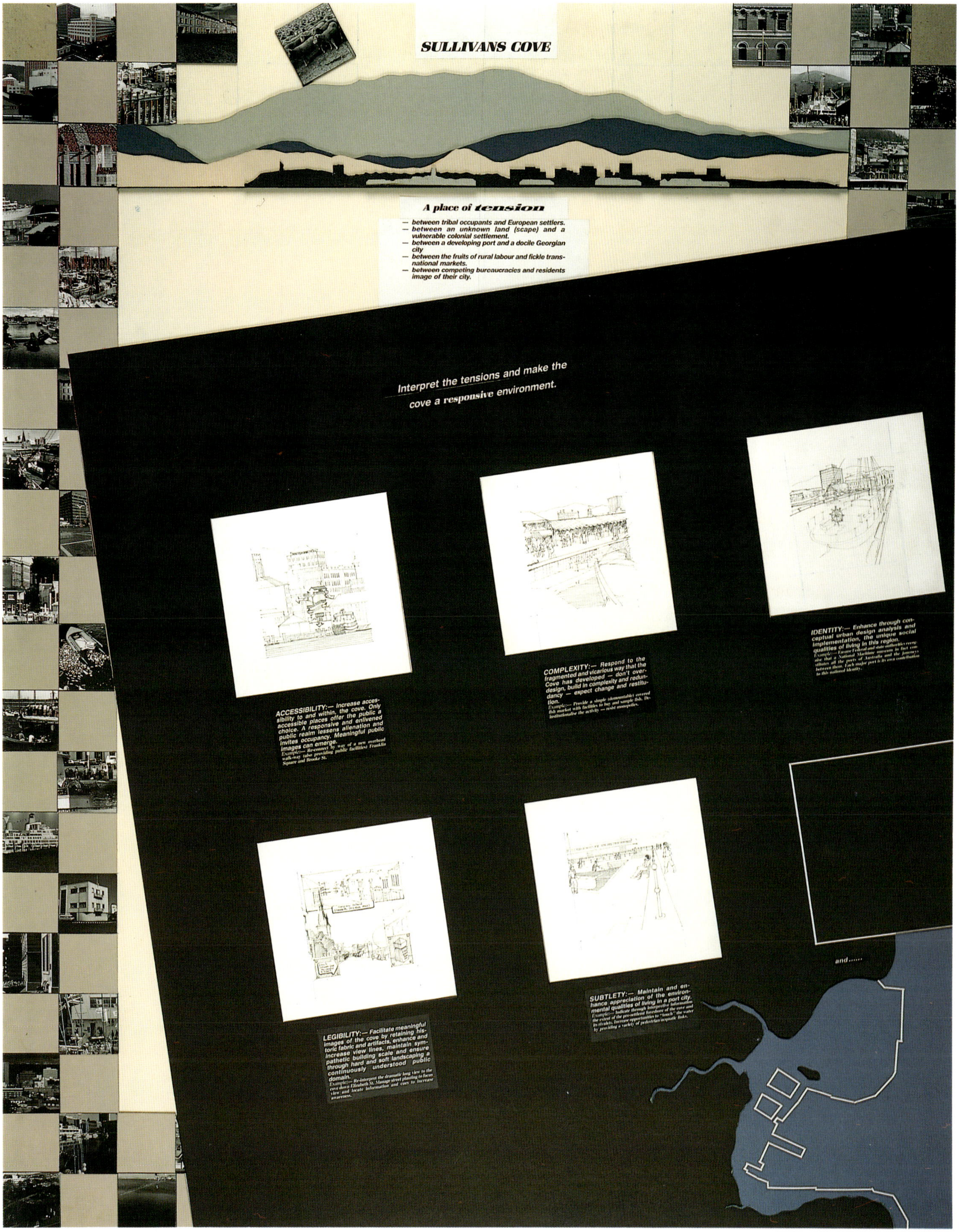
SULLIVANS COVE
A place of tension
— between tribal occupants and European settlers.
— between an unknown land (scape) and a vulnerable colonial settlement.
— between a developing port and a docile Georgian city
— between the fruits of rural labour and fickle trans-national markets.
— between competing bureaucracies and residents image of their city.
Interpret the tensions and make the cove a responsive environment.
ACCESSIBILITY:— Increase accessibility to and within, the cove. Only accessible places offer the public a choice. A responsive and enlivened public realm lessens alienation and invites occupancy. Meaningful public images can emerge.
Example:— Re-connect by way of a new overhead walk-way (also providing public facilities) Franklin Square and Brooke St.
COMPLEXITY:— Respond to the fragmented and vicarious way that the Cove has developed — don't over-design, build in complexity and redundancy — expect change and restitution.
Example:— Provide a simple (demountable) covered fish market with facilities to buy and sample fish. De-institutionalise the activity — resist monopolies.
IDENTITY:— Enhance through conceptual urban design analysis and implementation, the unique social qualities of living in this region.
LEGIBILITY:— Facilitate meaningful images of the cove by retaining historic fabric and artifacts, enhance and increase view lines, maintain sympathetic building scale and ensure through hard and soft landscaping a continuously understood public domain.
Example:— Re-interpret the dramatic long view to the cove down Elizabeth St. Manage street planting to focus view and locate information and cues to increase awareness.
SUBTLETY:— Maintain and enhance appreciation of the environmental qualities of living in a port city.
Example:— Indicate through interpretive information the extent of the pre-settlement foreshore of the cove and its rivulets. Increase opportunities to "touch" the water by providing a variety of pedestrian/aquatic links.
and......

ARCHITECTURAL REVIEW/HEUGA INTERNATIONAL IDEAS COMPETITION – LONDON ENGLAND 1987 DONALDSON + WARN ARCHITECTS

Design Architects:
Richard Donaldson,
Geoff Warn and
Richard Black
Drawing Artist: Geoff Warn
Size: 840 x 590 mm
Date: 1987

In 1987 *Architectural Review* held an international ideas competition to convert a disused industrial warehouse in London's Royal Docks into a Maritime Museum. The brief called for the display of a very varied collection of material including a Thames barge, 'The Kathleen', small wooden vessels and skiffs, arrangements of tools for traditional crafts such as rigging and sail making, and an extensive collection of smaller objects such as photographs, postcards, stamps, letters and coins. The large objects were required to be on permanent display while the small artifacts would be frequently changed with the huge collection held in storage. The brief also called for reception, theatre, bookshop, restaurant and administration facilities. The permanent displays were located in the original warehouse building over a ground floor of storage, thereby referencing the structure's earlier function. The smaller dynamic displays were confined to the smaller gallery spaces in the water-bound structure. The museum could be accessed from the land or the water, with circulation 'journeys' meeting at 'The Kathleen' exhibited in the grand, vaulted chamber. Our response was to explore nautical themes and evoke the 'mysteries of cargo and visitors from foreign lands' through a large vaulted roof over 'The Kathleen' and a dynamic ship-like structure extending from within the original warehouse out into the water.

The building was drawn with 0.35 and 0.5 mm technical pens on an A1 sheet of tracing paper. The water was produced with a charcoal stick and a soft graphite pencil. On completion the image was printed onto quality heavyweight art paper, using the Balfact process.

BRIDGEWATER MILL – SOUTH AUSTRALIA   WOODS BAGOT

The original Bridgewater Flour Mill was constructed in 1860 in the Adelaide Hills and was the only fully productive watermill used in South Australia until its closure in 1960. In 1985 Petaluma Pty Ltd purchased the derelict building and commissioned Woods Bagot to revitalise the old mill for use as a wine maturation cellar with facilities including tasting, sales, restaurant and entertainment. The mill was restored to its original condition. The new additions were to have transparent connections with the old structure in order to allow a clear expression of the original form. Stone, glass, exposed concrete and raw timber were selectively used to complement colours, tones and textures of the existing building. Any visual presentation should reflect the spirit and intentions of the designed scheme. The conversion of the Bridgewater Mill was designed as a sensitive response to both the beauty of the old building and its sylvan setting. The Mill lies nestled in a valley on the bank of a stream and is surrounded by trees. Light flickers through the leaves and the sound of running water fills the air. The presentation visual was designed to capture the quality of light and the sense of movement, whilst reflecting the importance of Nature and natural materials to the scheme. This was achieved through the elimination of hard lines and the building up of the image through a series of sensuous pencil strokes. Faber Castell pencils gave an intense colour to the presentation and a smooth satin grade paper enhanced line quality.

Project Architect: Rex Gray
Drawing: Karen Griffin
Size: 841 x 594 mm
Date: 1986
Photographer: unknown

WOLLONGONG FISHERMENS CO-OPERATIVE – WOLLONGONG – NEW SOUTH WALES BRUCE AND JANE EELES ARCHITECTS

Design Architect: Bruce Eeles
Model Artist: Tim Allison
Size: 1:200
Date: 1984
Model Photographer:
Jill Crossley

This building was designed in 1984 and completed in 1987. The site is adjacent to the fishing fleet mooring on the very beautiful quayside of Wollongong Harbour. The functional brief was to design a commercial building containing fish processing and handling areas as well as lettable spaces for raw fish shops, food outlets and a 100-seat seafood restaurant. Cost was a prime consideration. Hence the spare nature of the finishes (concrete block, timber and steel). The aggressive nature of the saline environment dictated the use of simple junctions which could be easily accessed for maintenance. Stainless steel was used generally to connect concrete and other elements.

The main idea of the design is the walkway (or through site link). This connects the upper level shops and restaurant to the adjacent upper-level car park and the waterfront promenade and beach at the lower level. This walkway weaves in and out of the building allowing marvellous northerly ocean views (almost to Sydney) from every shop and the restaurant. The building has made waterfront urban linkages which were not present before and provided popular attractions on the way.

As with virtually all designs prepared by this practice models were built in the early stages of design to test hypotheses and to ensure that there were no nasty surprises at completion of the project.

An interim model of the Restaurant was also made to enable close examination of the layering of a very complex space. Issues such as views, intimacy, table groupings etc, related to restaurant design could be tested long before drawings were finalised.

The models were made of cardboard.

ARIZONA CAFE – NORTH SYDNEY – NEW SOUTH WALES   JAHN ASSOCIATES ARCHITECTS

Design Architect: Graham Jahn
Drawing Artist:
Conception – Graham Jahn, and execution – Mark Cashman and Anne Hooton
Size: 650 x 450 mm
Date: 1989
Photographer: Ross Honeysett and Graham Jahn

Arizona is located in downtown North Sydney in the ground floor retail space of a new office building. The room is dominated by two elements – central bar and a deeply etched mural along the entire northern party wall. It creates a social setting for loud, young professionals to yee-ha.

The expressive nature of this type of drawing sometimes provides for a clearer feeling of the architect's intention for the space rather than a set-up perspective. The drawing communicates the textural and emotive quality of the design in a far more encompassing manner. The perspective drawing is a freehand bird's-eye view loosely projected from the plan. Sometimes this form of view is the only way of capturing such a large space, allowing one to take in the plan along with an informative feeling for the spatial quality. Materials included 4B pencil – Faber Castell on detail paper. Pastels – Faber Castell, Polychronios pastels, Compressed charcoal - Alphacolor CharKole, Acrylic paints – Liquifer (artist quality), Teton paper supplied by Allied Reprographics, image transferred onto Teton by means of large format Xerox photocopier.

Rather than painstakingly constructing an interior by paint or pencil, it was appropriate to adopt a gestural and expressive rendering technique. This was already apparent in the line drawing. The line work had a vitality which could have been overwhelmed by large areas of colour, therefore a balance needed to be created. One does not have to cover an image completely in colour as the viewer's eye can effectively fulfil that function. The underlying paint washes of broad brushstrokes provide movement throughout the space, except where the movement is arrested by the areas of solid paint. These painted elements help to create resting points for the eye to fix upon and to highlight areas of importance. The pastels and charcoal are the final stage of the rendering which again generate movement, tying in all the areas and directing the eye around the space. The end result is a dynamic shorthand which captures the integrity and legibility of the design.

When working with a photocopied image on textured Teton paper one must be aware that the line work does not fuse completely onto the paper and is therefore easily damaged. It must be worked upon with great care.

ARIZONA

RETAIL CENTRE AND NIGHTCLUB – SYDNEY – NEW SOUTH WALES **KEN MAHER AND PARTNERS**

Initially Ken Maher and Partners were engaged to prepare design proposals for an eight-storey retail and food centre in this prominent George Street strip site. The client finally decided to build a short-life building with only three levels.

The building was designed to respond to its active and youth oriented location. A perforated steel screen has been applied to the street frontage of a simple masonry box containing a nightclub on the first floor and shops on the ground floor and in the basement. The screen which comprises a grid of self-rusting steel panels punctuated with square holes of varying sizes is lit from behind and at night-time presents an abstract representation of the city pattern. The screen is detailed to reveal its nature as a veneer over the building surface.

A large video screen is incorporated into the street façade and this screen will add to the lively night-time quality of the street, displaying rock and experimental videos.

A steel-framed corner tower marks the entry to the nightclub and gives the building a scale appropriate to its immediate neighbour. The rest of the building is faced with coloured and polished sawn concrete blocks inset with bands of polished granite. A steel cornice element caps the masonry building walls.

This elevation was one of a series drawn to illustrate the façade treatment to the client. A line elevation was photocopied onto bond paper and then hand rendered using coloured pencils – Derwent Artist and Faber Castell Polychromos. The background colour was applied by hand pressure pack spray using automotive touch-up paint.

Design Architects: Ken Maher,
Everard Kloots and
Robin McInnes
Drawing Artist: Everard Kloots
Size: 840 x 594 mm
Date: 1990
Photographer: Ken Maher

THE EXCHANGE HOTEL, OXFORD STREET - SYDNEY - NEW SOUTH WALES   LIPPMAN ASSOCIATES

Design Architect:
Ed Lippmann
Drawing Artist:
Su Keong Cheah
Size: 841 x 594 mm
Date: 1989
Photographs: John Gollings

The site of this hotel is in the inner city precinct of Darlinghurst. The hotel is one of the first buildings situated along Oxford Street which is characterised by its busy and colourful street-life and commercial activity. The project confined itself to the interior of the lower two floors of the building. While the façade of the upper floors remains unaltered the old street level elevation was replaced with a wall of glass, porthole entry doors and galvanised steel panelling. The new bar areas, dance floors, staff, client amenities and service zones were seen as an intrusion of a highly serviced technological interior plugged into a robust Victorian infrastructure. Representation of axonometric projections are useful as they illustrate volumes within a spatial composition. Sections are cut away revealing surfaces and finishes at different depths which describe the layering of the spatial form. The original was drawn on A2 plastic film in ink. A 0.25 Rapidograph is used to achieve the required clarity.

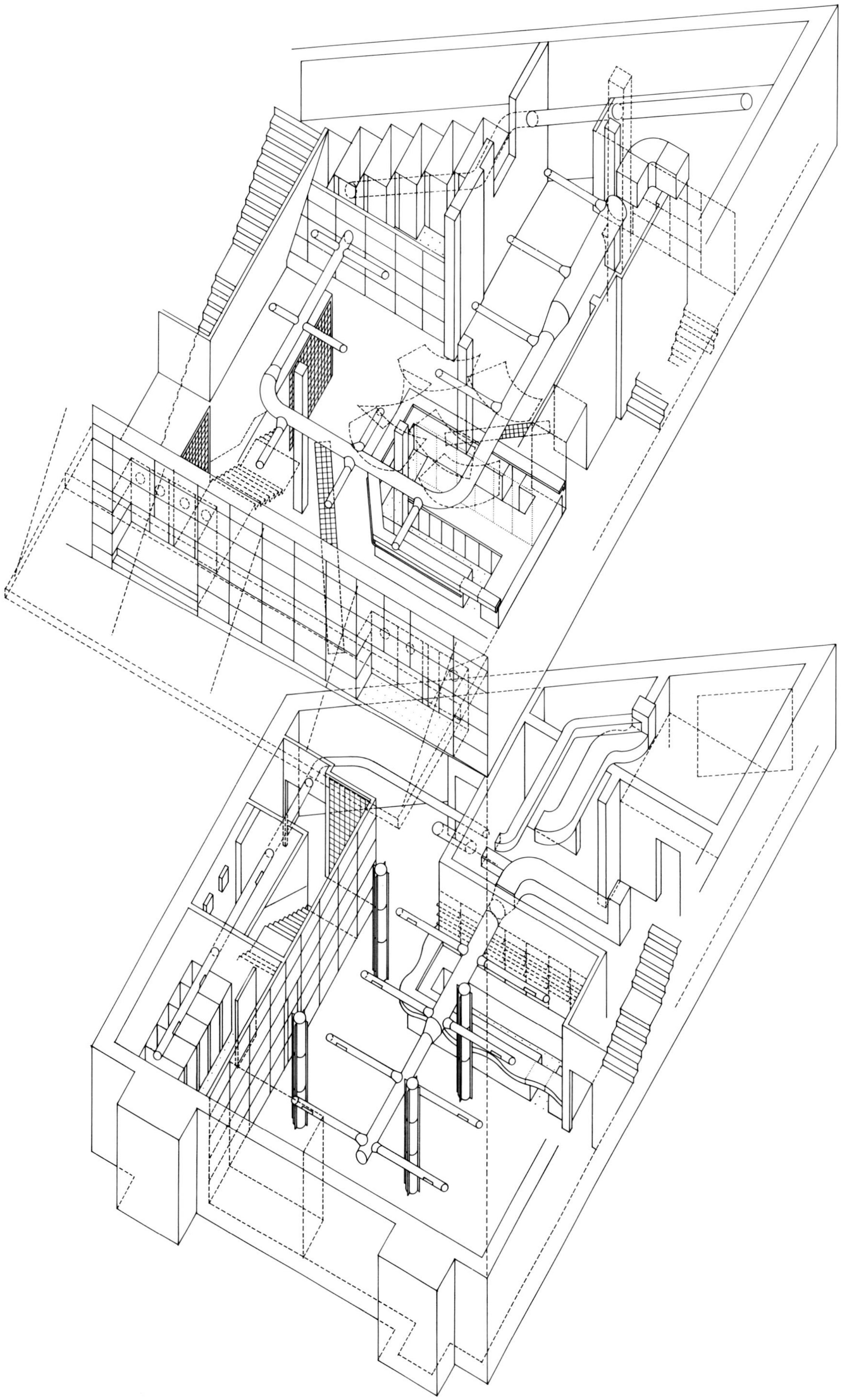

BARTON CAFETERIA – BARTON – AUSTRALIAN CAPITAL TERRITORY DENTON CORKER MARSHALL

In association with
Robert Peck YFHK
Design Architect:
Denton Corker Marshall
Drawing Artist:
Barrie Marshall,
Denton Corker Marshall
Size: 650 x 580 mm
Date: 1984
Photographer: John Gollings

This is a public service cafeteria in Canberra set within a grassed and treed park-like setting, with a number of three to five level buildings close by. The brief required a red terracotta tiled roofed building in sympathy with nearby 'Canberra-style' buildings of the 1930s; pitched roofs, large overhangs, detailed surfaces.

It is a single-storey construction, with two projecting dining wings flanking an entry courtyard and outdoor dining area. It is elevated on a coloured concrete podium, with the roof supported by structural timber fabricated columns set at the eaves line, with fully glazed or panelled timber frame walls set back to form a colonnade to the full perimeter.

It was also proposed to be made available for special functions during non-working hours, and hence was required to have as 'friendly' and non-institutional a character as possible.

The perspective was set-up by eye/guesswork, and traced through with lead pencil onto the paper over a light table. The plans, sections etc, were drawn directly onto the paper. Final line work was then drawn with sepia ink, pencil set-up removed, and the drawing coloured.

The drawing is a composite showing the building from 'dogs-eye' level, axially along the front entry from the street; a plan setting out the major dining and entry areas overlaid with a roof plan, and a cross-section through the external wall. The perspective is a distorted wide-angle lens view with accentuated verticals and horizontals vanishing to both sides.

It was produced specifically for magazine publication (*International Architect*), although the perspective view was based on an earlier drawing. This drawing aims to tell the idea of the building in a single composition, without other visual explanation. The wide perspective emphasises the axial/symmetrical composition, the park-like setting, and the importance of the podium base and the red-tiled roofs held precariously on the timber columns. The technique used was coloured Derwent (Cumberland) pencil on Fabriano Watercolour cold pressed 300 gsm paper.

BARTON CAFETERIA
CANBERRA
PDCM

COMMUNITY ARCHITECTURE

THE NATIONAL MEMORIAL TO THE AUSTRALIAN VIETNAM FORCES – COMPETITION ENTRY – CANBERRA – AUSTRALIAN CAPITAL TERRITORY   BLIGH VOLLER ARCHITECTS

Design Team:
Shane Thompson,
Chris Clarke, Michael James,
Alison Taylor, Megan Tracy
and Michael Stewart
Drawing Artist:
Gregory Rogers
Size: 594 x 420 mm
Date: 1989

The proposed design seeks to symbolically recreate the environment and conditions in which Australian Service Personnel served in Vietnam, evoking a sense of empathy between those who served and the viewer. The scale and the proximity of the poles, not only implies the relationship between man and Nature, but creates a sense of jungle, enclosure, protection and fear of what is unseen. The 365 poles clustered in the form of an ellipse, represents the '365 days and a wakey' that all Service Personnel were required to serve as a 'Tour of Duty' in Vietnam. The elliptical form is a classical symbol and makes oblique references to the cycle of time, and the continual cycle of life. The shadows cast by these poles would create the effect of broken light of the jungle canopy, as well as providing a dynamic visual dimension to the form.

A central clearing was to be formed within the ellipse, which would serve as a private place of contemplation and reflection on dedications and other textual information. The focus of this space and indeed the whole monument is a pole of light, symbolic of the Eternal Flame, which is created by using either gas or laser technology. This not only bears reference to the original ANZAC Eternal Flame, but contributes to the sense of spiritual reflection of those who died. The names of those killed in Vietnam would be entombed under this central pole of light.

Viewing the monument from the front would reveal the word *Vietnam* created by alternating the texture or angle of the poles. Thus the composition addresses the ceremonial avenue. The power of the word *Vietnam* coupled with the power of the repeated vertical poles would make the Memorial striking from a distance. It would express the dichotomy of the war in Vietnam through the jungle imagery, and the war in Australia through the strong *Vietnam* headline.

This interpretative drawing needed to convey not only a sense of 'being there' but also the mood that the designers envisaged would be apparent in its built form. It also had to be perspective accurate. To do this a three-point perspective plot had to be drawn using the architectural plans, a maquette of the memorial and site photographs as reference.

Graphite pencils ranging from HB to 6B were used for the illustration on white Canson Mi Teintes paper. The hardest pencils were used first for the set-up plot and the Memorial details, working toward the softer pencils for the darker tones. The rigidity of the composition was relieved and contrasted by the use of evocative loose tonal and linear areas in the background and sky, these being rendered in the softer pencils.

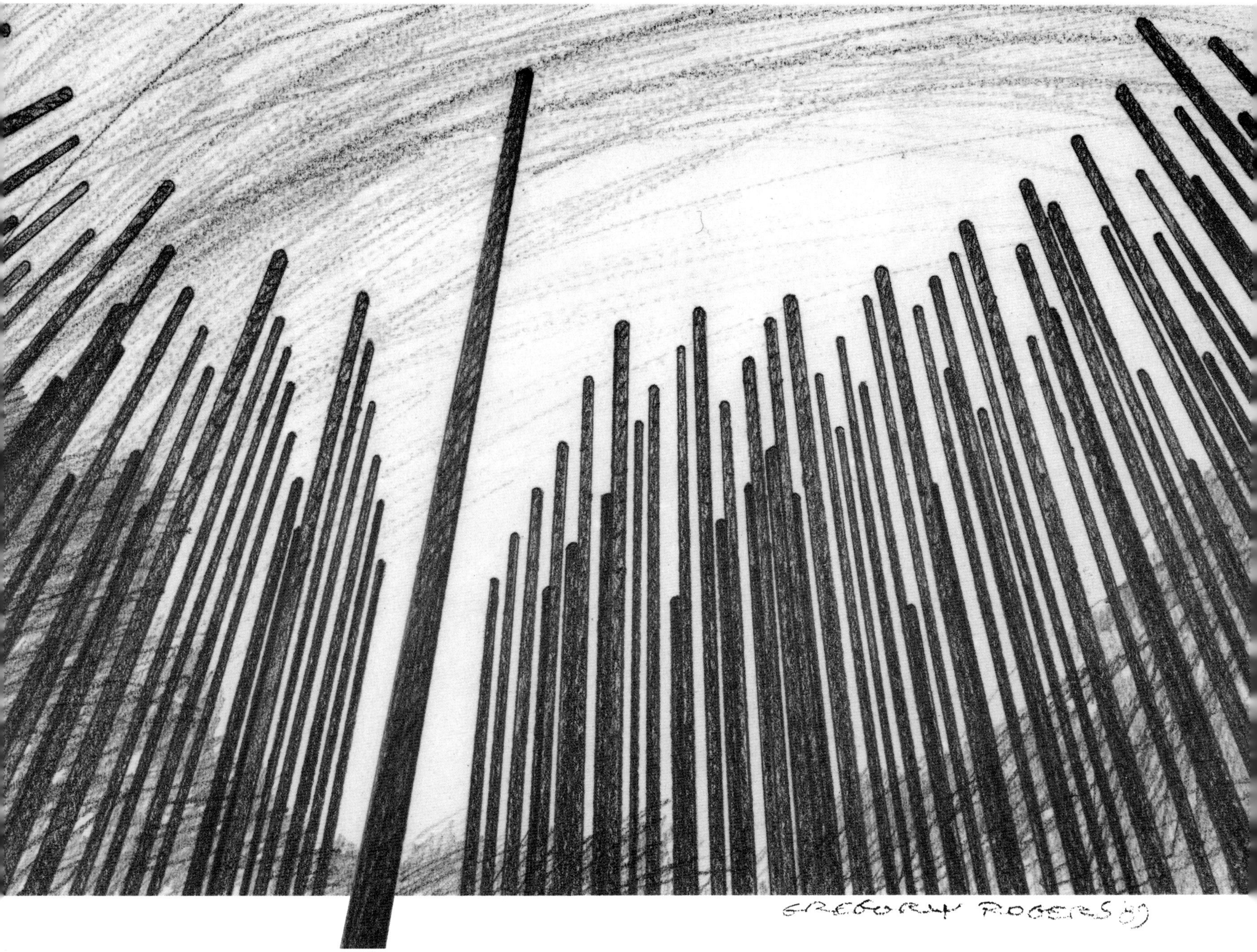
GREGORY ROGERS 89

NATIONAL MEMORIAL TO THE AUSTRALIAN VIETNAM FORCES - CANBERRA - AUSTRALIAN CAPITAL TERRITORY TONKIN ZULAIKHA HARFORD ARCHITECTS AND KEN UNSWORTH

Design Architect: Peter Tonkin and Ken Unsworth
Drawing Artist: Peter Tonkin
Size: 1189 x 841 mm
Date: 1990

A National Memorial to the Australian Vietnam Forces must reconcile the Australian peoples' reaction to the war and the important requirements of those who served, aspects which are sometimes in conflict. It must be a fitting civic element, at the ceremonial focus of Canberra.

The design for the Memorial by Tonkin Zulaikha Harford Architects with Ken Unsworth AM sculptor, was selected after an extensive three stage open competition. The client is the National Capital Planning Authority. Construction has been financed by donations raised by the Vietnam Veterans.

The Memorial is conceived as an open structure, constructed with three complex geometrical forms in concrete, inspired by ancient standing stones and by the classical Greek stelæ. The stelæ have acutely pointed edges, producing a contrast of shape and scale. They stand in a moat which is bridged by the entry ramp and stairs.

The interior is the subtle, dramatic centre of the work, uniting directly representational images with abstract symbols. As the 'roof' of the Memorial is a ring or halo of stone, recalling the sacrifices made by those who fought and died. Facing the entry, across the face of the western stelæ, is the major representational icon. Etched into black granite, the larger-than-life image is directly photographic, avoiding any artistic reinterpretation. On the right of the entry is a series of quotations selected from the letters and writings of the Veterans.

The drawings shown are all on tracing paper, and were prepared for various stages of the competition. An interior view is in soft pencil, and was executed very quickly to fulfil an urgent jury request. It is set up by eye only, using estimated vanishing points. The highly contrasting pattern of dark and light is used to emphasise the drama of the interior.

The remaining drawings are in technical pen, and combine a variety of stick-on tones and photographic images produced with the office photocopier. The exterior perspective was set up with six pairs of vanishing points, and slightly distorted to allow more view into the interior.

THE AUSTRALIAN/HELLENIC MEMORIAL – CANBERRA – AUSTRALIAN CAPITAL TERRITORY
ANCHER, MORTLOCK AND WOOLLEY

The Australian/Hellenic Memorial was won in a limited competition in 1986. The monument is an important urban design marker element in a huge scale landscape, relating to the Australian War Memorial and Anzac Parade. Its concept as a memorial is the universal destruction over history of symbols of civilisation and cultivation by war and by time. A grove of cypresses and olives contain an amphitheatre in which a partly buried and ruined doric column contrasts with twisted riveted steel beams, the ruins of modern war. The floor is a mosaic map of Greece from which rises jagged rocky mountains.
As an urban design element, the scale and siting of the massive buried column are directed at the enormous scale of the Anzac Parade vista from the Australian War Memorial axis, where the Hellenic Campaign Memorial forms the leading architectural element in a landscape composition. The orientation of its elements relate to the diagonal view from the War Memorial and its pedestrian approach, from the south, leads through a gap which frames the War Memorial beyond.
Planting, which is based on a Greek landscape of olives and cypresses, needs a lot of time to mature in the Canberra climate so as to establish the intended balance with the solid elements.
The executed work is identical to the competition, apart from the incision of a Greek cross in the form of a defacement of the ruined ancient column and the use of riveted steel columns from a wrecked building in Sydney, instead of the boiler plate originally proposed. As intended, this steelwork from the period of World War II was further damaged by gunfire, provided by courtesy of the Australian Army. A mosaic pavement is the map of the peninsula and archipelago of Greece, on which this haunting ensemble resides. The mosaic pavement was carried out by Mary Hall.
The presentation technique is one which has evolved in this office over a number of competitions in a period of ten years or more. The primary aims are to convey the essential concept and background thinking in the design with clarity, economy and speed with capacity to convey this sensitivity and feeling of the design. It is also required that the drawing be reproducible by quick, in-house techniques to avoid time problems at the end of competitions. A number of smaller drawings is preferred, if allowed, to enable several people to work in the same limited period before submission. Usually the drawings are to be coloured, so line work and shading has to be printable and photocopiable, to read on its own but also to work with colouring. For this reason pencil drawings on film are used with standardised line weights and densities, pencil shading when required, then prints are finished with coloured pencils. Basic medium: Mylar film, matt finish, heavy weight; pencils: ordinary Caran D'Ache clutch pencil lead, range of softness.

Design Architect: Ken Woolley with Wally Barda
Mosaic Artist: Mary Hall
Drawing Artist: Wally Barda
Size: 1189 x 841 mm
Date: 1986
Photographer: Michael Nicholson and Ken Woolley

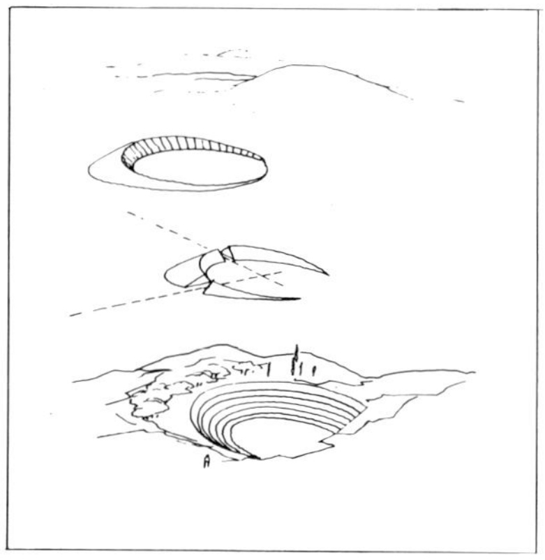

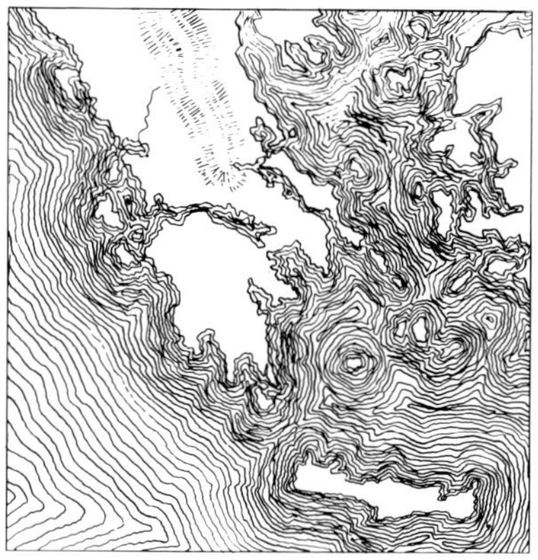

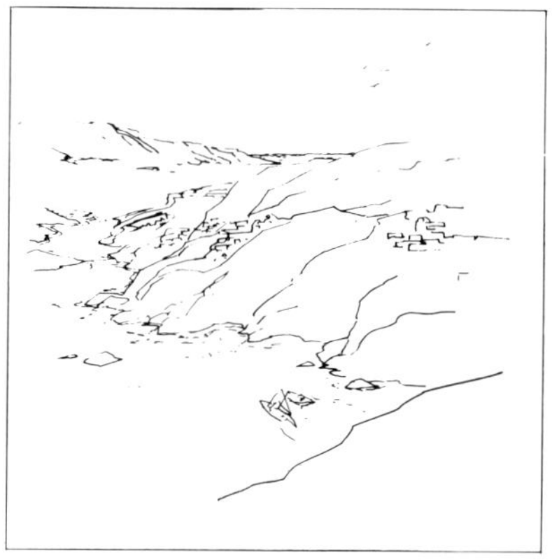

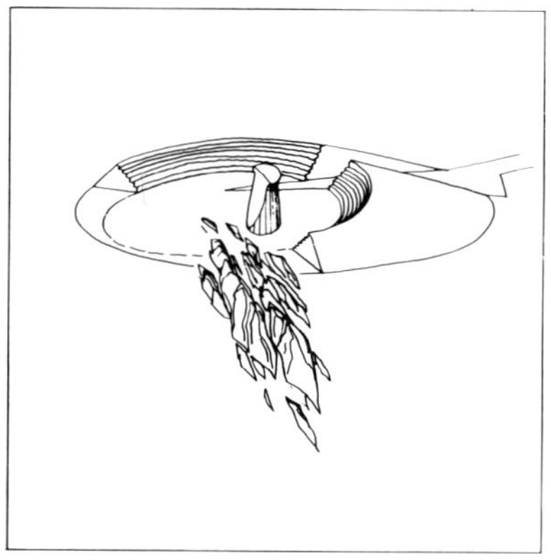

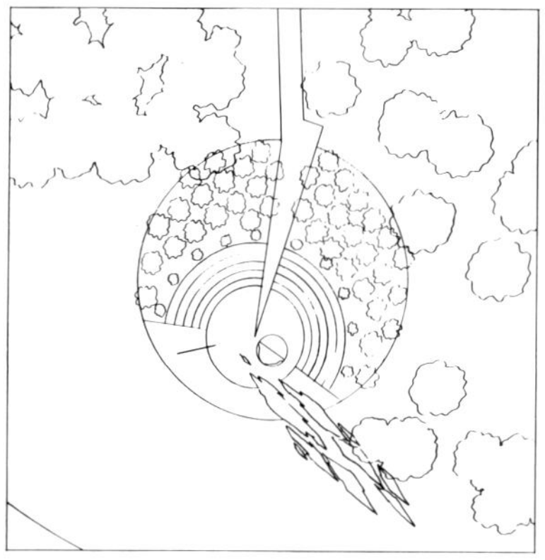

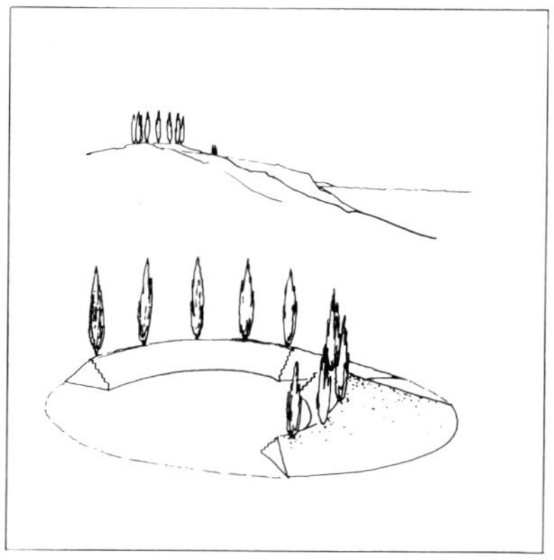

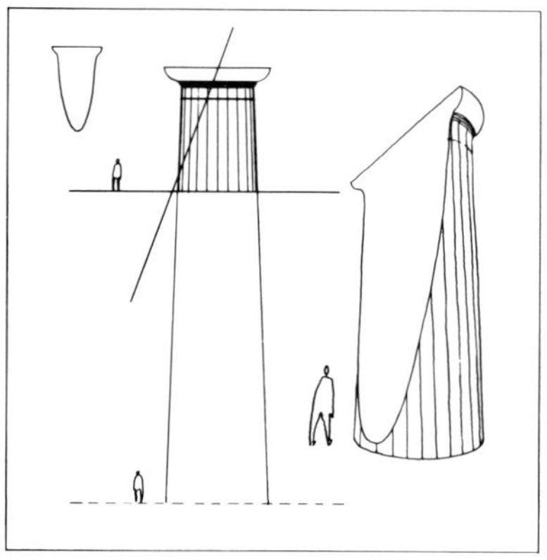

Palimpsestos - rubbed smooth to write again, history written over and over again on the same ancient ground. The monument is a palimpsest.
The harsh but beautiful landscape across which the soldiers fought and died has, since the beginning, contrasted with man's artifacts of civilisation, cultivation and war. Man has destroyed and so has time. But the antiquities in this landscape symbolise man's spirit as well as his struggles with nature and his own land. The most noble monument to man's spirit is the doric column. The most futile is the rusting, shell-torn fragment of modern conflict. These pieces emerge from the ground, implying vast buried relics of both civilisation and conflict. This ground is the most placid of places, an amphitheatre of seats where an audience contemplates this Greek tragedy. Like an ancient glade, the arc of seats resides in an olive grove and the formal cypresses stand evidence of a sacred place. The names of ancient and modern battles are inscribed in the faces of the amphitheatre. Various scales contrast - the column is oversized and cut by clear imagination, not the wear of time. The rocks, as sharp as flint, are also seen as mountains. A mosaic pavement is the map of the peninsula and archipelago of Greece, on which this haunting ensemble resides.

The column is white concrete, the war fragment is heavy rivetted steel plate, rusting and with a real shell fired through it. The rocks/mountains are harsh flint stone. The amphitheatre is white concrete and the paving is a tesselated mosaic of dark blue/black and white tile fragments. Construction is simply by assembling the various objects broughi together, pouring in situ concrete elements and by landscape works.

Mounting, walls, kerbs	$	25,000	Flagpole stands	1,000
Paving		80,000	Power and lighting	8,000
Amphitheatre		35,000	Inscriptions	12,000
Rocks		33,000	Planting	10,000
Steel plate		10,000	Water and drainage	18,000
Doric column		28,000	Fees	40,000
			At November 1986	$300,000

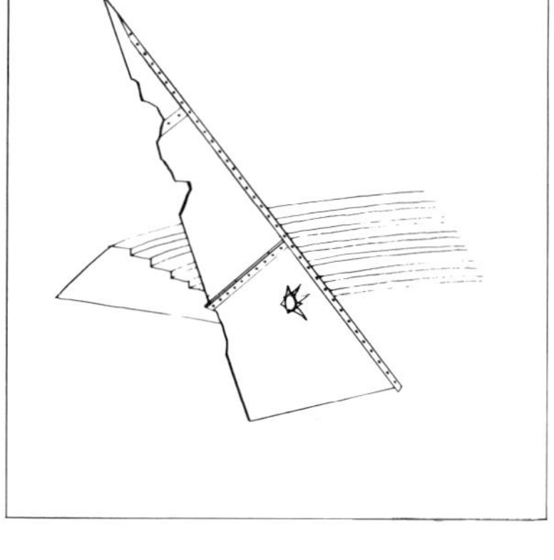

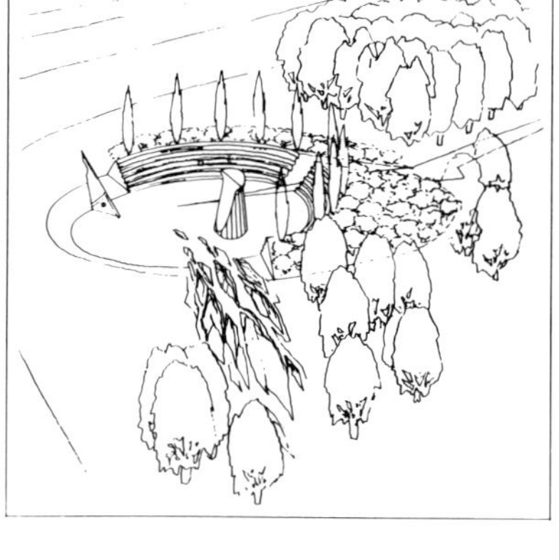

THE AUSTRALIAN HELLENIC MEMORIAL COMPETITION - CANBERRA - AUSTRALIAN CAPITAL TERRITORY KEN MAHER AND PARTNERS

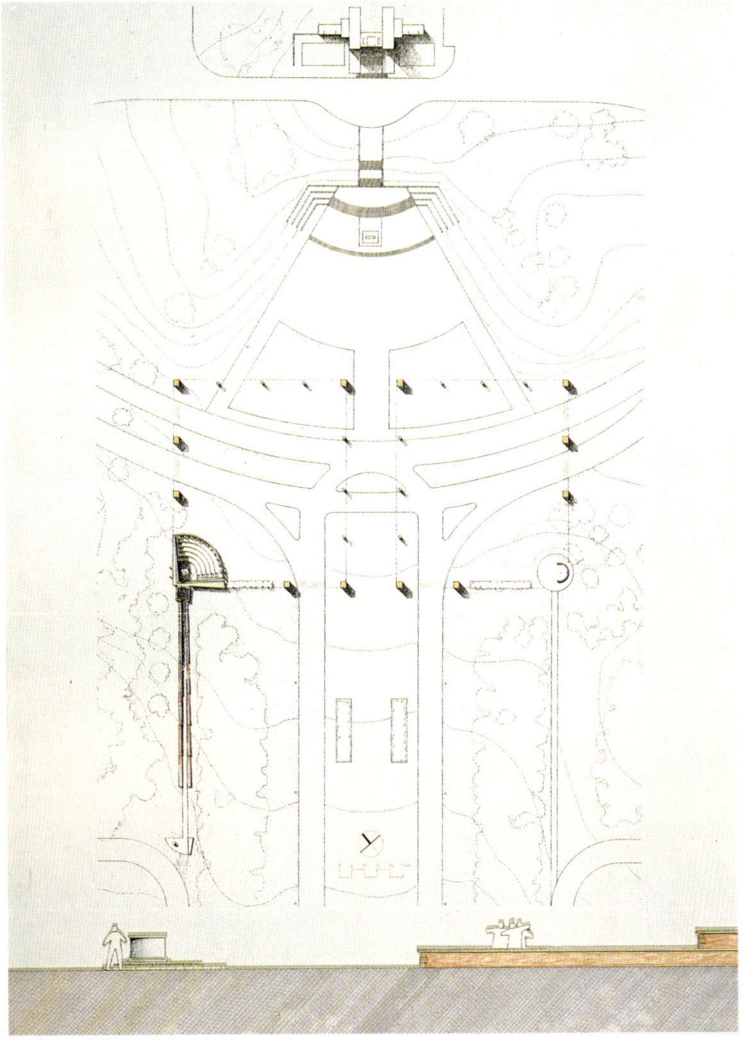

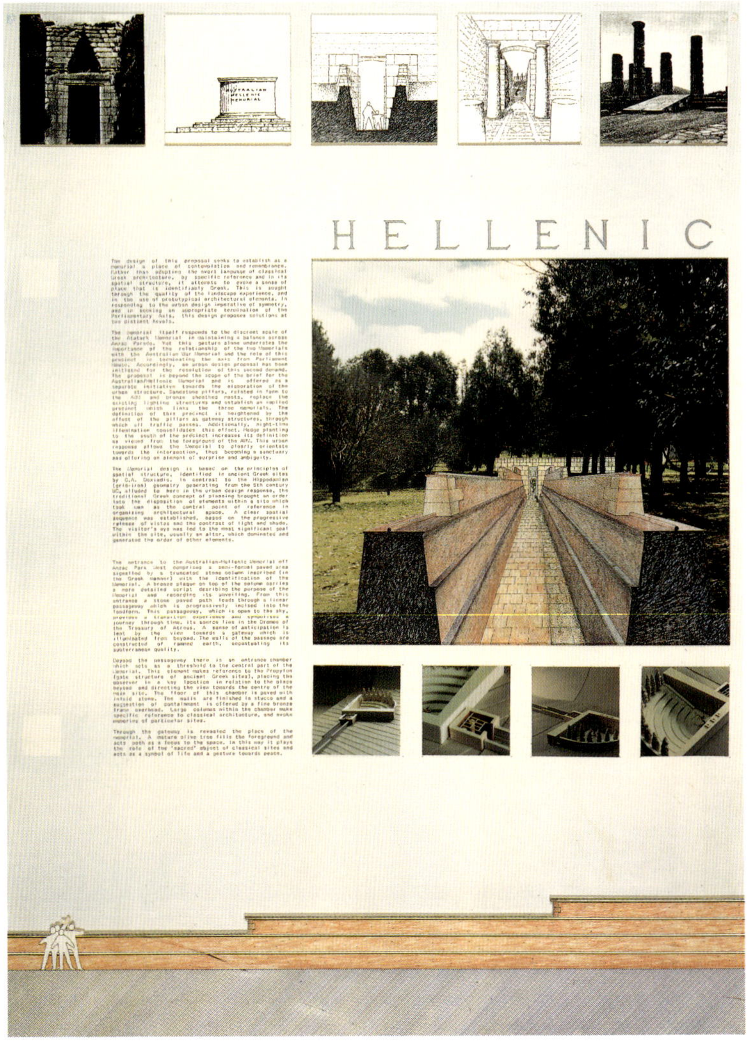

The design proposal seeks to establish the memorial as a place of contemplation and remembrance. Its spatial structure and specific elements evoke a sense of place that is identifiably Greek. The memorial is part of an urban ensemble, joining with the Australian War Memorial and the Attaturk Memorial to terminate the Parliamentary Axis at the end of Anzac Parade. The proposal includes a series of sandstone pillars and bronze masts which define a precinct and provide a visual link to the Australian War Memorial, while allowing the Hellenic Memorial to maintain a modest scale and an introversion fitting to its contemplative intent.
The entrance to the Memorial is off-the-street, adjacent to Anzac Parade. A forecourt leads to a linear passageway, open to the sky, which provides a transition experience and implies a journey throughout time. Its source lies in the dromos of the Treasury of Atreus. The walls of the passage are constructed of rammed earth, accentuating its subterranean quality. An entrance chamber acts as a threshold to the central space, in the manner of the propylon of Ancient Greek sites, placing the observer in a key vantage point directing the view towards the centre of the main site.
Through the gateway, a mature olive tree plays the role of the sacred object typically within classical sites, and acts as a symbol of life and peace. The amphitheatre-like central space is constructed by masonry elements and finishes, an allusion to the barren Greek landscape. A single water source penetrates the site from the east at the southern wall, providing a symbolic link to the world beyond, and representing the life sustaining support given to the Australians by the Greek people.
This limited competition entry was presented on four A1 panels, hung vertically to form a single narrative. Images and drawings were mounted onto the panels to give a sense of depth, and to give a

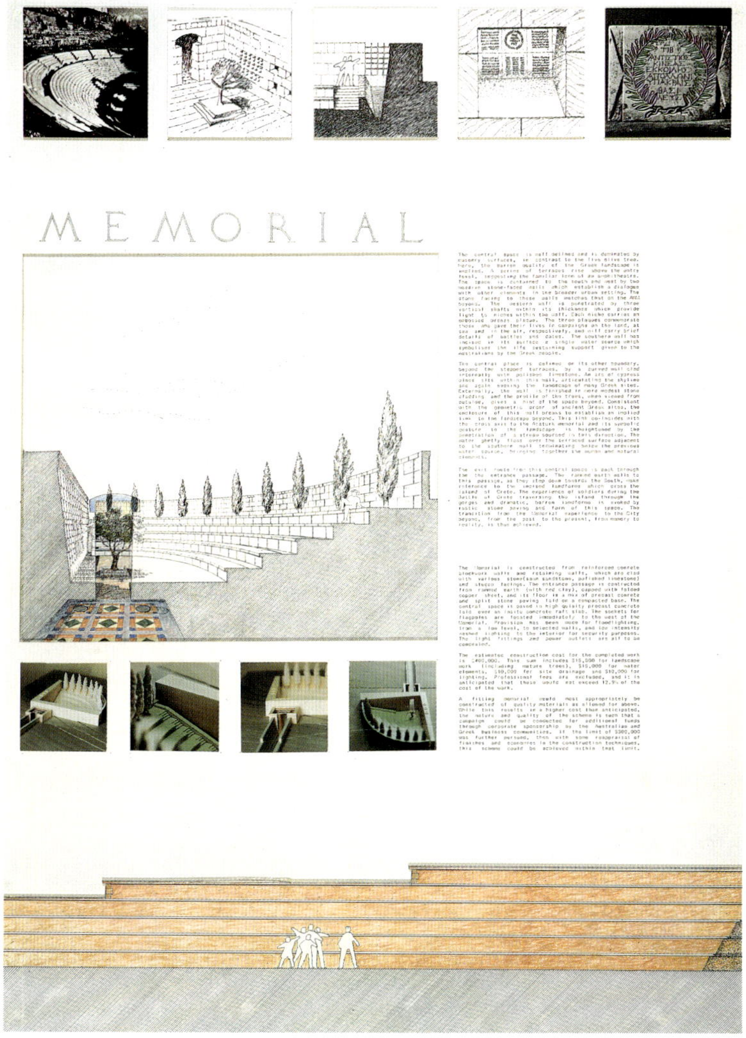

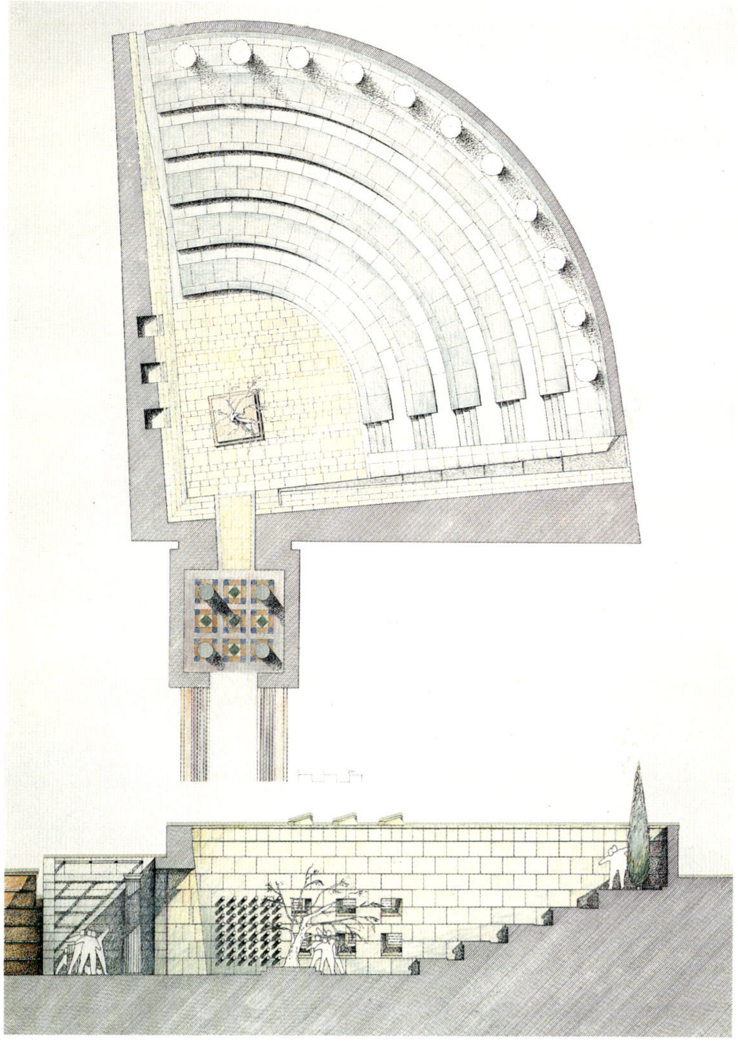

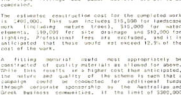

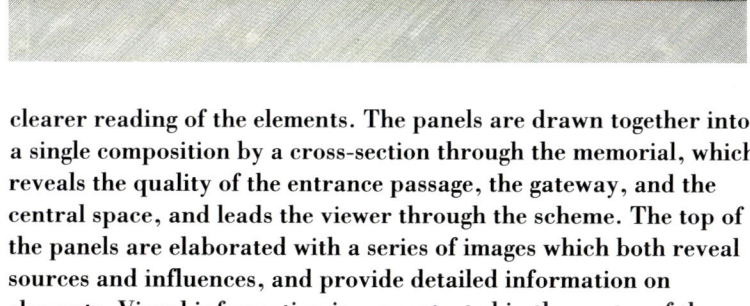

clearer reading of the elements. The panels are drawn together into a single composition by a cross-section through the memorial, which reveals the quality of the entrance passage, the gateway, and the central space, and leads the viewer through the scheme. The top of the panels are elaborated with a series of images which both reveal sources and influences, and provide detailed information on elements. Visual information is concentrated in the centre of the display, while a contextual plan commences the narrative on the left, and a detailed plan completes it on the right. Text is used to separate the images.

Techniques used include ink on film, photocopy reproduction on bond, hand rendered with colour pencils (Derwent Artists and Faber Castell Polychromos). Background overspray using mechanical and brush. Small sketches were ink and Artline 200 Fine 0.4 felt-tip pen on bond and detail paper, photocopy reproduction on bond. Photomontage – ink on film, photocopy reproduction on bond, overlaid on photographic print, hand rendered in colour pencil and reproduced in cibachrome.

Design Architects: Ken Maher and Everard Kloots, assistance from Amanda Burgess, Janelle Plummer, Luigi Rossell, Vladimir Sitta and Phillip Thalis
Drawing Artists: Site plan drawn by Vladimir Sitta and panel designed by Ken Maher.
Detail plan drawn by Janelle Plummer. Sectional perspective drawn by Luigi Rossell. Section drawn by Everard Kloots.
Rendering by Everard Kloots and Janelle Plummer. Small sketches drawn by Ken Maher. Air-brush by Simon Palmer
Size: 4 x 1189 x 841 mm
Date: 1986

WARLAND RESERVE DESIGN COMPETITION – SOUTH AUSTRALIA   WOODS BAGOT

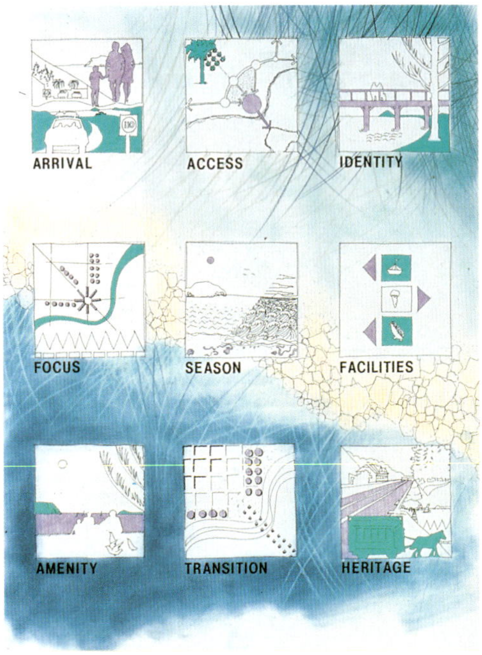

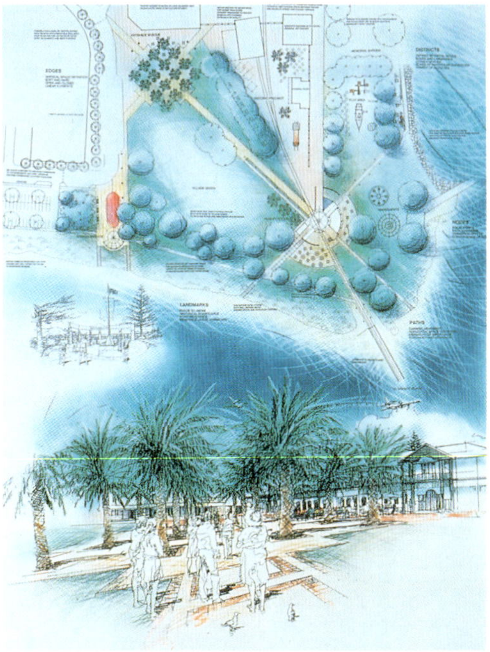

Warland Reserve's 'sense of place' is enhanced by the reinforcement of its axial links and existing focal points. Key elements include a grid of palm trees relocated from the existing foreshore car park, defining the area of transition from the main street to the reserve. The structure is essentially transparent, retaining and framing axial views, while catering for the functional need of a very public space.

In the design of presentation visuals two important considerations are: the mode of exhibition and the nature of those to whom they are to be exhibited. This particular scheme was one of approximately 30 competition entries to be mounted on mobile partition screens, to be judged by a panel of local councillors and designers. It was designed to be both clear and visually arresting. The colours were vibrant and the format bold. An axonometric view of the site gives a dynamic and three-dimensional form to the master planing proposal. The base colour was applied using a mixture of crushed pastels blended into the paper and overlaid by pastel and pencil shading.

Project Architect: Mark Dunstan
Drawing: Karen Griffin
Size: 1189 x 841 mm
Date: 1987

CIRCULAR QUAY REHABILITATION – SYDNEY – NEW SOUTH WALES ALLEN JACK & COTTIER

In 1986 Allen Jack and Cottier were commissioned to design the eastern foreshore to Circular Quay including a new covered walkway to the Opera House, and the restructuring of the Circular Quay railway station and ferry wharfs. The existing 1950s Railway building was to be 'opened' at its base to reconnect the city and harbour. New restaurant and retail facilities were planned to enliven the concourse, the Ferry Wharfs were stripped back to reveal their nautical bones and all facilities were relocated to the wharf's sides so as to open their waiting areas to the wonderful aspect of Circular Quay.

The perspective was created in the very early stages of the design and was therefore done as an impression, its brief was to capture an atmosphere.

The initial set-up was worked over a large format photograph that established massing and proportion. A butter paper rough was done from this, filling in the 'characters' and detail. A final drawing was done in ink on film. This was then photocopied onto heavy weight coloured paper and finally coloured using Caran D'Ache water based crayons.

Design Architects:
Peter Stronarch, Victor Lake,
Cesar Perrazzo and
Robert Willoughby
Drawing Artist: Peter Ireland
Size: 473 x 370 mm
Date: 1986

FLINDERS STREET RAILWAY STATION PROJECT - MELBOURNE - VICTORIA JOHN ANDREWS INTERNATIONAL

Architectural integration and public amenity are the two key principles which inform JAI's joint submission for the redevelopment of Flinders Street Railway Station.
The proposed building exhibits a strong industrial character, establishing its own identity but complementing the handsome Victorian station. The new structure presents a stepped profile in two dimensions: horizontally, following a line of the Yarra River, and vertically on the southern edge, providing terraces which extend from restaurants. Portal frames define the form of the roof in the curve of a wave.
The building's public amenity is enhanced by a conservatory at the river walk level. Internally, the building focuses on a central mall, three storeys high, with shops on the lower two levels. The top floor is devoted to restaurants, nightclubs and community facilities. A market is planned for a major hall, between the existing station buildings and the shopping centre.
The complex task of building over a busy rail centre is accomplished by the use of a simple steel module, enabling the station to remain fully operational throughout construction.
We prepared preliminary drawing in pencil or a computer outline. This drawing has all the information of the final drawing and is to establish the view and to provide a drawing for assessment and checking. The line drawing is prepared by tracing the preliminary pencil drawing onto tracing paper using a 0.25 Rapidograph or Isograph pen with black drawing ink. The style of line work is necessarily seen to be compatible with the elevations and plans being prepared by the architect for the same presentation.

Design Architect:
John Andrews and Greg Deas
Drawing Artist:
David Wardman
Size: 1198 x 841 mm
Date: 1988

Tea Centre
FLOWERS

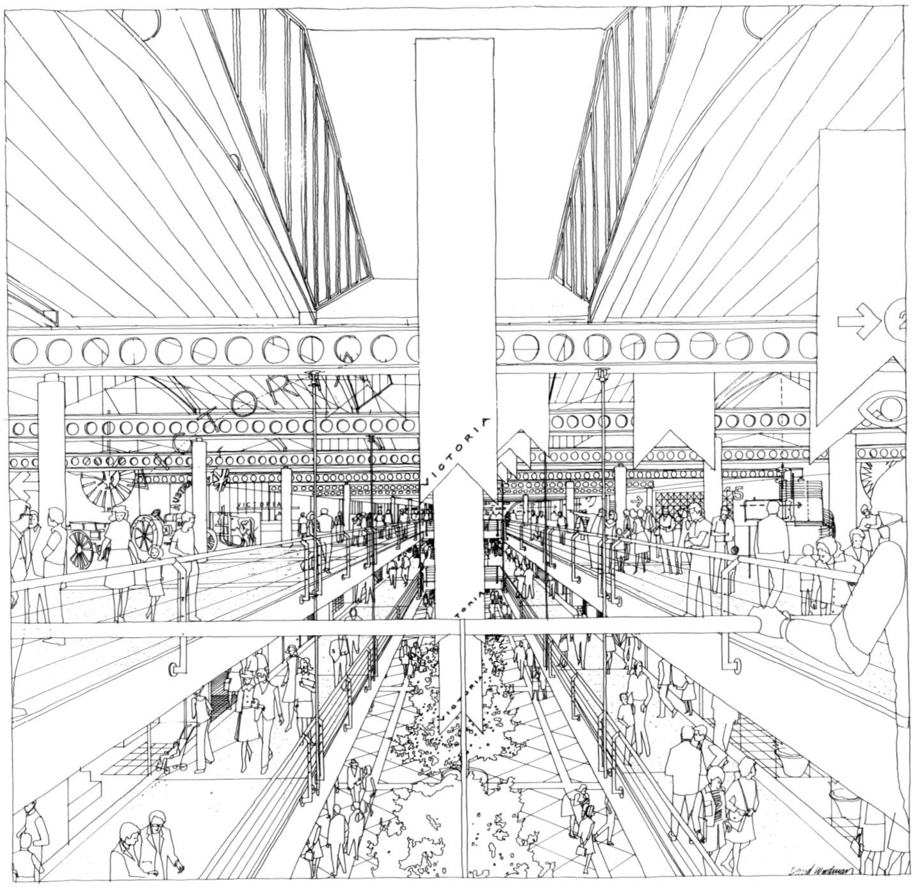
VICTORIA

PALM PAVILION – DARLING HARBOUR, SYDNEY – NEW SOUTH WALES McCONNEL SMITH & JOHNSON ARCHITECTS, THE MSJ GROUP

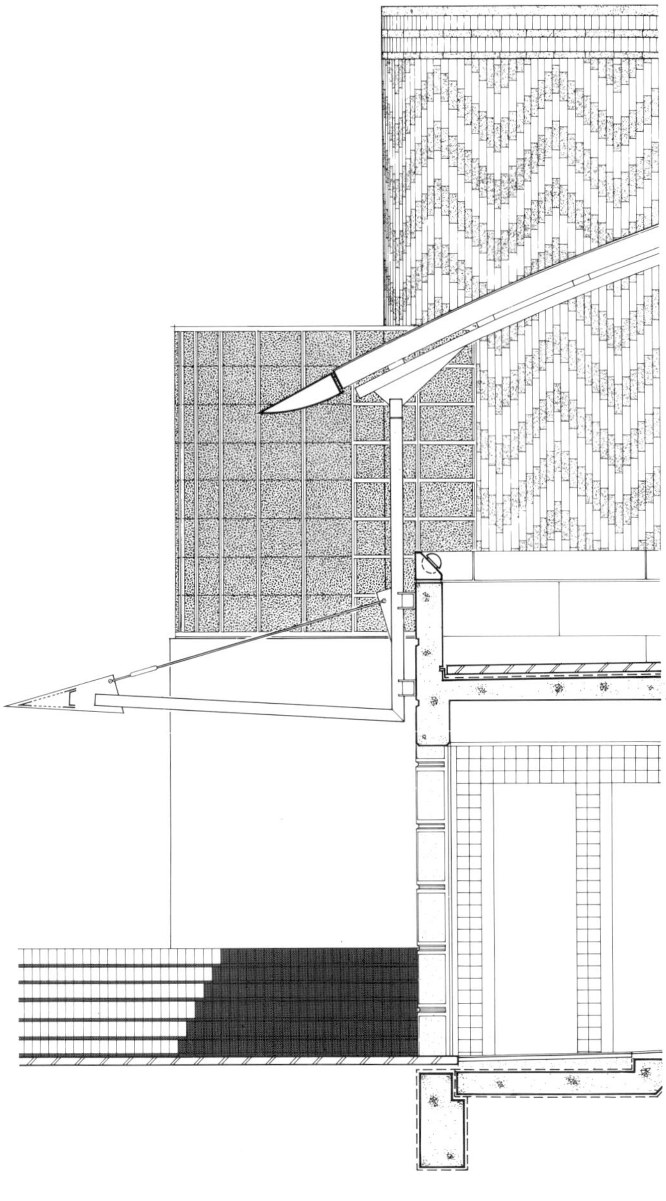

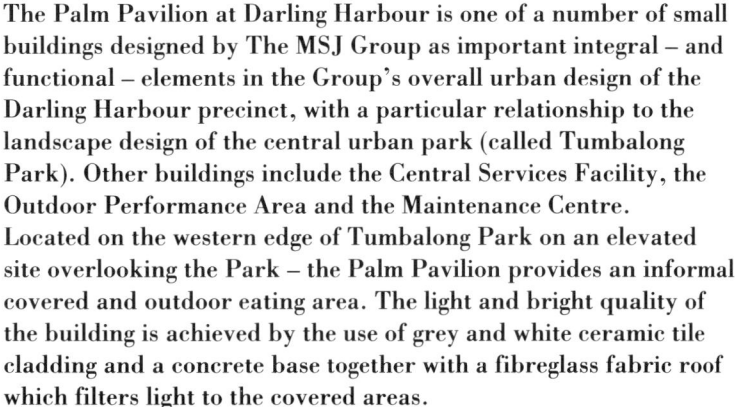

The Palm Pavilion at Darling Harbour is one of a number of small buildings designed by The MSJ Group as important integral – and functional – elements in the Group's overall urban design of the Darling Harbour precinct, with a particular relationship to the landscape design of the central urban park (called Tumbalong Park). Other buildings include the Central Services Facility, the Outdoor Performance Area and the Maintenance Centre.

Located on the western edge of Tumbalong Park on an elevated site overlooking the Park – the Palm Pavilion provides an informal covered and outdoor eating area. The light and bright quality of the building is achieved by the use of grey and white ceramic tile cladding and a concrete base together with a fibreglass fabric roof which filters light to the covered areas.

By integrating the stepped back terraces and the landscaping, the Palm Pavilion contributes to the transition of scale from Tumbalong Park to the massive size of the Exhibition Building.

The drawing is an oblique elevation parallel to the blade wall and was chosen to describe the wing shape of the canopy's structure and the significance of the planting screen in defining the eating area around the central drum. Ink drawing on film using pen sizes 0.18/0.25/0.5/0.85, Letratone LT936 and Pantone Black on reverse side of film.

Palm Pavilion – detail shows section through the eaves bracing and the steel connections of the canopy with an indication of the bush – hammered face to in situ concrete. The double tube used to support the canopy was chosen as an alternative to a single tube of larger dimension. Ink drawing on film using pen sizes 0.18/0.25/0.35/0.5/0.7, Letratone LT28(70%)LT305/LT935 on back of film.

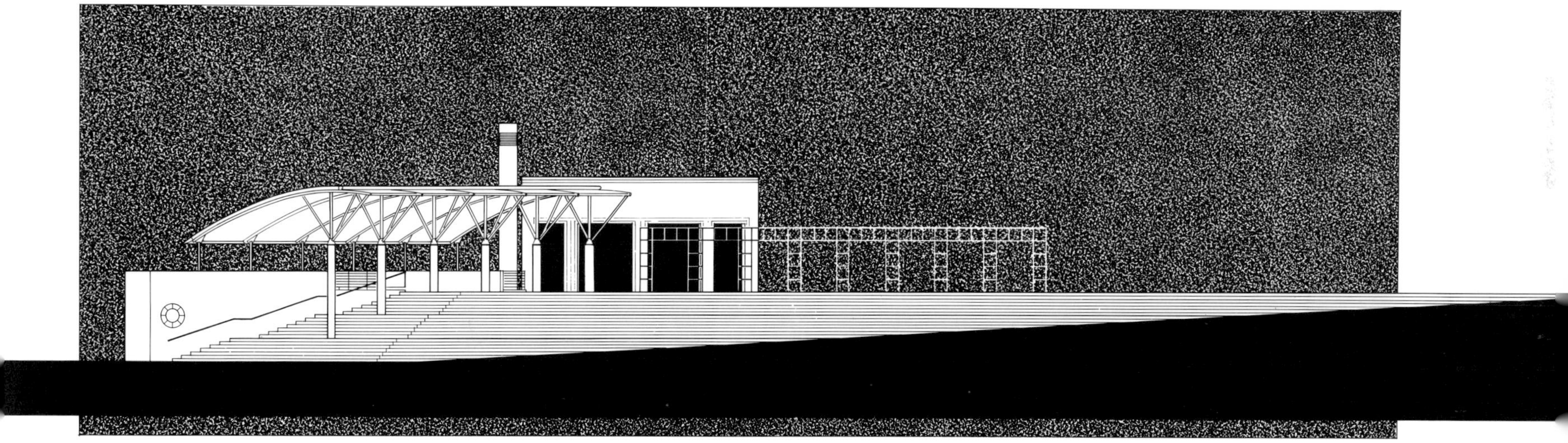

Design Architect: Mark Willett
– McConnel Smith & Johnson
Drawing Artist:
Vahan Hekimian
Size: 500 x 300 mm
Date: 1988
Photographer:
Michael Nicholson

CAULFIELD TOWN HALL - CAULFIELD - VICTORIA IVAN RIJAVEC ARCHITECTS

Design Architect: Ivan Rijavec
Drawing Artist:
Zbigniew Jaworski
Size: 1090 x 760 mm
Date: 1989
Photographer: Trevor Mein

Like many Town Halls of its genre, the Caulfield Town Hall has been extended and renovated at various intervals to accommodate new and expanded Community Service departments.
Typically, each alteration was characterised with the architectural expression of its time and like many other Town Halls, the side and rear of the building became a collage of architectural expressions ranging from Victorian, Edwardian and Early through to Late Modern Architecture.
A new Municipal structure comprising 3800 square metres of floor area, was officially commissioned in early 1989, following a limited competition between 12 invited participants.
The brief required that the hotchpotch of municipal accommodation which had been dispersed ad hoc around the Town Hall, in housing and an assortment of relocatable structures adjoining one another, be rationalised into a new building to be constructed on the west of the original building.
Our winning solution proposed a four-storey composite of elements which by way of abstract allusion proposed a transition from Victorian Eclectic, to Modern.
Media: pencil, coloured pencil, ink tipped pens, applied to both sides of detail paper. (The artist's general statement which elucidates some of the concerns specific to his work can be found outlined under the heading of the Manifold Residence by Ivan Rijavec Architects.)

IVAN RIJAVEC ARCHITECTS
CAULFIELD MUNICIPAL OFFICES EXPANSION

PARLIAMENT HOUSE - CANBERRA - AUSTRALIAN CAPITAL TERRITORY MITCHELL/GIURGOLA & THORP ARCHITECTS

The concept of the building is not as a monumental structure imposed on the landscape, but rather one which is closer in spirit to the Greek monumentalisation of an acropolis, in which there is a continuity from the most minute elements of the architectural order to the massive form of the building itself, yet all of which is congruent with the landscape. In an architectural design of this magnitude, there is a sense of the grandiose. But it is the architect's intention in the development of the design to resist this connotation of the architectural gesture, and instead to nurture and refine the simple sense of monumentality, in concert with the honest, natural landscape.

The hill is of utmost importance. For centuries, man occupied its crest with structures as signs of possession and power. It was felt that the hilltop should be left clear of visible constructions with only the flag, which has been there since the city's foundation, present as a permanent rallying-point or symbol for the citizens. This flag is supported by a structure which is an integral outgrowth of the entire complex.

The hill is also a characteristic geological configuration of the region, with its clustered trees and marble colours of sunlight and shade. For the hill of the Capital, these connotations of the natural landscape are emphasised so that the built structures made of complementary materials nestle within it and restate the gradual slope of the hill.

The profile of the complex has been purposefully arranged to complete geometry of the Parliamentary Triangle, thus accomplishing Griffin's intentions for the massing of buildings. However, rather than imposing a building on the hill which terminates the Land Axis, the solution allows the mall to extend to areas beyond. While the transparent mast structure supporting the flag provides visual engagement and unity, the roof monitors over the two Chambers are clearly expressive of the bicameral system of government.

The foyer's primary function is to facilitate the movement of visitors to other parts of the building. The fine craftsmanship and natural materials serve as the visual focus in an area is partly illuminated by natural light from the north-facing gallery and skylights in the roof and public terrace.

The drawings are the result of several sequential steps and by several sets of hands. The original drawings were done as measured perspectives on rag-based paper and then transferred in graphite onto a textured rag-based illustration board. The figures of people, works of art etc, were added first in pencil then in sepia ink. The ink line work was then executed, followed by an initial overall colouring with Derwent pencils. The drawings were then given highlight and focus by some additional line work and finally the spatial character, due to both artificial and natural daylight provided by final colour density and graduations.

Design Architect:
Romaldo Giurgola
Drawing Artists:
Kate Montgomery,
Romaldo Giurgola, and
Harold Guider
Size: 710 x 510 mm
Date: 1984
Photographer: John Gollings

AUSTRALIAN EMBASSY – TOKYO – JAPAN DENTON CORKER MARSHALL

As Australia's new Embassy in Tokyo, this building inevitably makes an architectural statement about the image Australia wishes to present to Japan. It does not draw on any obvious 'Australian' imagery, but instead presents a contemporary and dynamic form, making maximum use of materials and technology available specifically in Japan. Hence, materials are stainless steel, pre-coated aluminium, galvanised steel; factory components assembled with expressed fixings or as panelled elements.

The drawing shows the main entry (to the Chancery) from the street, which is approached through an opening below the high level sloping canopy and via an open courtyard. The Chancery building is flanked on each side by residential apartments.

The drawing aims to show how the Chancery will establish a strong presence despite its integration with the apartments. The technique used was lead pencil (Staedler Mars) B/2B on 53 gsm Fenton C30 detail paper, a full-sized photocopy print was later made on bond paper 80 gsm OCE and coloured with Derwent (Cumberland), Venue (Spectracolor), Berol (Eaglecolor), as they come to hand. The drawing was set up (by hand) by the artist as a two-point perspective, defining only the major elements, planes, etc. This was then used as an underlay beneath the detail paper, and the final drawing sketched freehand over the top, in lead pencil line only. The underlay was then removed and areas of lead pencil shading applied, and a photocopy taken and coloured.

Design Architect:
Denton Corker Marshall
Drawing Artist:
Barrie Marshall,
Denton Corker Marshall
Size: 1189 x 841 mm
Date: 1988
Photographer: John Gollings

Australian Embassy, Tokyo. View from Mita Avenue.

MOWBRAY COLLEGE – MELTON – VICTORIA **NORMAN DAY ARCHITECT**

Design Architect:
Norman Day
Drawing Artist:
Marc Raszewski
Size: 1682 x 1189 mm
Date: 1990
Photographer:
Sebastian Gollings

Mowbray College is a new school located some 38 kilometres from Melbourne in the satellite town of Melton. The architecture is designed to symbolise the school community's hopes, aspirations and spirit – it is representative of buildings they know and those they do not. The school has a small city pattern with side streets, lanes, arcades and so on, where individual classrooms are arranged as 'houses' (or homerooms) and larger facilities for community foci. The library is a circular, spiritual central building, which at the moment remains a singular, until more buildings surround it, but the notion is that the building remains a central position (with a drum-like Renaissance form) to locate the school centre. It is the formal urban focus.

It is set apart from its drum by adopting free-form adjacent architectural elements which infiltrate it. There was the fundamental desire to build Mowbray's functional and educational program (in a spiritual way) into our buildings, which we interpreted as the character of the school and which produces not only a library (which also operates as classrooms) but also in the one building a reading room for toddlers, a senior study room (on top of the drum), a meeting room for parents, and a debating chamber. It is also used for drama. Mowbray buildings need to be more than a mere single purpose facility.

The library drum is concealed as a Mannerist building (the Tempieto comes to mind) and therefore the centre of the school will never be entirely visible or understandable until you are in it.

Our presentation drawings are designed to show the design intention, to describe to the viewer what we are planning to achieve in the design process. By including the plan of the building, the elevation and some perspectival elements, we are trying to describe how the building is conceived. We have deconstructed the building into a graphical diagram showing the plan, some elevation, structure and perspective elements. Three-dimensional form is indicated by shading, but the intention was for the drawing to read as a colourful diagram as much as a representation of design ideas. (The technique is air-brush on card and each drawing [approximately 1 metre by 3/4 metre] takes about ten days to produce).

LAKE GINNINDERRA COLLEGE – BELCONNEN – AUSTRALIAN CAPITAL TERRITORY
DARYL JACKSON PTY LTD

The principal design objective for Lake Ginninderra College was to develop a massing of building which extended the urban context of Belconnen and at the same time strike a balance with the natural land and water context.
A further design idea was to produce (via shape and mass) differing and therefore distinctive expression, externally and internally to the various teaching disciplines which are represented by the articulated blocks which form the College. The overall intention was to produce an image of urban precinct (ie, a collection of building forms tightly arranged and juxtaposed) which would signify and consolidate a Collegiate model.
Viewed from the Lake and John Knight Park the building forms are modulated to create receding solid terrace areas, and overhanging lightweight forms that provide sheltered places for recreational activity. These also assist in sunshading lower parts of the building. Four vertical concrete stair towers are used to establish a strong pattern of access. They have also been designed to represent the fundamental elements of life and learning as understood by the ancient philosophers: earth, air, fire and water. Strong colours painted within each tower depict each of these four themes. A series of shaped skylights afford separate identity to each tower. The real function of these drawings is to assist in the pattern of thinking. They are usually done on yellow trace using Pentel Sign Pens. The sketches encapsulate Daryl Jackson's primary working method and communication medium in conveying his ideas to both employees and clients. Ideas are usually conveyed in plan and section although three-dimensional form studies are also used as a way of representing the intention.

Design Architect:
Daryl Jackson and
Bob Sinclair
Drawing Artist: Daryl Jackson
Date: 1987

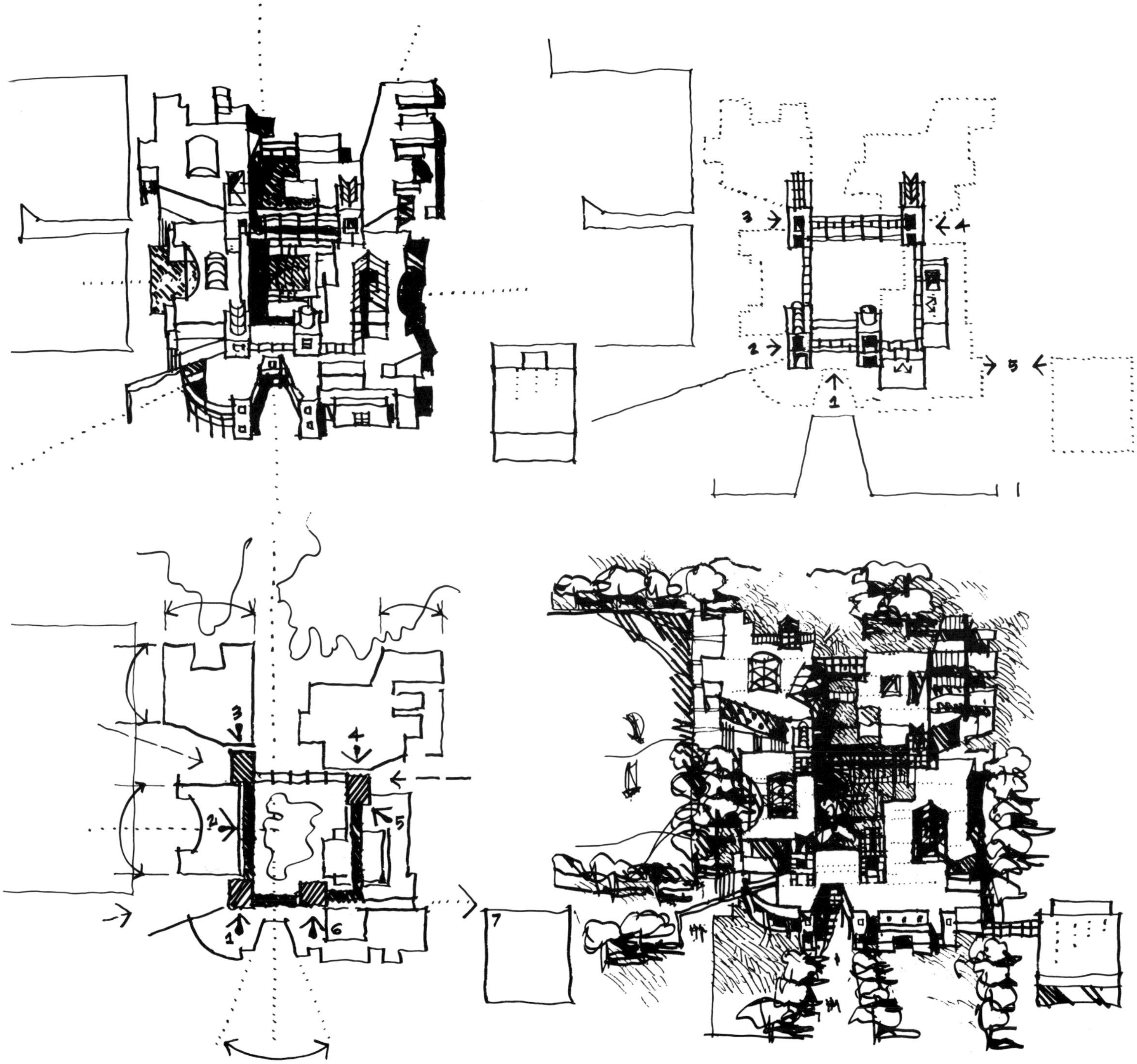

LAKE GINNINDERRA COLLEGE - BELCONNEN - AUSTRALIAN CAPITAL TERRITORY
DARYL JACKSON PTY LTD

The graphic style, illustrated here, is that developed by Jaro Safer, an associate director with Daryl Jackson Pty Ltd. Fine ink drawings, 0.3 Rapidograph, are a conclusive representation of a building; an assemblage of the 'known' design images and a compositional designation of parts. This is the use of the drawing format as a metaphor for architecture and seen as art. They are usually made when the design process is complete as a recording. These drawings are not easily read for they are an intended abstraction, there for the eye to explore. The basic formula for the Safer drawing is to show the buildings in plan with their elevations projected onto one or two faces as a geometric portrayal of the inner volume. Around this centrepiece, other elevations may be drawn as a border, usually related to each side of the plan, which means that in some cases the elevation appears upside down. These drawings resemble the familiar drawings of children before they learn about rules of perspective and the singular, or exclusive viewpoint. Children's drawings of houses show an astonishing wholeness of understanding. Their two-dimensional, yet complex constructions (as drawings) clearly show basic volumes and forms as collage.

Each object depicted is given meaning via its association, there is no beginning and no end. In a parallel sense, the Cubists endeavoured to incorporate such things as 'time', and 'the other side of the moon', in their works, and traditional artists in places such as Rajasthan and Bali produced a similar form of inclusive painting as 'allegory'.

Design Architects:
Daryl Jackson and Bob Sinclair
Drawing Artist: Jaro Safer
Size: 1000 x 707 mm
Date: 1988
Photographer: John Gollings

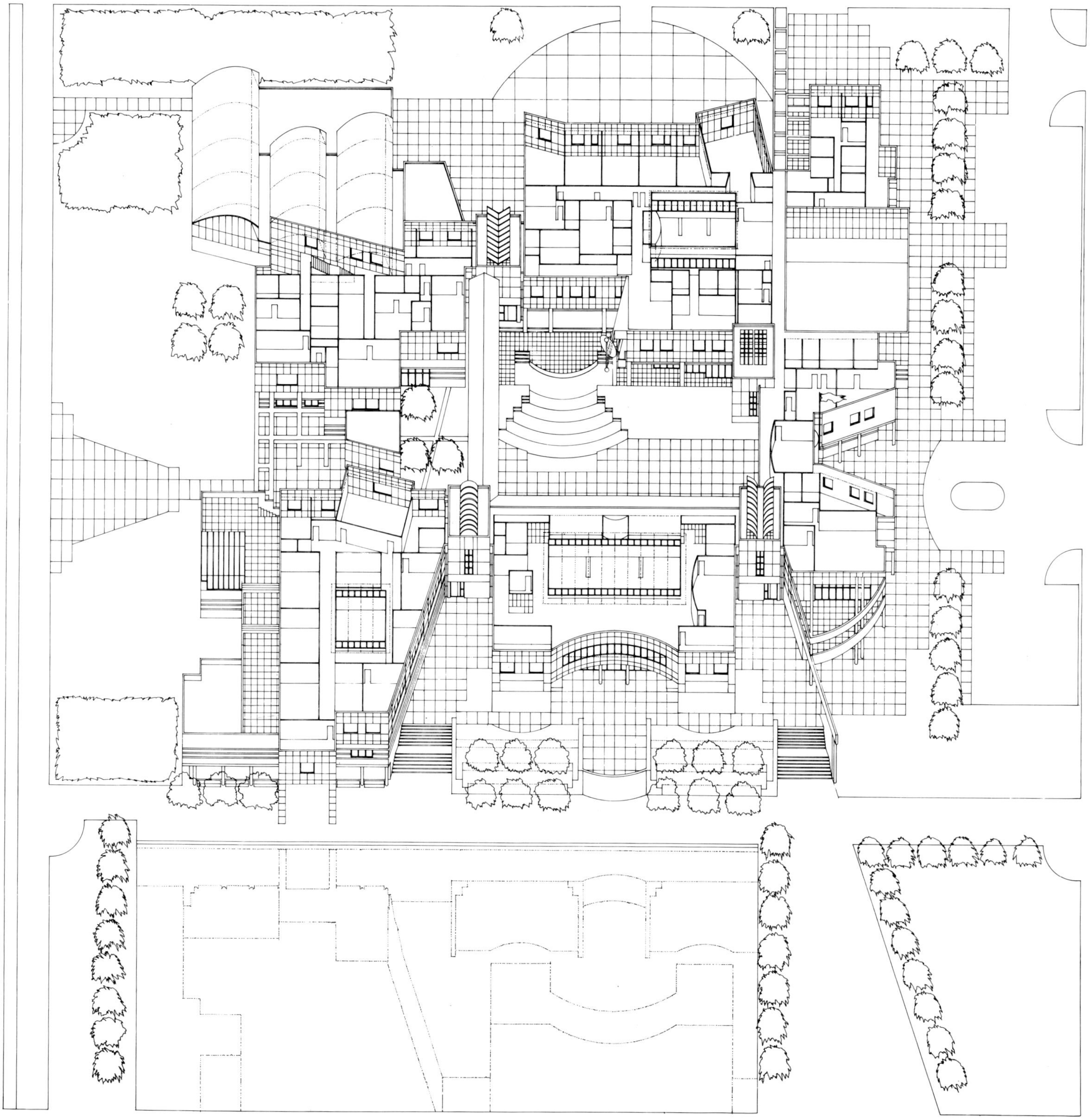

MENINDEE CENTRAL SCHOOL – MENINDEE – NEW SOUTH WALES PUBLIC WORKS DEPARTMENT, NEW SOUTH WALES

Menindee is a small town in outback NSW 80 minutes drive from Broken Hill. The new Central School caters to the townships primary and secondary age education needs. An existing classroom block is kept and refurbished for historic reasons and serves as the visual focus at the southern edge of a newly formed school assembly area.

Two of the new buildings parallel the orientation of the existing building and frame the edge to the upper level of the new assembly area. The other blocks shift axis by 18.5 degrees in order to retain a stand of existing trees for a newly created shade court at the southern side of the new library. All buildings are oriented in a north-south direction for maximum sun protection.

In outback Australia, which is typified by a limitless horizon, the predominant visual sign for a building in the landscape, is the impact of its roof form. At Menindee the school's different functions can be identified by their roof.

Classroom blocks have the same roof type while the administration wing, performance hall and library each have their own distinctive roof profile. A covered way runs across the plan from east to west and serves as the linkage element for all the buildings. The grouping of the blocks around this link is designed to provide a series of outdoor courtyards. The heat in Menindee during a good part of the year can be extreme, so wide roof overhangs and covered ways are designed not only as wet weather protection but as shaded circulation paths as well.

A large mural painted by the architect occupies the entry foyer, a colourful school sign visible at night from afar.

Perspective 1: The aerial perspective is a stylised portrayal of Menindee's outback location with the blue-green of the Menindee Lakes off on the horizon. A limited range of intense colours give the painting its vivid quality. Original: colour pencil Faber Castell polychromos, Rotring ink and Marabu Buntlak Spray Colours acrylic spray paint (CFC free) on plastic film.

Design Architect: Keith Pike
Drawing Artist: Keith Pike
Size: 900 x 600 mm
Date: 1990
Photographer:
Michael Nicholson

Keith Pha 88

NURSING SCIENCES UNIVERSITY OF CANBERRA FOR AND ON BEHALF OF THE ACT PUBLIC WORKS – AUSTRALIAN CAPITAL TERRITORY MITCHELL/GIURGOLA & THORPE ARCHITECTS

Project Architect:
Robert Richards
Drawing: Harold Guida,
Design Partner
Size: 1600 x 500 mm
Date: 1991
Photographer: Harold Guida

The new Nursing Sciences building consolidates facilities previously housed in several location both on and off the campus. It is sited near the top of a rise at the north-east corner of the campus where it may be seen from a great distance as one approaches the University.

The brief required spaces of two distinct types: quiet, private and administrative rooms and teaching spaces which, by their very nature, are active, public and interactive. Due to the differing module and character of the briefed spaces, the design gathers 'like functions' together into two individual structures which best serve the activities, and provide economies of structure and services. The building is composed of a western three-storey 'student' wing and a 'rotated' eastern faculty and administration wing of the same height. The rotation of this wing creates generous and evident entry locations and offers a long view to Mount Majura. At the entry, which is the point of junction of the two geometries, there is a small two-storey foyer which serves as a circulation focus.

The drawing by Harold Guida is a freehand ink on Mylar. The drawing was done over construction documents and is simply tonal so as to show the relationships between the banded brickwork of the new building and the horizontal, recessed, continuous window of the School of Management. Additionally the drawing conveys the strong relationship of the several horizontal profiles, yet the unique character of the new building with its divergent shadow pattern.

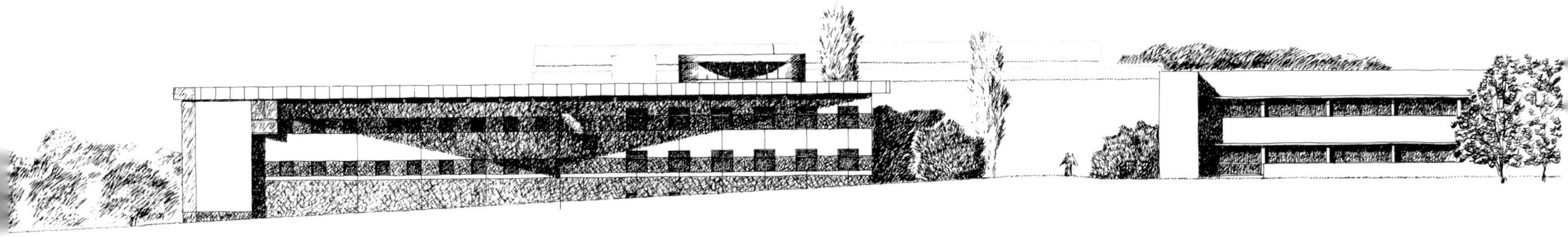

PERTH INSTITUTE OF CONTEMPORARY ARTS - PERTH - WESTERN AUSTRALIA DONALDSON + WARN ARCHITECTS

The former school, designed in the early part of this century and attributed to eminent Western Australian architect George Temple-Poole, is now located in the Perth Cultural Centre. The building has been assigned the home for the Perth Institute of Contemporary Arts and Donaldson + Warn Architects have been commissioned by the Building Management Authority to adapt the structure to its new use.

The cultural centre precinct location, the historical significance of the building, the fascinating and evolving character of contemporary art, the modest budget, and the difficulties of adapting a 'Victorian' school building to accommodate a complex and dynamic artistic program, makes this an exciting and extremely challenging project.

The design philosophy is one of meeting the client's need with resourceful and pragmatic solutions whilst hinting at a possible relationship between architecture and the contemporary arts.

The illustration shows a structural frame and truss which supports a first floor gallery, enabling the removal of the existing ground floor structural walls to create a performance space below. The truss has been designed in small components to be assembled and tensioned within the space prior to completing the demolition of the internal walls. Bow trusses spanning across the space are made up of V members cast in ductile iron and tensioned together with threaded rods. The cast components also support a lighting grid. Additional to their structural, functional and lightweight aesthetic appearance, the ductile iron refers to cast iron often used in local buildings constructed in the same era as the original school building.

This finished drawing was generated from two A1 size originals drawn at 1:50 scale on drafting film using a 0.7 mm minimum size technical pen. A base drawing was prepared in pencil on tracing paper and the various components (truss, internal screens, staircase, cafe counter and figures) arranged accordingly. The figures were photocopied from magazines and books and enlarged to suit the composition of the drawing. The figures were printed onto clear film and arranged onto an overlay sheet of drafting film. A selection of the new design components (staircase, truss and lighting grid, etc) were drawn in ink onto the film overlay sheet. The plan and part of the clock tower were drawn onto a separate sheet of film, producing an underlay drawing. The wall zones were inked in solid. Both originals were then photographically reproduced resulting in two A4 size 'inter-negs'. The 'inter-negs' were then combined to produce a duplicate negative with the underlay image reproduced with a dot screen. A black and white bromide 'original' was then printed from the duplicate negative. The coloured planes were generated from overlays produced in the printing process, making the image in this book the colour original.

Design Architects:
Richard Donaldson,
Geoff Warn and Richard Black
Drawing Artists: John Smart
and Geoff Warn
Size: 790 x 575 mm
Date: 1989
Photographer: Michael Annear

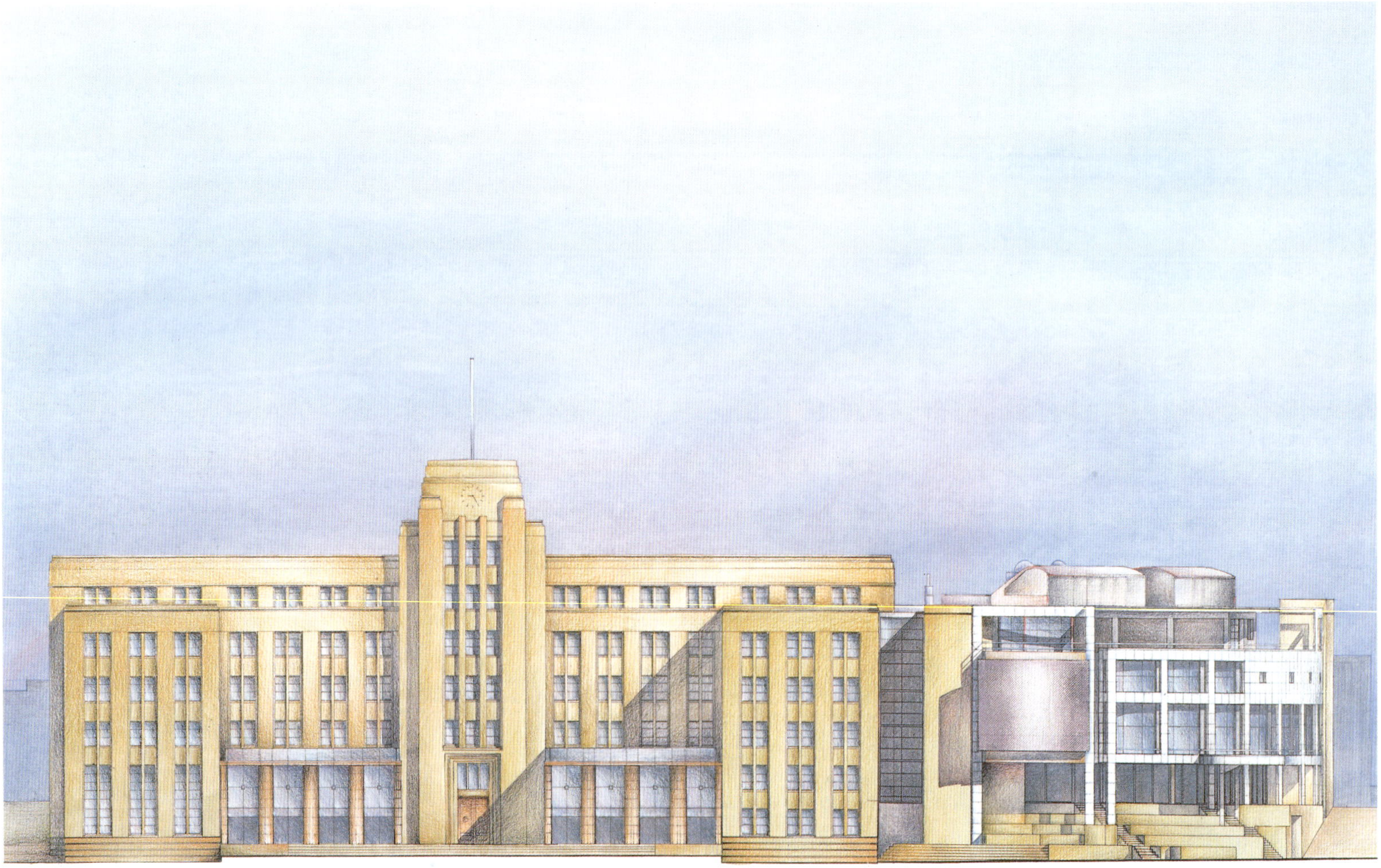

Design Architect: Tom Rivard
Director in Charge:
Andrew Andersons
Drawing Artist: Tom Rivard
Size: 594 x 420 mm
Date: 1991

Inspired by the architectonic possibilities inherent in the subject matter, the building deliberately evokes cinematic structure and visual processing in its formal qualities, framing, focusing and exposing both subject and object through a sequence of architectural interpretations of screen, lens and aperture. These signs and systems are used to construct and articulate an environment whose spaces and forms reflect use, site and an enhanced level of awareness, perception and discourse. The building becomes a cinematic presentation and representation of its users, its contents and its context.

The quarter circle geometry terminates the MCA complex. In scale and detail the building mediates with the context, as well as framing the orientation of the complex to Circular Quay with its maritime and civic qualities.

In the resultant void between the two theatres, radiating circulation and stairs progress through the building, gradually focusing participants on Sydney Harbour, Circular Quay and the Opera House.

On the exterior a ten metre screen, transmission camera and satellite link will establish interactive communication with other urban centres around the world. The images transmitted via live video and audio links will broaden the context of the cinematheque to a global one.

Composite conceptual diagram of building organisation includes a small scale location plan over which is superimposed abstracted museum and cinematheque elevations, plan fragment and graphic linking building with cinematographic and visual operations.
Materials – impasto acrylic and gesso background applied with palette knife on illustration board. Elevation frames – tinted gesso painted through cardboard templates. Plan inked in white, lenses and site buildings applied with adhesive film and visual corridor oversprayed with toothbrush.
Secondary images – on dyeline print ink-based marker on solid or dense areas. Pastel scraped and rubbed in broad colour washes over masked out larger areas and colour pencil to develop texture, shadow and detail. This drawing attempts to express both the content and inspiration for the cinematheque on a variety of levels, evoking both the architectural and cinematic properties of the building and their interrelationship. A simple collection of abstracted architectural elements is composed in a geometric organisation reflecting the site, its use and its interpretation. The wilful abstraction and transposition of scales makes the drawing, rather than the depiction of a singular aspect, a more comprehensive representation of both the initial conception and final perception of the building and its context.

THE NATIONAL SCIENCE AND TECHNOLOGY MUSEUM – CANBERRA – AUSTRALIAN CAPITAL TERRITORY LAWRENCE NIELD AND PARTNERS

Design Architects:
Lawrence Nield and
Warwick Simmonds
Drawing Artist:
Warwick Simmonds and team
Size: 1189 x 841 mm
Date: 1987
Photographer: John Gollings

The site for the National Science and Technology Centre is on the Parliamentary Triangle. It holds an important urban position where the design must mediate between the buildings within the triangle while creating a sense of place and excitement and revealing the centre's public nature.

The building houses exhibition galleries and workshops for interactive science exhibits. The internal organisation of the centre has a 'voyage of discovery' theme, leading visitors up a great ramp to the top gallery and letting them spiral down through the gallery sequence. The building's circulation, using a large ambulatory, is organised around a rotunda.

The galleries were the building blocks of the design. Optimum gallery sizes and arrangements were investigated and a 25 by 25 metre gallery with four columns became the preferred solution. Each gallery required a different ceiling height with overhead servicing and lighting cat-walks. A layout based on three cubes evolved to house five galleries, a two-level workshop, and loading dock/storage area. It was also decided that ramps should be used for transporting large crowds to the galleries.

The drawing uses ink on drafting film and is coloured with watercolour using air-brush technique.

MUSEUM OF SCOTLAND COMPETITION – EDINBURGH – SCOTLAND FLIGHTPATH ARCHITECTS

The principle objectives of the competition were to design a new building 'which will form a distinct part of the existing Royal Museum of Scotland ... to provide display space for the Scottish collections of the National Museums of Scotland and accommodation for other museum facilities; and for the integration and effective operation of the whole museum complex'.
The new building is situated on Edinburgh's 'Bridges of Culture', a route connecting the new part of Edinburgh to the older University area. These 'Bridges' connect Edinburgh's major cultural buildings including Edinburgh Castle and the Museum of Scotland. The new addition is situated directly on this path. The addition is integrated with the existing Museum, conceptually, functionally and architecturally. Architecturally, the provision of a major space is an abstract interpretation of the existing main hall. The axis of this space continues, extrapolated from the main hall where the intersection of the existing building's major axes form an anchoring point for new addition. The ordering principle which determines the pattern of the façade is taken from the existing building and transcribed onto the new building. Drawings were completed in ink on tracing paper at A3 and A4 size. They were then enlarged or reduced by photocopier and copied onto sheets of Letraset Letracopy. These were then stuck down in a desired position on the background sheet of tracing paper. The background photograph of the existing Museum building was supplied with information from the organisers. This was enlarged to the appropriate size and graininess and photocopied onto white cartridge paper to be rendered. The red space is rendered in layered colour pencil Derwent No 20 Crimson Lake. Conceptually the red space represents the architectural void. The strong colour is designed to make the drawing stand out from its neighbouring entries. Discrete use of Derwent No 38 Kingfisher Blue as a highlight colour added relief and contrast to the composition.

Design Team: Anthony Coupe,
Sam Hosking, Cynthia Curtis
Drawing Artist: Anthony Coupe,
Sam Hosking, Cynthia Curtis,
Douglas Alexander and
Richard Woods
Size: 1682 x 1181 mm
Date: 1991

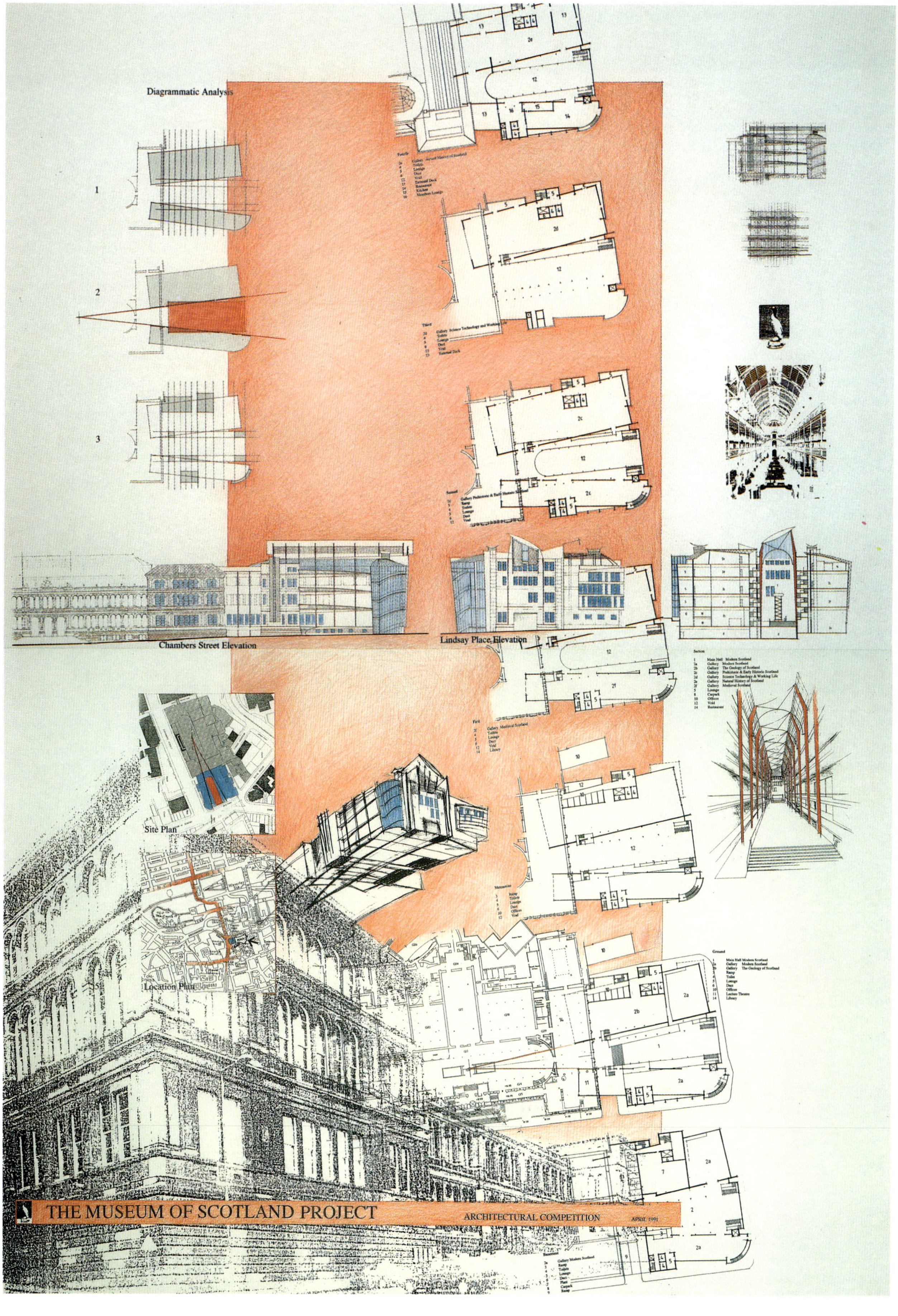

Diagrammatic Analysis
1
2
3
Chambers Street Elevation
Lindsay Place Elevation
Site Plan
Location Plan
THE MUSEUM OF SCOTLAND PROJECT
ARCHITECTURAL COMPETITION
APRIL 1991

USA GALLERY – AUSTRALIAN NATIONAL MARITIME MUSEUM – SYDNEY – NEW SOUTH WALES
BURLEY KATON HALLIDAY

The project was the result of a limited competition to design the interior fitout of the USA Gallery in the Australian National Maritime Museum. The floor space was handed over in shell form and work included all services, display lighting, object placement and graphics. The approach taken is intended to be permanent and to sympathise with and enhance the collection. The space can be entered from either end and while display is broadly chronological, direction of circulation is optional. The older parts of the collection are heavily object based with items such as maps, charts, paintings and models resulting in a high need for show cases. The newer section relies more on photography, film, television and interactive displays.
The presentation drawings were done in ink using Rotring pens size 0.5, 0.35 and 0.18, and Derwent coloured pencils on 110 gsm drafting film. This technique produces a delicate result which we believe suggests quality and tends to become an object in itself.

Project Architect:
Ian Halliday
Drawing Artist: Bruce Nockles
Size: 594 x 594 mm
Date: 1990

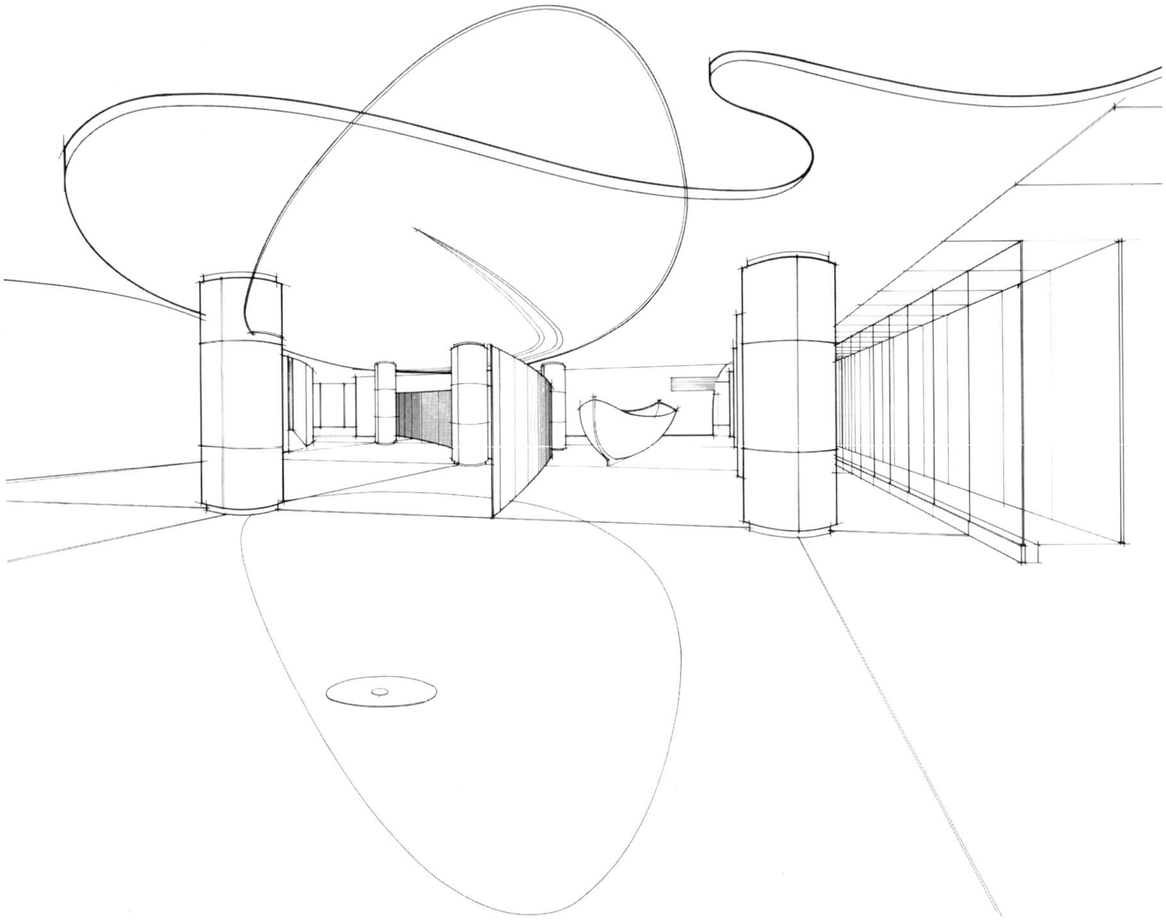

3 U.S.A GALLERY PERSPECTIVE

2
AXONOMETRIC
1:100

MANYUNG RECREATION CAMP - VICTORIA   IVAN RIJAVEC ARCHITECTS

This facility proposed for a bayside youth recreation camp comprises administration facilities, a commercial kitchen and large dining and recreation hall. This project proposed to be constructed predominantly of prefabricated steel element alludes to a host of maritime images. The concept relies on the rotation of the curvilinear roof form above a Miesian plan to achieve a definite sensation of movement.
An exploded perspectival overview dominates the graphic. Around this image plans and elevations which demonstrate the rotation of form, complete the picture. Media: pencil, coloured pencil, ink tipped pens, applied to both sides of detail paper. (The artist's general statement which elucidates some of the concerns specific to his work can be found outlined under the heading of the Manifold Residence by Ivan Rijavec Architects.)

Design Architect: Ivan Rijavec
Drawing Artist:
Zbigniew Jaworski
Size: 850 x 690 mm
Date: 1989
Photographer:
Zbigniew Jaworski

IVAN RIJAVEC ARCHITECTS

SYDNEY FOOTBALL STADIUM – MOORE PARK, SYDNEY – NEW SOUTH WALES   PHILIP COX, RICHARDSON, TAYLOR AND PARTNERS

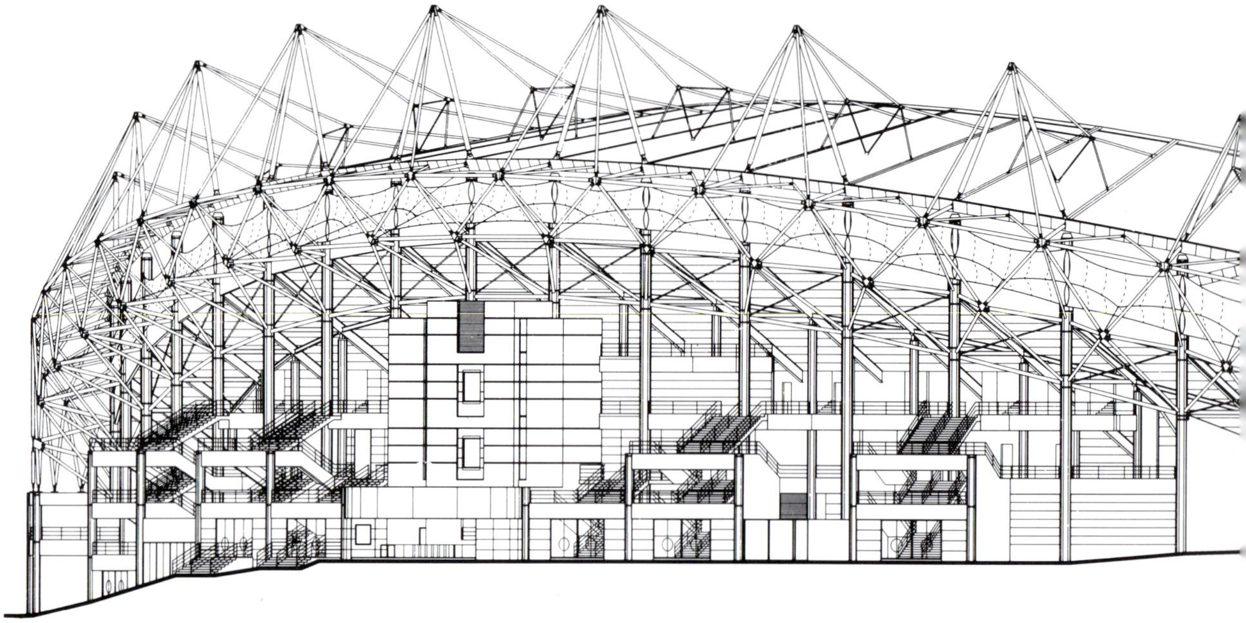

Design Architect: Philip Cox, Richardson, Taylor and Partners
Drawing Artist: Philip Cox, Richardson, Taylor and Partners
Size: 2 x 1682 x 1189 mm
Date: 1986
Photographer: Paul Simcock

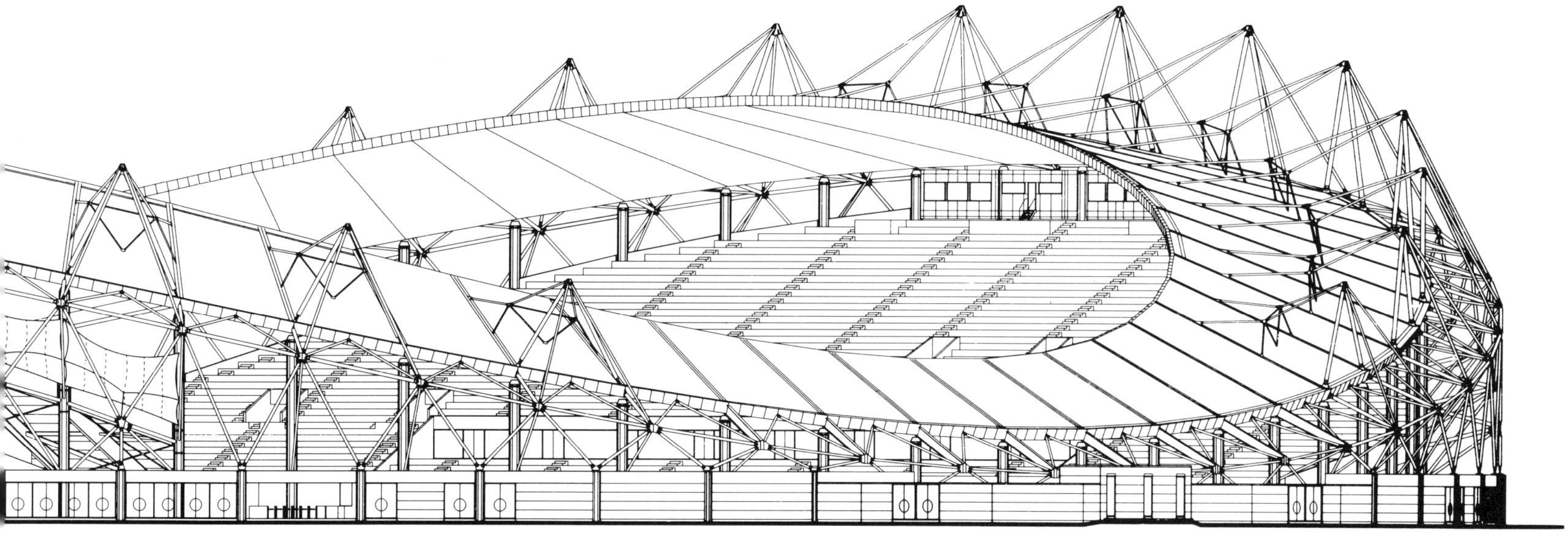

The Sydney Football Stadium is a large 40 000 spectator capacity facility, primarily for football, but also for outdoor entertainment events. Its unusual shape is determined by a number of planning and contextual issues: the relationship of rectangular field to circular perimeter produces a higher seating level at the field's centre line than at the ends; the circular perimeter responds to the existing SCG and Showground shapes, and relates well to external spaces; there was a contextual need to reduce the building scale adjacent Moore Park's residential area.

It was considered desirable to have a continuous roof encircle the stadium both to maximise cover and to create a true 'bowl' enclosure for atmospheric reasons. Absence of columns is a mandatory requirement of modern stadiums, requiring development of a structural system capable of hanging the roof. Elimination of any need for light towers, with their undesirable spill of light onto surrounding areas, also generated the continuous roof form with lighting incorporated into the leading edges at particular heights for television optimisation. The 'bowl' approach to both arena and roof also provided a means of acoustic control.

The system of masts and rods was further developed to create qualities of drama and strength appropriate to use, and they accentuate the roof form as its cantilever depth increases toward the field centre.

While it is relatively easy to communicate such a roof and arena shape by loose conceptual sketches, it is virtually impossible to accurately draw the form manually. No elevation is true, nor does a roof plan accurately communicate true shape (see Site Plan). CAD techniques were therefore essential for both design development and documentation. Throughout the project, models ranging from 1:200 overall to 1:10 detail were continuously used to refine the form and details, and CAD operators directly translated these three-dimensional ideas into computerised working drawings. The large long elevation illustrated was computer generated using Autocad on two joined AO sheets to demonstrate roof form, exposed structure and substructure.

WOLLONGONG HOSPITAL – WOLLONGONG – NEW SOUTH WALES KEN MAHER AND PARTNERS

Ken Maher and Partners were engaged by the NSW Public Works Department to work with them on the design of a new Cancer Care Centre, as part of major extensions to Wollongong Hospital. A design proposal was developed which isolated the existing main hospital building from both the Cancer Care Centre, and the new Clinical Services facilities. The new buildings were sited to allow a reordering of the circulation through the site, and to establish a new entrance and orientation space to serve the hospital as a whole. The dominant form of the existing hospital building was mediated by a transition in scale established through the siting of the two new buildings.

The new Cancer Care Centre has a direct address to the street, in recognition of its community funding and its day care function. Its forms are elemental, its materials are diverse, and more fragmented in scale than the existing buildings, to reflect the position and role of the new building. The building is divided into two formal and functional elements by a central circulation and entry component. This isolates the primary forms, and provides views towards the nearby mountains for those entering or waiting in the building. Other formal elements, such as lifts, stairs and the main radiotherapy treatment bunker, are expressed clearly, allowing a further articulation of the mass. The roof is designed to be viewed over from within the site, and specific elements are accentuated further articulating the main building form.

Detailed plans and elevations were prepared for the new building which illustrated the proposed materials and colours, and coloured study drawings were used in developing the design of the building through to a detail level. Elevations developed from base computer plot drawings on bond paper. These were hand rendered in coloured pencils – Derwent Artists and Faber Castell Polychromos. The background colour was applied by hand pressure pack spray using automotive duco touch up paint.

Design Architects: Ken Maher and Everard Kloots with assistance from Colin Small and Yarek Alexander.
Health Planning by Debbie Wyatt from the Public Works Department of New South Wales.
Drawing Artists: Rendering by Nicky Ross and Julie McKenzie under the direction of Everard Kloots
Size: 840 x 594 mm
Date: 1989
Photographer: Ken Maher

OUTPATIENTS DEPARTMENT WESTMEAD CHILDREN'S HOSPITAL – WESTMEAD – NEW SOUTH WALES McCONNEL SMITH & JOHNSON ARCHITECTS, THE MSJ GROUP

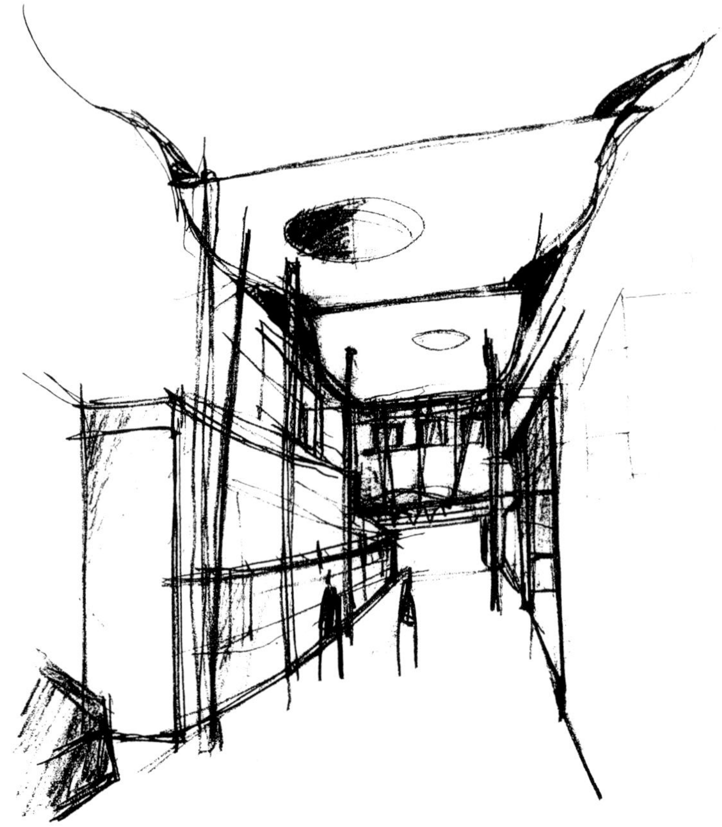

The hospital has been cooperatively designed by four architectural firms. McConnel Smith & Johnson is responsible for the design of the Outpatients Wing which flanks the main entry.
The Wing has been conceived as a set of pavilions connected to a series of courtyards related to the various Outpatient Departments. The juxtaposition of colonnades and steel covered-ways along the edge of the building, connecting the car park with the entrance, reinforces the illusion of discrete pavilions.
The height of the building has been kept to a maximum of three storeys and the scale has been consciously diminished to create a human environment for children and families in what is fundamentally a very large hospital.
The pitched white metal roof over the central mass of the Outpatients Building forms a backdrop to the pavilions like a small hill and gently curves towards the entrance of the hospital. Accordingly, the composition of the windows and coloured render of the façades have been designed to inflect the visual weight of the building towards the entry.
The rendered perspective depicts the street approach to the Outpatients Building from normal eye level and was produced to study the three-dimensional effects of the composition of the forecourt elevation. Technical information: pencil drawing on drafting film; Liquitex acrylic rendered on reverse side of film. Detail is applied before large areas of loose painting. Faber Castell coloured pencil highlights applied to face of film. Ink drawing on film using pen sizes 0.25/0.35. Letratone LT936 and Pantone Black on side of film. Pencil sketches of interior and courtyard spaces. Originals were produced at approximately 75 mm square in 0.7 mm B clutch pencil and bromided.

Design Architects:
McConnel Smith and Johnson
Drawing Artists: Mark Willett,
Mark Gerada
Size: 840 x 840 mm
Date: 1991

MEDITATION CHAPEL PROJECT – RICHMOND – VICTORIA GREG BURGESS ARCHITECT

With such a proliferation of violence, greed, corruption, poverty and alienation world-wide, the human race is in desperate trouble. The preparation of a meditation chapel would seem a timely consideration. There is an urgent need to integrate the life of the world and the life of the spirit within us.
The site chosen for this submission is in Richmond – an old inner Melbourne suburb. In close proximity to Richmond's heart it is also a precinct of remarkable peace and beauty – the inherent power which drew me to it. Perhaps significantly the site is on a hill overlooking Richmond and Melbourne proper – and is within a short distance of five churches.
The sense of the living earth here is surprising in such a generally harsh urban scene. Three large and very old peppercorn trees bound the site from the southern approach. A church, manse, row of 19th century terrace houses and a three-storey warehouse (now art gallery) share Waltham Place with the Chapel.
Lead Pencil, Derwent colour pencil on tracing paper. Pencil was chosen for its suitability to enter the play between light and darkness. One of the key themes explored in this submission was the balance and movement between polarities.

Design Architect:
Greg Burgess
Drawing Artist: Peter Jensen
Size: 400 x 400 mm
Date: 1981

ST THOMAS ACQUINAS CHURCH – CHARNWOOD – AUSTRALIAN CAPITAL TERRITORY MITCHELL/ GIURGOLA & THORPE ARCHITECTS

Project Architect:
Robert Thorne
Drawing: Romaldo Giurgola, Design Partner
Size: 840 x 580 mm
Date: 1988
Photographer: John Gollings

St Thomas Acquinas Parish Church at the Canberra suburb of Charnwood, was constructed within a limited budget to seat a congregation of 400 people and is adjacent to an existing presbytery and Catholic School. The Church was a community focus for the parishioners who participated in its fit-out in collaboration with commissioned craftspeople and artists. The Church is designed around an itinerary of discrete events. The simple timber columns of the entry court establish the sacred ground and prepare in mind and spirit those about to enter. The intimately-scaled narthex forms a quiet transition space, a threshold to the nave which is the primary space of assembly and the place of revelation. The itinerary culminates in the sanctuary, the place of celebration of the sacrament. The most important architectural concept of the Church's design is the presence of the soaring white brick wall of the sanctuary whose division into three identifiable parts represents the Trinity and reflects the most important elements of the ritual: the altar, the blessed sacrament and the place of baptism. The drawing by Romaldo Giurgola is pencil on Crystalline and was executed as a freehand sketch in order to capture the spirit of the space, the handmade character of the building and the handcrafted character of the ceramic tiling in the tabernacle area of the Blessed Sacrement Chapel within the Church.

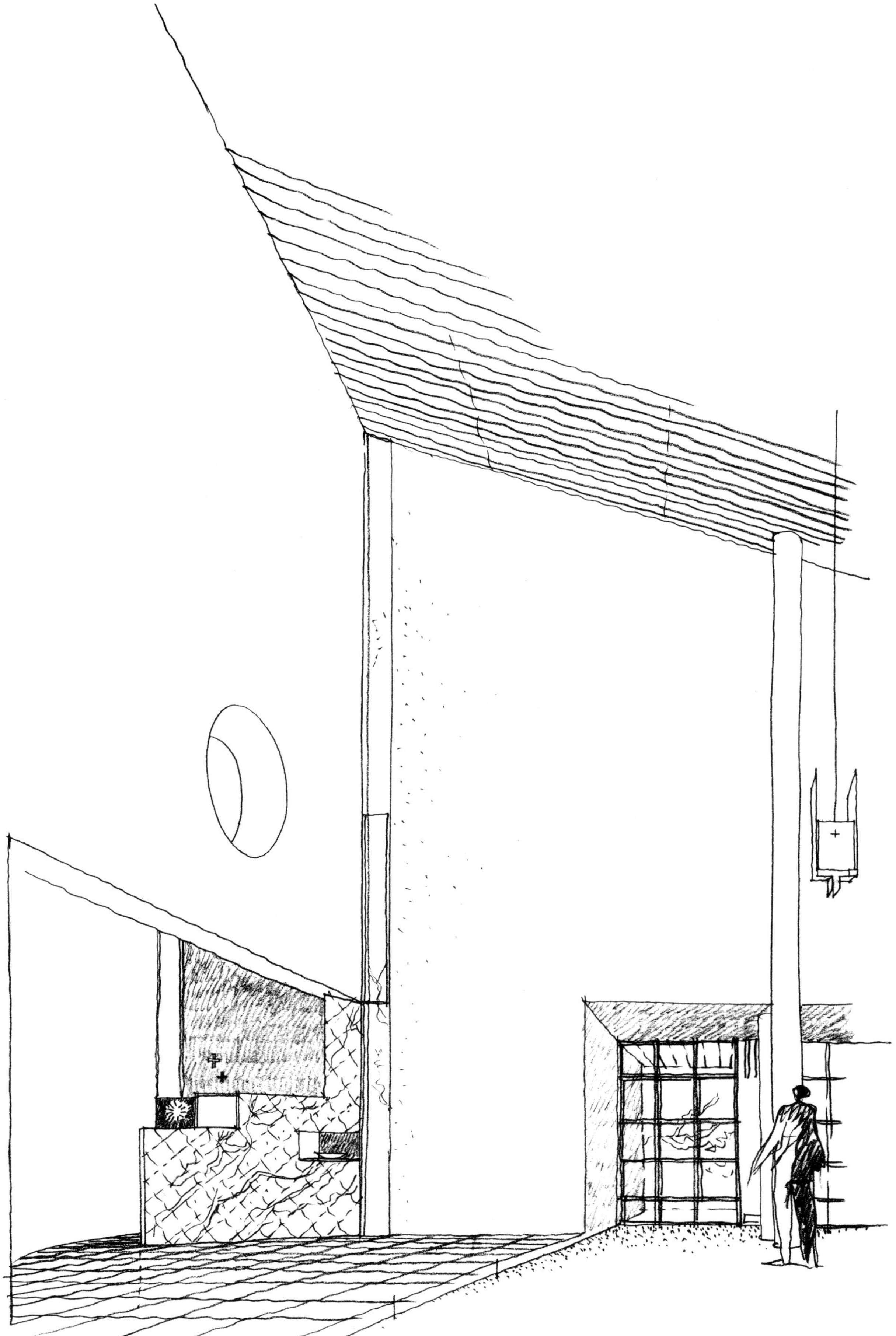

BRAMBUK LIVING CULTURAL CENTRE – GRAMPIANS NATIONAL PARK – VICTORIA
GREG BURGESS ARCHITECT

The Brambuk Project was initiated to protect the many enigmatic rock art sites in the Grampians from vandalism and weather. It subsequently evolved through the five responsible Aboriginal communities into a much larger vision of an integrated living cultural centre. This is a place where visitors can experience, through the building, its activities and displays, the richness and wisdom of Aboriginal culture and through personal contact with its people, discuss the aspirations, problems and issues facing them today. For 18 months we have been working with five Aboriginal communities from western Victoria and representatives from the Ministry of Conservation, Forests and Lands, Victorian Archaeological Survey, Victorian Tourist Commission and the Ministry for Planning and Environment, to develop this building and landscape as a focus for Aboriginal cultural activities in Western Victoria.
The site for the building is beside Fyans Creek in the centre of a dramatic valley between the Wonderland Range and Boronia Peak, just south of Halls Gap. The evolution of the building through the many workshops was guided by the communities' poetic sensitivity to the natural environment; and pride in the remains of groups of semi-permanent stone dwellings built at Lake Condah by their ancestors some 8 000 years ago. Highly sophisticated and extensive weir and canal systems (also built of stone) for the seasonal catching of eels and other fish have been discovered nearby. A garden surrounding the building for observation, discussion and learning about medicinal and edible plants will provide an introduction to Koorie bushcraft.
Sketch carried out in felt tip pen on butter paper. Documentation drawings were black ink, Letratone on tracing paper. This was needed for crisp but delicate reproduction emphasising roof pattern.

Design Architect:
Greg Burgess Architect
Drawing Artist: Greg Burgess
and Ian Khoo
Size: 1189 x 841 mm
Date: 1989
Photographer: Trevor Mein

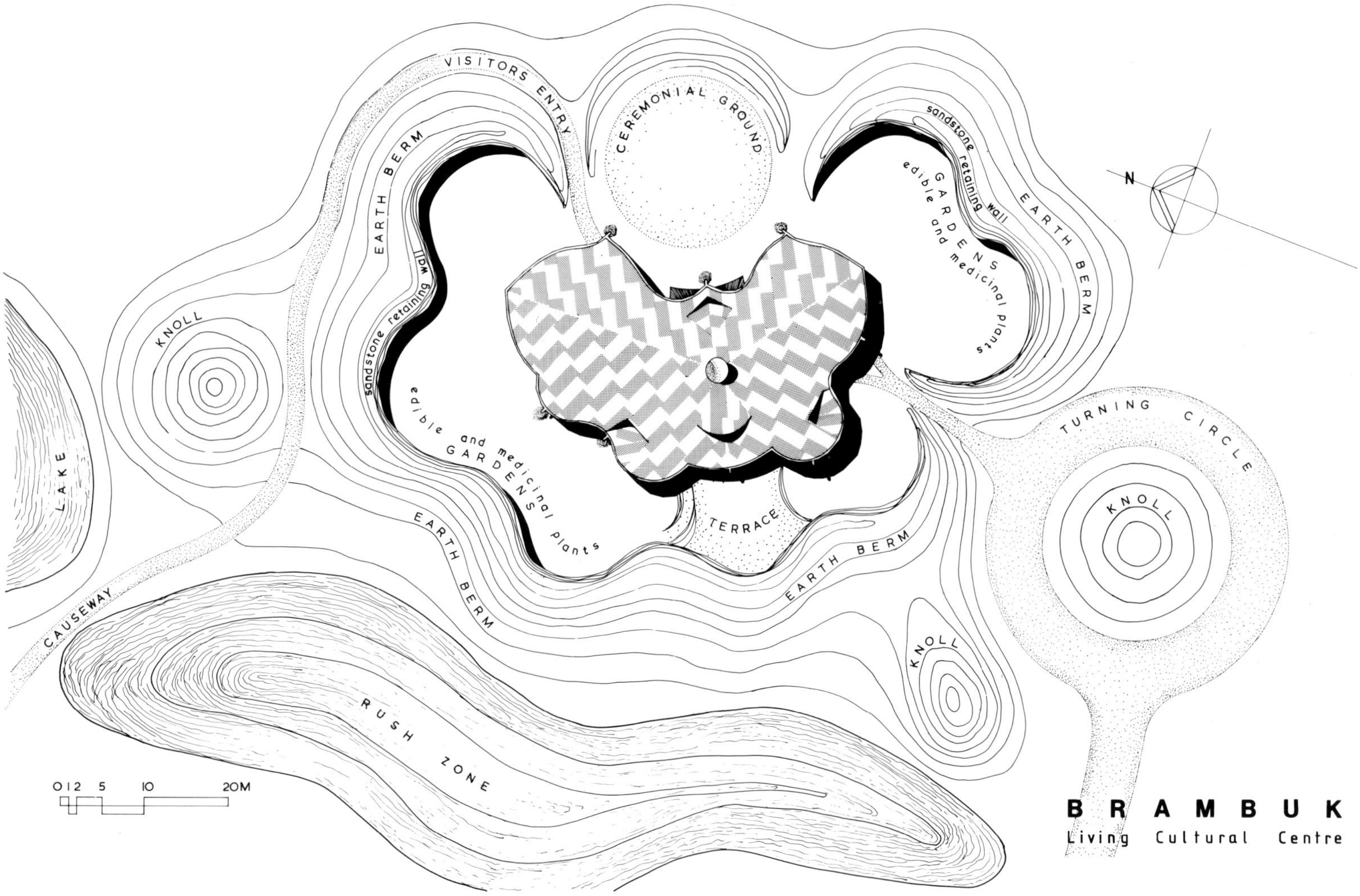
VISITORS ENTRY
CEREMONIAL GROUND
sandstone retaining wall
EARTH BERM
GARDENS
edible and medicinal plants
KNOLL
LAKE
TERRACE
TURNING CIRCLE
CAUSEWAY
RUSH ZONE
N
0 1 2 5 10 20M
BRAMBUK
Living Cultural Centre

JOHN BELL SHAKESPEARE TRAVELLING INSTALLATION D4 DESIGN

Design Architect:
D4 Design Pty Ltd
Drawing Artist:
Michael Scott Mitchell
Size: 1189 x 420 mm
Date: 1991
Photographer: Branco Gaica

The brief from John Bell, director of *Hamlet*, Carol Woodrow, director of the *Merchant of Venice* and the Elizabethan Theatre Trust as producers, was to provide two completely different 'performance platforms' within the Silver Brothers' Circus tent – whilst maintaining a seating capacity of 800 on the flat. The staging was to be designed with touring in mind with the specific capability of 'changeover' from *Hamlet* to the *Merchant* within four hours.

John Bell's specific directive for *Hamlet* was to provide a central stage with an ancillary area attached and quick access for actors through the audience. Conceptually, *Hamlet* was to be a 'bare boards' production. Carol Woodrow's requirements differed significantly. Where *Hamlet* was to be concentrated at the centre of the tent, in the round, *Merchant* was to open out and use the entire width of the tent – in essence, traverse staging.

Broadly the staging is concerned with spatial dynamics. Very little of the structure is visible at any given moment, consequently the placement and movement of actors – horizontally and vertically is of paramount importance.

The production is currently being remounted to suit proscenium theatres – as well as ongoing use of the tent.

The drawing is a working drawing and as such is ink line using Rotring pens 0.5, 0.35 and 0.18 on 90 gm drafting film.

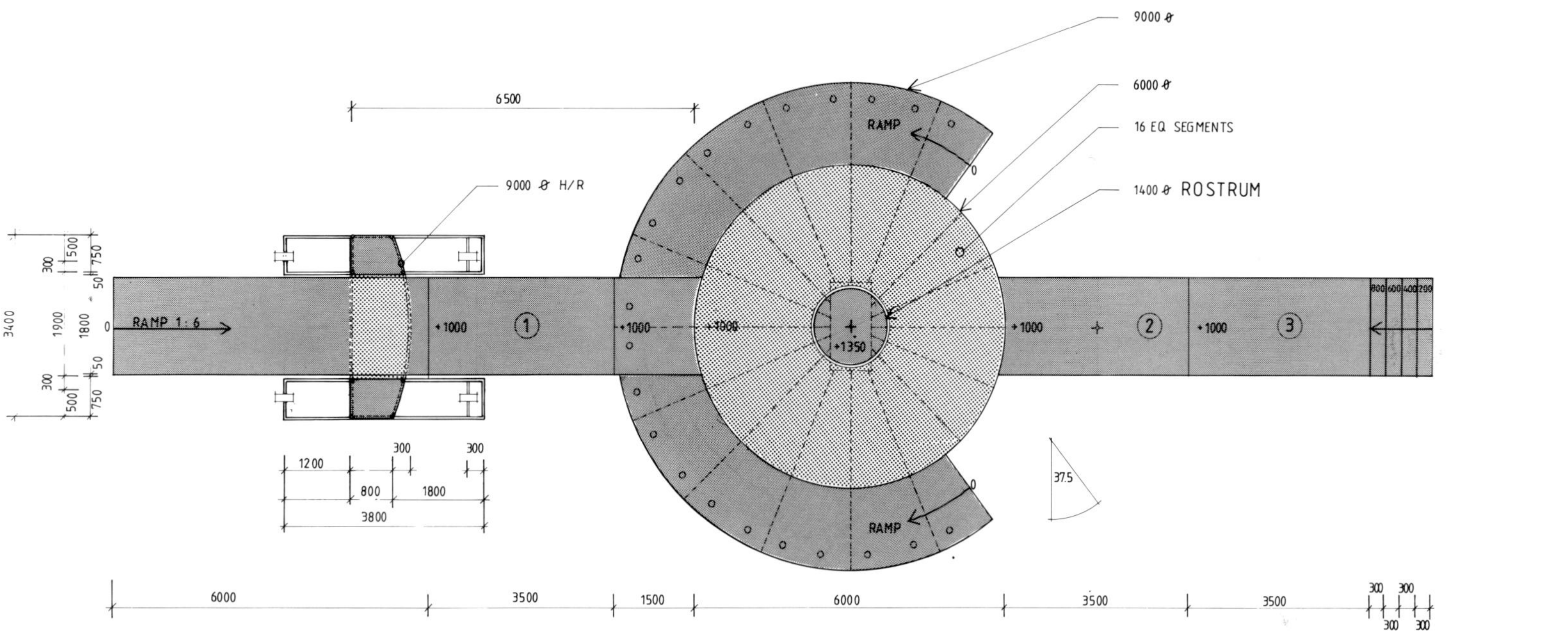

PLAN

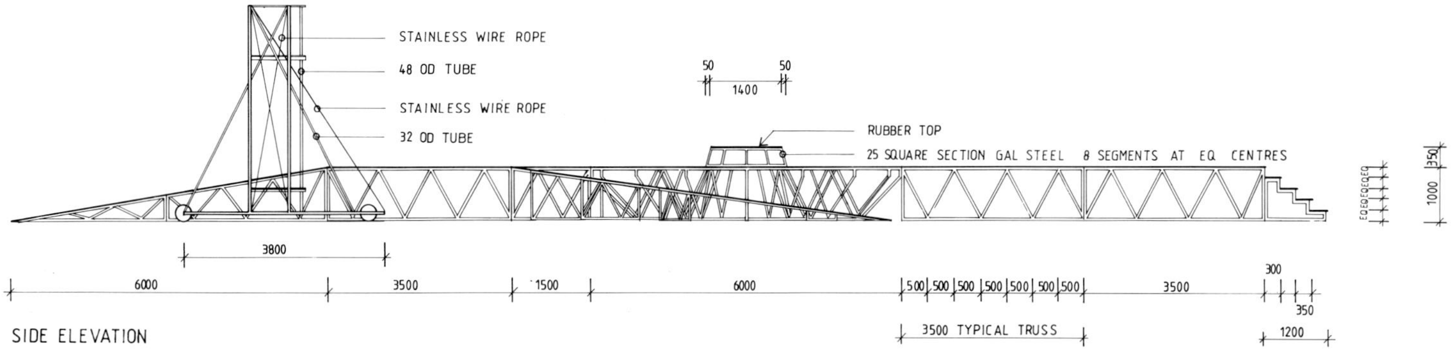

SIDE ELEVATION

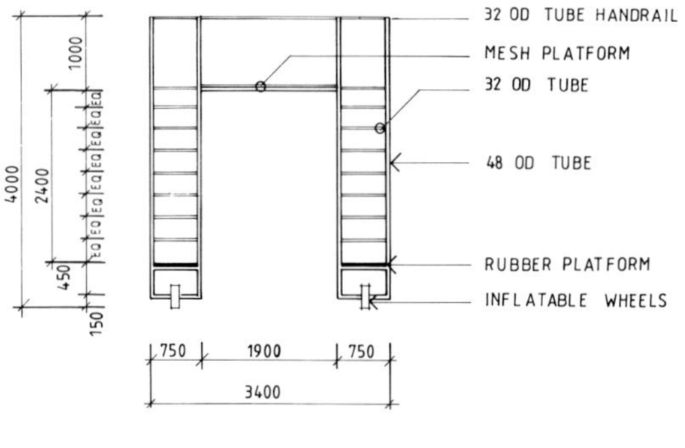

TOWER FRONT ELEVATION

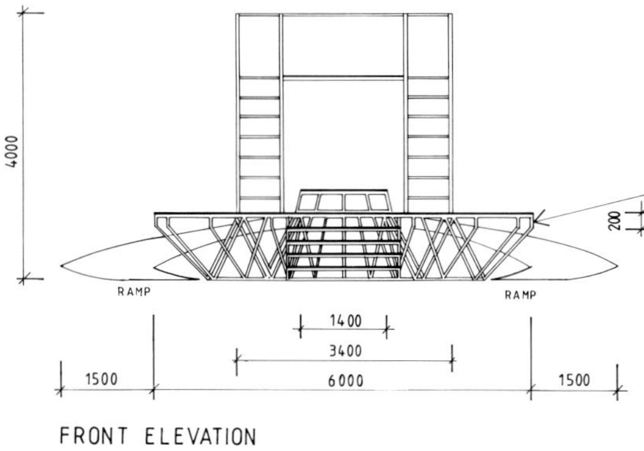

FRONT ELEVATION

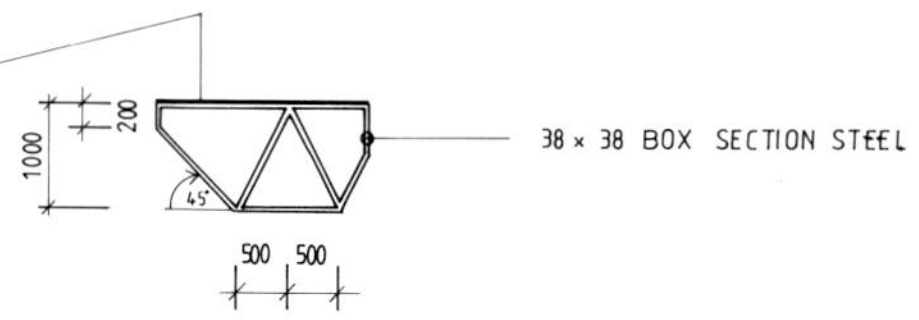

TYPICAL CENTRE TRUSS

BIBLIOGRAPHY

SELECTED BOOKS ON AUSTRALIAN ARCHITECTURE 1981–91

Apperly, R, Irving, R and Reynolds, P, *A Pictorial Guide to Australian Architecture: Styles and Terms from 1788 to the Present*, Angus and Robertson, 1989.

Beck, H, Parliament House, *Canberra: A Building for the Nation*, Collins, Sydney, 1988.

Beck, H and Cooper, J, *Australian Architects: Denton Corker Marshall*, Royal Australian Institute of Architects, Red Hill ACT, 1987.

Beck H and Turnbull, J, *Critiques I*, University of Melbourne, Department of Architecture and Building/Invicta Foundation, Melbourne, 1987.

Boyd, R (Howells, T, revised edition), *The Walls Around Us: A Popular History of Australian Architecture*, Angus and Robertson, Sydney, 1982.

Carrick, J and Rumley, K, *Expressing Australia: Art in Parliament House*, Parliament House Construction Authority, Canberra, 1989.

Drew, P, *Leaves of Iron: Glenn Murcutt, Pioneer of an Australian Architectural Form*, The Law Book Company, Sydney, 1985.

Dunster, D, *Key Buildings of the 20th Century, 2: Houses 1945–1989*, Butterworth, London, 1990.

Edquist, H, *Reasons to be Cheerful*, George Paton Gallery, Melbourne, 1988.

Fitzgerald A, *Canberra and the New Parliament House*, Lansdowne Press, Sydney, 1983.

Gollings, J, Hopkins, T and Greene, P, *Melbourne*, William Heinemann, Melbourne, 1990.

Griggs, M and McGregor, C, *Australian Built: Catalogue to a photographic exhibition of Recent Australian Architecture*, 1985.

Hudson, N and McEwan, P, *That's Our House: A History of Housing in Victoria*, The Ministry of Housing, Melbourne, 1985/86.

Irving, R, *History and Design of the Australian House*, Oxford University Press, Melbourne, 1985.

Jackson, D, *Daryl Jackson Architecture: Drawings and Photographs*, McMillan, Melbourne, 1984.

Johnson, C (ed), *The City in Conflict*, Law Book Company, Sydney, 1986.

Judd, B and Dean, J, *Medium Density Housing in Australia*, Royal Australian Institute of Architects, Canberra, 1983.

Lee, T, *Building on Tradition: Nine Designs for the Victorian State Library and Museum Architectural Competition*, Emery Vincent, Melbourne, 1986.

Mitchell, E and Giurgola, R, *Mitchell/Giurgola Architects*, Rizzoli, New York, 1983.

Ogg, A, *Architecture in Steel: The Australian Context*, Royal Australian Institute of Architects, Education Division, Canberra, 1987.

Parliament House Construction Authority, *Australia's New Parliament House*, Parliament House Construction Authority, 1986.

Paroissen, L and Griggs, M, *Old Continent New Building: Contemporary Australian Architecture*, David Ell and the Design Arts Committee of the Australia Council, Darlinghurst, 1983.

Pegrum, R, *Australian Architects: Australian Government Architects*, Royal Australian Institute of Architects, Canberra, 1988.

Pegrum, R, *Details in Australian Architecture*, Volumes 1 and 2, Royal Australian Institute of

Architects, Education Division, Canberra, 1984, 1987.

Royal Melbourne Institute of Technology, Students, *Aardvark: A Selected Guide to Contemporary Melbourne Architects*, School of Architecture, Royal Melbourne Institute of Technology, Melbourne, 1990.

Saunders, D and Shigeru, Y, *Modern Australian Architecture*, Process Architecture, Tokyo, 1981.

Shaw, AGL, *Victoria's Heritage*, Allen and Unwin, Melbourne, 1986.

Sinclair, R, *et al.*, *Australian Architects: Ken Woolley*, Royal Australian Institute of Architects, Canberra, 1985.

Smith, D, *Interpreting the Art and Design of Parliament House: A Guide for Senior Secondary Schools*, Royal Australian Institute of Architects, Education Division, Canberra, 1989.

Taylor, J, *Architecture in Australia Since 1960*, 1st and 2nd Editions, Law Book Company, Sydney, 1986, 1990.

Taylor, J and Andrews, J, *Architecture as a Performing Art*, Oxford University Press, Melbourne, 1982.

Towndrow, J, *Philip Cox, Portrait of an Australian Architect*, Viking, Melbourne, 1991.

Turnbull, J, *Critiques 3*, University of Melbourne, Department of Architecture and Building/Invicta Foundation, Melbourne.

Webber, G.P, *The Design of Sydney*, The Law Book Company, Sydney, 1988.

JOURNALS INCLUDING AUSTRALIAN ARCHITECTURE 1981–91

Agenda; Architect (RAIA Vic); *Architect* (RAIA WA); *Axis 39–021; Architecture* (AIA); *Architecture and Design; Architecture and Urbanism; Architecture Australia; Architecture New Zealand; The Architecture Show; Architectural Journal; Architectural Design; The Architectural Review* (London); *Art and Architecture; Arkitektur* (Sweden); *Art* (RAIA Vic); *Art and Australia; Artlink; Australian Art Review; Australian Business; Australian Concrete Construction; Australian Home Beautiful; Australian Home Journal; Australian House and Garden; Australian Project Manager; The Bulletin* (RAIA NSW); *Belle; Blueprint; BOMA; Builder: New South Wales; Building Design; Building Ideas; Building Journal; Building Services Australia; Building Today; Casabella* (Italy); *Casa Vogue* (Italy); *Connections; Constructional Review; Corporate and Office Design; Corporate Design and Realty; Craft Australia; Design World; Designer's Journal; Dimensions* (Hong Kong); *Domus* (Italy); *Express Australia: Contemporary Arts and Popular Culture* (NY); *Good Housekeeping; Interior Design; Interiors; Landscape Australia; Laras* (Jakarta); *Metal Building News; Modo* (Italy); *New Zealand Architect; Nikkei Architecture* (Japan); *Panorama; Pataphysics; Plenty; Process: Architecture; Progressive Architecture; Royal Institute of British Architects Journal* (Britain); *Space Design* (Japan); *Space and Society* (Italy); *Steel Profile; Tension; Timber Trader; Today's Living; Transition; UIA International Architect; Vision* (Hong Kong); *Vogue Entertaining Guide; Vogue Living; Wind: World Interior Design* (Japan); *Women Australia; Wood World.*

INDEX OF NAMES